TEACHING
AT ITS
BEST

TEACHING AT ITS BEST

A RESEARCH-BASED RESOURCE FOR COLLEGE INSTRUCTORS

SECOND EDITION

Linda B. Nilson

ANKER PUBLISHING COMPANY, INC.
BOLTON, MA

Teaching at Its Best
A Research-Based Resource for College Instructors

Second Edition

ISBN 1-882982-64-9

Cover design by Frederick Schneider/Grafis

Anker Publishing Company, Inc.
176 Ballville Road
P.O. Box 249
Bolton, MA 01740-0249 USA

www.ankerpub.com

ABOUT THE AUTHOR

Linda B. Nilson has been the founding Director of Clemson University's Office of Teaching Effectiveness and Innovation since 1998. She came to Clemson from Vanderbilt University, where she directed the Center for Teaching for five and a half years. In addition to managing OTEI and its staff, she holds individual consultations with faculty, consults on instructional and assessment issues on grants and to committees and departments, and designs and conducts faculty development workshops at Clemson and other universities across the country.

Dr. Nilson's workshop repertoire includes comprehensive course design by student-learning objectives, interpreting student evaluations, peer assessment of teaching for promotion and tenure, interactive lecturing, learning styles, getting students to do the readings, case study design and debriefing, problem-based learning, cooperative learning, discussion management, questioning techniques, student-peer feedback instruments, developing a graphic syllabus, techniques for grading writing, and designing tests and assignments. In 1998, Anker Publishing released the first edition of *Teaching at Its Best: A Research-Based Resource for College Instructors* and has just released the second. It is the most up-to-date and comprehensive teaching methods book on the market.

For the previous three and a half years, she directed the Teaching Assistant Development Program at the University of California, Riverside, and designed and taught a very popular graduate seminar on college teaching. In addition, she developed the "disciplinary cluster" approach to training TAs, a cost-effective way for a centralized unit to provide disciplinary-relevant instructional training. This approach received coverage in the *Chronicle of Higher Education*. She similarly structured TA training at Vanderbilt.

Since moving to the South, Dr. Nilson has been very active in the Southern Regional Faculty and Instructional Development Consortium (SRFIDC). She served on its Executive Committee for five years, including three years as Chair, and organized and hosted the 1994 conference. She is also active in the Professional and Organizational Development (POD) Network in Higher Education and the Society for Teaching and Learning in Higher Education (STLHE).

Dr. Nilson entered the area of instructional and faculty development in the late 1970s while she was on the sociology faculty at UCLA. After distinguishing herself as an excellent instructor, her department selected her to establish its Teaching Assistant Training Program. She supervised it for four years, and it still follows her original organization.

In addition to *Teaching at Its Best: A Research-Based Resource for College Instructors,* Dr. Nilson has written three book-length instructional handbooks her employing universities. She has also published articles and book chapters on the graphic syllabus, improving student-peer feedback, teaching large social science courses, mentoring graduate students, TA training, critical thinking, and designing and publishing research on teaching. As a sociologist, she conducted research in the areas of occupations and work, social stratification, political sociology, and disaster behavior.

Dr. Nilson's career also included several years in the business world as a technical and commercial writer, a training workshop facilitator, and business editor of a Southern California magazine.

A native of Chicago, Dr. Nilson was a National Science Foundation Fellow at the University of Wisconsin, Madison, where she received her Ph.D. and M.S. degrees in sociology. She completed her undergraduate work in three years at the University of California, Berkeley, where she was elected to Phi Beta Kappa.

CONTENTS

PREFACE

This second edition of *Teaching at Its Best* has basically the same goals as the first edition, but it aims to meet the needs of additional instructor audiences: those who teach adult and diverse student populations as well as those who teach more in more traditional contexts, and those who use considerable technology and multimedia resources as well as those who rely more on traditional classroom methods.

Among the many changes and revisions made in the second edition are completely new sections on how people learn, the adult learner, student diversity, the graphic syllabus, the learner-centered syllabus, getting students to read the syllabus, the "cognitive profile" learning-style model, parallels across learning-style frameworks, new writing-to-learn activities, student-peer feedback, and teaching with laptops. Several chapters were extensively revamped and updated, specifically those on copyright guidelines for instructors, preventing and responding to classroom incivility, experiential learning activities, instructional aids and technology, teaching science labs, and evaluating and documenting teaching. Two chapters are entirely new: the one on getting students to do the readings and the other on problem-based learning. Finally, one of the major parts of the book now addresses teaching problem solving in a number of different contexts and with several distinct methods.

Like the first edition, this revision is designed primarily for use in colleges and universities with high standards of instructional excellence, in particular at the undergraduate level. It addresses the concerns of new as well as experienced instructors who are sincerely dedicated to "teaching at its best" and have students committed to learning at its best. Teaching and learning that need little or no remediation provide fertile soil for innovation. So this book focuses on state-of-the-art techniques and formats designed to elevate college teaching to its highest potential.

The reader should use this book as a toolbox for both classroom and technology-enhanced instruction. It is a concise compilation of hundreds of teaching techniques and formats, classroom and electronic activities and exercises, suggestions to enhance instructor-student rapport, guidelines for assignments and papers, and tips for teaching any material more effectively. In considering this resource as a toolbox, the reader may recall the timeless advice of some mechanical sage: "Always use the right tool for the job." But in teaching, there may be several, even many "right tools" for a given teaching "job," and this book presents alternatives wherever appropriate.

Two objectives guided the decisions regarding its content, organization, and layout: 1) to enhance the credibility of the content by grounding it in the vast body of research on college-level teaching and 2) to make the content easily and quickly accessible.

The college-level teaching literature has expanded rapidly since the late 1960s, gaining high quality and developing into a thriving field of its own. The research encompasses not only the impact of different instructional methods—usually measured by student learning, satisfaction, and retention—but also recommendations on how to implement these methods most successfully. Of course, few instructors have the time to keep abreast of both their own area of scholarship and instructional research. This is why a concise summary of teaching options and innovations should be a particularly useful resource.

To ensure accessibility and to allow rapid reading, the writing style is concise and informal, the paragraphs are relatively brief, and the format is double-column. The thirty-one chapters are grouped into five major sections ordered roughly according to most instructors' chronological need for the material.

Part I: Sound Preparations addresses the tasks that need to be done before the term begins.

Part II: Good Beginnings focuses not only on what to say and do on the first day of class but also on how to set policies, tones, and a productive learning environment for the entire term from that that first day on.

Part III: Varieties of Learning and Teaching Styles presents an extensive and varied menu of the most effective teaching techniques and formats available at the college level. Most of them appeal to a range of student learning styles and are easily adaptable to any subject matter.

Part IV: Teaching Problem Solving for Today's World covers ways to teach open-ended, realistic problem solving using the case method and problem-based learning, then closed-ended quantitative problem solving, and finally truly challenging scientific problem solving in the laboratory.

Finally, Part V: Assessment/Measuring Outcomes offers guidance on, first, evaluating student learning, including testing and grading, and second, assessing instructor effectiveness, including documenting it for review.

Still, the organization of the book is flexible. The chapters need not be read in any order, and the text makes numerous cross-references to other chapters that elaborate on a given subject. In addition, the chapters are purposely short and generously divided into sections. Therefore, the reader can casually browse or quickly locate specific topics of interest.

The content is sufficiently rich and varied to offer something to instructors at all levels, from beginning TAs to seasoned full professors—a highly disparate audience. Experienced faculty can simply skip over the tools with which they have already achieved success.

Another feature of this book is that almost all of it is written in the second person. The new teaching books, including those published by major presses, are increasingly written in this form, and for good reason. It personalizes the information for the reader and makes it easier to read. In addition, certain techniques follow certain essential rules and formulae; some are even defined by a specific sequence of action (e.g., instructor does this, students do that, instructor gives a certain response). In other words, the directions resemble recipes or assembly instructions. Clearly, the second person is the most concise way to present such information.

Credit and thanks go to a group of 13 anonymous reviewers of the first edition who carefully identified what was missing, obsolete, and ripe for improvement. I also thank Sirisha Saripalli and Jennifer Alexander for preparing the index and proofreading the manuscript.

Researching and writing this second edition kept me at the computer after hours and on weekends for a number of months, and I am grateful to my sweetheart and husband, Greg Bauernfeind, for encouraging my efforts, celebrating my progress, and taking care of business on the home front. This edition is dedicated him and his two wonderful grown children, Kristin and Kimberly, who together have given me a fulfilling new life, my personal "second edition."

Linda B. Nilson
Clemson, South Carolina
2003

Part I.

Sound

Preparations

INSTRUCTIONAL SUPPORT SERVICES AND RESOURCES

Teaching well at the college level starts with becoming familiar with your institutional environment. Instructors, especially new ones, need to realize that they cannot and *should* not try to handle all the many challenges of their jobs single-handedly. Every college and university is a large, multilayered organization—a few rivaling small cities in size and complexity—each with its own unique subculture, norms and values, official power structure, informal power networks, and infrastructure of services and support units. Even seasoned faculty in a new institution feel unsettled as they anticipate unfamiliar policies, forms, procedures, expectations, and types of students.

Most colleges and universities offer a wealth of instructional support services and resources—the library and computer services being among the most obvious. But the instructional help available from some individuals and units may not be obvious from their titles or names alone. The people and campus offices described below are well worth your getting to know. The referral services they provide can save you countless hours, and the information they furnish can prevent costly, however innocent, mistakes.

Colleagues, especially senior ones, are perhaps the most conveniently located and sometimes the most knowledgeable sources of information on discipline-specific issues, including how best to teach certain material, what to expect of students in specific courses, how to motivate students in a given subject, how to locate appropriate guest speakers, how to prepare for tenure and other faculty reviews, how to obtain special services or funding, and what assistance to request from department support staff. Colleagues are also excellent sources of informal feedback on teaching; most will be happy to serve as a classroom observer or teaching videotape reviewer. (Also see the "teaching center" below).

Department chairs are special colleagues who can offer broader, departmental perspectives on the discipline-specific issues above. They are especially well informed on departmental curriculum matters and can advise on proposals to develop new courses and to revise established ones. They may also provide the best counsel on standards and procedures for promotion and tenure. Finally, since they have the opportunity to study the teaching evaluations of all the courses and sections in their department, chairs can help interpret the student ratings and written comments as well as suggest ways to improve them.

4

The *Dean's office* of your college, school, or division can advise you about promotion and tenure matters, student characteristics, curriculum issues, and course design/development from a still broader perspective. Demographic and academic data about the student body will prove particularly valuable in helping you decide on the objectives, design, content, and techniques for each of your courses. You will also need information about curriculum policies and procedures: Do your courses satisfy general education or breadth requirements? If so, roughly what percentage of students will enroll in that course for that reason alone? How do you propose and get approval for a new course? What components and assignments must a course have to qualify for "honors," "writing," or any other special designation? Finally, the Dean's office may be the place to turn for help with classroom matters—for example, if the classroom you are assigned doesn't meet your class size, ventilation, or technological needs, or if you need a room reserved for special class activities and sessions. In large universities departments may control a set of classrooms and handle such matters.

A *teaching, faculty development, or instructional development center* has become an increasingly common resource on research- as well as teaching-oriented campuses. It usually provides instructional consultation and training services to faculty and TAs, such as classroom videotaping, classroom observations, class interviews (often in a small-group format called a "small group instructional diagnosis"), midterm student evaluations, advisory consultations, orientations for new instructors, and teaching workshops. Often these centers also maintain a library, run lecture series, publish a newsletter and teaching handbook, consult to departments and colleges on curricula and assessment, and award mini-grants for teaching innovations. Some house language testing and training programs for International TAs.

On a number of campuses, these centers also offer consultations and training in instructional technology, such as the most effective pedagogical applications and the how-to's of available software (see Chapter 22). Certainly those with "instructional development" or "technology" in the title do. But such services may be found in media units, libraries, computer centers and laboratories, and distance learning facilities. The vast majority of campuses that have come to rely greatly on technology usually have specialized, stand-alone centers.

An *academic computing, information technology, or instructional technology center* is the most likely unit to handle the faculty's (and staff's) computing needs, from setting up email accounts to replacing old terminals. Its major functions are client support in both hardware and software and training workshops in commonly used office, technical, and instructional software. This support usually includes buying the software and licenses and installing the software on request. Increasingly, campuses are adopting one or more brands of course management software. (WebCT® and Blackboard® are currently the most popular.) A few campus technology centers have developed their own.

With the recent technological revolution in higher education, these centers have expanded their roster of services. Many have transformed traditional classrooms into "smart classrooms" equipped with software-rich computer terminals, LCD projectors, VCRs, CD-ROM players, and internet connections. Scheduling, maintaining, and updating these classrooms are a full-time job. Some centers oversee mandated or voluntary laptop programs, which often entail training the faculty in their technical and pedagogical use, training the students, leasing the laptops or negotiating purchasing deals, and servicing the laptops, as well as retrofitting classrooms with Ethernet or wireless connections.

Centers vary in how much instructional design they will do for faculty who are teaching wholly and partly online. On one extreme, some universities expect instructors to learn the necessary software for web-page design, animation, photo and video digitizing and editing, etc. in specialized workshops and on their own. On the other extreme are the institutions that employ instructional designers to do the technical work for the faculty. Most fall in between.

An *A/V or media center* furnishes classrooms with audio/visual equipment at your request. If the library does not, it may maintain a collection of instructionally useful videos and films. In some colleges and universities it also houses instructional technology equipment, training, and consultation. If no such center exists on your campus, your department or college may have its own A/V equipment.

A *women's center* often provides a wider variety of services than the lecture series, library, and support groups that you would expect. It is well worth asking if the one on your campus also sponsors self-development and health workshops, career planning forums, book and study groups, and writers groups. No doubt it offers legal and policy information about sexual harassment as well as emotional support for those who may have a complaint. However, complaints are probably processed by the "equal opportunity" unit described below.

Multicultural and racial/ethnic cultural centers similarly may be a richer instructional resource than one might expect—and an essential one on today's highly diverse campuses. They usually offer symposia and lectures on cultural topics and coordinate multicultural celebrations and commemorations. Many of them maintain libraries of print materials and videos—most valuable if you are teaching multicultural subjects—and a few sponsor art exhibits and musical performances. Typically they also provide support services for students of colors.

Of particular value to faculty and staff are their cultural awareness programs, including diversity training workshops. These centers can also answer your private questions about the minority student population on your campus and cultural differences between various groups. They will help you resolve any concerns about relating to students of color in the classroom.

An *international center* typically provides acculturation counseling and support for international students and their families, as well as legal advice on visas, work permits, taxes, etc. On some campuses, the international center is also responsible for ESL (English as a Second Language) testing and courses. It usually assists non-internationals as well, often serving as the primary information source on opportunities to work and study abroad and on social and cultural differences between Americans and natives of other countries.

An *equal opportunity center* may go by any number of titles, but you should look for key words such as "opportunity development," "affirmative action," "equality," "equity," and "civil rights." Its purpose is to coordinate state and federally mandated programs designed to ensure equal opportunities for minorities, women, individuals with disabilities, and other disadvantaged groups. It also serves as a source of information for students, faculty, and staff who may have questions or complaints related to equal opportunity in education, employment, and campus programs and activities. If a complaint is judged valid, it will also advise on grievance procedures.

Sexual harassment falls under the equal opportunity umbrella. Often in collaboration with a women's center (see above), an equal opportunity office disseminates information on the legal definition of sexual harassment, the institution's policy regarding it, specific types of harassment behavior, its prevalence, its prevention, procedures for filing a complaint or a grievance, and confidential support and counseling services.

A *disabilities center* identifies students with learning as well as physical disabilities and usually issues written certification of these disabilities for instructors. As required by the Americans with Disabilities Act (ADA) of 1990, this type of center ensures that people with disabilities have equal access to public programs and services. Therefore, it also recommends the special accommodations, if any, that instructors should make for identified students in their teaching and testing.

Most accommodations are minor (e.g., an isolated test environment and/or a longer test period), and the center may provide special facilities for them (e.g., proctored testing rooms). In any case, it will advise the instructor about exactly what accommodations are needed. For the hearing-impaired classroom student, the instructor may have to stand or sit where the student can lip-read. For a visually impaired classroom student, you may have to vocalize or verbally describe any visual materials you present or distribute to the class. Appropriate testing may require your making a large-print copy of the exam or allowing the students to use a reader, scribe, or typewriter during the test.

Online learning demands more extensive adaptations, but usually the student's own specialized computer hardware and software will take care of most access problems. Still, instructors must be mindful to keep web pages uncluttered and to provide captions or transcripts for audio materials and text alternatives for visual materials.

The centers above may serve your own or your students' needs. Let's consider now the units and individuals that specialize in serving students. Students seeking general academic counsel should be referred to their academic advisers; those requesting information or assistance with respect to a specific course should be sent to the instructor or the department. At times, however, students need help with other problems, some that most instructors are ill-equipped to address. These include learning disabilities, math or test anxiety, severe writing problems, poor study and test-taking skills, weak academic backgrounds, emotional difficulties, and career planning questions. These cases call for a referral to a unit in the next group.

Almost all campuses have a facility designed to help students improve their academic skills. It is often called a **learning, learning skills, learning resources, academic assistance,** or **academic support center**, and its services typically include individual counseling in academic skills, individual and small group tutoring, workshops in learning strategies (e. g., reading skills, study skills, note-taking, test preparation, and test-taking). Some tutoring may be geared to specific courses or subject matter that are known to give students trouble, such as calculus, chemistry, physics, biology, economics, and foreign languages. This type of center may also offer ESL testing and courses.

A **writing or communication program** may be housed in a learning center or comprise its own stand-alone unit. It is likely to provide individual and/or small-group tutoring in the mechanics of grammar and punctuation as well as the structure of exam essays, short papers, critical papers, and research papers. It may even schedule formal writing workshops. Staff are trained not to outline or edit student work, but rather to show students how to master the

stages of the writing process on their own.

If "communication" is in the title, the unit may be one of a small but growing number of centers that also help students improve their public speaking and presentation skills. These are usually associated with an active speaking- or communication-across-the-curriculum program.

A **psychological** or **counseling center** is the place to refer students who manifest any type of psychological or emotional disorder. As they usually show signs of trouble only in more private environments, Chapter 9 on office hours lists the behaviors to watch out for. This type of unit gives free individual counseling for psychological, emotional, and sometimes academic problems, and it may coordinate group programs for personal growth, self-improvement, and self-awareness. If it is associated with a medical facility or it has a physician on staff, it may also prescribe psychotropic drugs.

A **career center** helps students identify and achieve their occupational goals. It typically provides assessment tests in skills and interests and resources for career exploration as well as information on internship opportunities and summer jobs. Workshops on job search strategies, résumé preparation, communication and decision-making skills, and job interview techniques may also available.

All of these campus units will welcome your requests for further information and will point you to their web page or mail you their brochures, newsletters, and any other materials they furnish for students. They are well worth

8

learning about as they are "service centers" with a service orientation. They exist to meet your and/or your students' needs, whether they be instructional, professional, or personal. Unless their resources are already stretched beyond capacity, they actively pursue and benefit from increasing usage. So if they can make your life as an instructor easier or more fulfilling, if they can save you class and office-hour time, if they can handle any of the many student requests and problems that pass through your office door, by all means take advantage of their invaluable services.

Understanding Your Students

Whenever we prepare an oral presentation, a publication, or letter, one of the first issues we consider is our audience. The person or people to receive our message influences our content, format, organization, sentence structure, and word choice. The same holds true in teaching. The nature of our students—their academic preparation, aspirations, and cognitive development—affects our choices of what and how to teach. Try to think of your job not as teaching art, biology, English, history, math, psychology, etc. but as teaching *students*.

Your Undergraduate Student Body Profile

If you're not already familiar with your student audience, or your recent experience tells you that its composition is changing, your institution's admissions or student affairs office can provide the type of student data you need. At a minimum, you should find out the distributions and percentages on these variables: age; marital and parental status; race and ethnicity; full-time and part-time employed; campus residents versus commuters; native versus international; geographical mix; and special admissions. If your students are primarily young, on-campus residents, you can afford to make more collaborative out-of-class assignments.

You also need to know your students' level of academic preparation and achievement. You can assess your institution's selectivity by comparing the number of applicants each year with the number of those accepted (a 2:1 ratio or above is highly selective). For each entering class, you can find out about its average scholastic test scores (SATs and ACTs), the percentage that ranked at varying percentiles of their high school graduating classes, the percentage of National Merit and National Achievement Finalists (over 5% is high), and the percentage that qualified for advanced placement credit (over a third is high). For several hundred American colleges and universities, almost all this information is published every September in the "America's Best Colleges" issue of *U.S. News and World Report*.

If your student body is largely young and traditional, ask about the high school leadership positions and activities of a given class. Your institution's career center should also have on file the percentage of students planning on different types of graduate and professional educations, as well as the immediate employment plans of the next graduating class.

How People Learn

Whatever your student body profile, certain well-research principles about how people learn will apply.

1. People are born learners, beginning with an insatiable childhood curiosity. They absorb and remember untold billions of details about objects, other people, their language, and things they know how to do (Spence, 2001).

2. People learn through "elaborative rehearsal," which means connecting new knowledge to what they already know (Tigner, 1999).

3. People learn socially by constructing knowledge in a group (Stage et al, 1999), but they otherwise learn one-on-one and on their own (Spence, 2001).

4. People *don't* learn well when their major learning context is "teacher-centered"—that is, they passively listen to a teacher talk (Spence, 2001).

5. People learn when they are actively engaged in a life experience (Bonwell and Eison, 1993; Spence, 2001).

6. People learn when that life experience evokes *emotional* and not just intellectual or physical involvement. In other words, people must be *inspired* to want to learn a certain content. This learning pattern mirrors the biological basis of learning, which is the close communication between the frontal lobes of the brain and the limbic system. From a biological point of view, learning entails a change in the brain, the establishment of desirable new synapses (Leamnson, 1999, 2000).

These key learning principles have some complementary teaching principles, most of which will echo through later pages of this book:

- Hold your students to high expectations. (But be reasonable; very few students will choose the life of the mind as you have.)
- Start where your students are. Find out what they already know (and don't know), and become familiar with their life styles. Then relate the new content, skills, and abilities you are teaching to what is familiar to them, both cognitively and experientially. Use examples and analogies out of their lives and generation.
- Assign creative, inventive, and challenging tasks to small groups and more routine learning tasks, such as first-exposure reading and standard problem sets, as individual homework. Some students will need tutoring after their individual attempts at learning, which you, a TA, or group members can provide. Reflection and writing are also individual learning activities, even though they can be very challenging and creative.
- Use active learning techniques, and when you do lecture, do so interactively (with frequent breaks for student activities).
- When possible, use experiential methods, those which place students in real-life problem-solving situations, simulated or genuine.
- Motivate learning with emotions. Make a learning experience dramatic, humorous, surprising, joyous, maddening, exciting, or heart-wrenching. Any emotion will aid learning by inducing changes in the brain.

The Adult Learner

Adults learn the same way as

traditional-age students, but they respond somewhat differently to certain instructor behaviors, teaching strategies, and content emphases. They are less forgiving about an instructor being poorly prepared, having questionable expertise, and not having suitable supplementary materials. They value their own life experience (for good reason) and want to share and discuss it in small groups and as a class. As they know the world to be complex, they expect to learn multiple ways of solving problems and to have discretion in applying the material. They need the opportunity for reflection after trying out a new application or method. Rote learning just won't work with them. Finally, adult learners are practical and are usually quite disinterested in theory. They demand that the materials have immediate utility and relevant application (Wlodkowski, 1993; Vella, 1994). None of this implies that they are difficult learners. In fact, they are often highly motivated, eagerly participatory, and well prepared for class.

Inclusive Instructing

Age is but one variable on which your students vary. Another one we addressed in the first chapter is disability, along with the accommodations instructors should make. Add gender, race, ethnicity, national origin, sexual orientation, and religion. Time was when only white males attended college in the U.S. In 2001 54 percent of all undergraduates were female, 11 percent African American, 8 percent Hispanic, and 6 percent Asian American (Trower and Chait, 2002).

While all people learn by the same basic processes described above, some of these groups educationally thrive under circumstances

that are not always typical in the American classroom. In addition, they often share distinctive values, norms, background experiences, and a sense of community that set them apart and make *them* feel set apart—and not always in a positive way. Certainly, traditionally underrepresented groups are more likely to struggle emotionally in college and to leave before attaining a degree.

As an instructor, you are also an ambassador of the academy to these groups, and you are close enough to them to reach out and include them. How you relate to these students has a powerful impact on their performance and retention (Ferguson, 1989; Kobrak, 1992; Grant-Thompson and Atkinson, 1997). Here are some guidelines:

- Assign and mention the scholarly and artistic contributions of diverse groups, where appropriate (Toombs and Tierney, 1992).
- Call a group by the name that its members prefer.
- Develop a personal rapport with your African American, Native American, Hispanic, and female students. Their style of thinking and dealing with the world tends to be "relational" and "interpersonal," which means intuitive, cooperative, holistic, subjective, relationship-focused, motivated by personal loyalty, interested in discussion to reconcile disagreement and find common ground, and oriented to socially relevant topics (Anderson and Adams, 1992; Baxter Magolda, 1992). This style contrasts with the "analytical," which values analysis, objectivity, logic, reason, structure, sequence, the abstract, debate, challenge, competition, and practicality. It

is prevalent among European and Asian American males, and in the academy in general (Anderson and Adams, 1992). How closely and easily you relate to your diverse and female students will strongly affect their motivation to learn, their trust in your intentions for them, and their overall satisfaction with college (Nettles, 1988; Allen et al, 1991; Kobrak, 1992; Grant-Thompson and Atkinson, 1997; Gonsalves, 2002).

- Be aware that most international students stand closer to others than do Americans, that most Asian-American women are taught to avoid eye contact, and that many Asian Americans and Native Americans have learned to listen quietly rather than jumping into discourse.

- Don't avoid course-appropriate topics related to diverse groups because they are sensitive, controversial, or applicable to only a minority of people. Some students will see your avoidance as prejudicial.

- Don't avoid giving timely, constructive feedback to diverse students about their work out of fear of injuring their self-esteem or being accused of racism. Indeed, diverse students *may* interpret your criticisms as racially motivated disrespect, so you should bring up this possibility yourself and explicitly ask them, rather than sweeping the issue under the rug. Be very sure that the students really understand your criticisms and recommendations for improvement (Gonsalves, 2002).

- Don't make so much of their successes that you imply you didn't expect them to succeed.

- Don't let any students get away with insensitive remarks in class. Such incidents open up "teachable moments" for you to lead an open discussion about cultural differences and stereotyping.

- Don't ask diverse students to speak in class as representatives of their group. Whatever the group, it is too diverse to be represented by one or a few members.

Now let us return to common qualities and patterns in students.

The Cognitive Development of Undergraduates

No matter how bright or mature your prospective students may be, do not expect them to have reached a high level of cognitive maturity in your discipline. Almost all students, especially freshmen and sophomores, begin a course of study with serious misconceptions about knowledge in general and the discipline specifically. Adult learners are no exception. Only as these misconceptions are dispelled do students mature intellectually through distinct stages. As an instructor, you have the opportunity—some would say the responsibility—to lead them through these stages to epistemological maturity.

Psychologist William G. Perry (1968, 1985) formulated a theory of the intellectual and ethical development of college students (see Table I). The research supporting it accumulated rapidly, making Perry's the leading theory on the cognitive development of undergraduates. Baxter Magolda's (1992) four levels of knowing—absolute, transitional, independent, and contextual—roughly parallel Perry's, but most females follow a "relational" pattern and most males the "abstract."

Table I

PERRY'S STAGES OF UNDERGRADUATE COGNITIVE DEVELOPMENT

1. **DUALITY**: Uncertainty doesn't exist. Authorities hold the right answers.

2. **MULTIPLICITY a)**: Uncertainty exists due to incompetent authorities OR instructor is just leading an intellectual exercise.

3. **MULTIPLICITY b)**: Uncertainty exists only temporarily while authorities seek answers.

4. **RELATIVISM a)**: Uncertainty is inherent and pervasive, rendering all opinions equal in value.

5. **RELATIVISM b)**: Relativism is qualified—not for purely factual and special contexts (e.g., moral).

6. **COMMITMENT a)**: Relativism weakens under qualifications and internal contradictions. Commitment is sought.

7. **COMMITMENT b)**: A tentative personal commitment to a certain viewpoint is made.

8. **COMMITMENT c)**: The meaning of commitment and its trade-offs are examined.

9. **COMMITMENT d)**: Making and adjusting commitments becomes part of the life-long pursuit of personal growth and wisdom.

Understanding Your Students

14 While Perry's framework of development applies across disciplines, a student's level of maturity may be advanced in one and not in another. So we shouldn't assume, for example, that a sophisticated senior in a laboratory science major has a comparable understanding of the nature of knowledge in the social sciences or the humanities.

The more elaborate version of Perry's theory posits nine positions through which students pass on their way to cognitive maturity. (Perry also developed a simpler model of four stages, which are referred to in italics below.) How far and how rapidly students progress through the hierarchy depends largely on the quality and type of instruction they receive. It is this "flexible" aspect of Perry's theory that has made it particularly attractive and useful. The schema suggests ways that we as instructors can accelerate our undergraduates' intellectual growth.

Let us begin with position 1, the cognitive state in which most freshmen arrive. (Of course, some sophomores, juniors, and seniors are still at this level.) Perry used the term *dualism* to describe students' thinking at this stage because they perceive the world in black-and-white simplicity. They decide what to believe and how to act according to absolute standards of right and wrong, good and bad, truth and falsehood. Authority figures, like instructors, supposedly know and teach the absolute truths about reality. Further, all knowledge and goodness can be quantified or tallied, like correct answers on a spelling test.

At position 2, students enter the general cognitive stage of *multiplicity*. They come to realize that since uncertainty exists, so does a multiplicity of opinions. But to them the variety merely reflects that not all authorities are equally legitimate or competent. Some students don't even give these competing opinions much credence, believing them to be just an instructor's exercise designed ultimately to lead them to the one true answer. As they advance to position 3, they accept the notion that genuine uncertainty exists, but only as a temporary state that will resolve once an authority finds the answer.

Entering position 4, which marks the broader stage of *relativism*, students make an about-face and abandon their faith in authority's ability to identify "the truth." At this point, they either consider all views equally valid or allow different opinions within the limits delineated by some standard. In brief, they become relativists with no hope of there ever being one true interpretation or answer.

Students at position 5 formalize the idea that all knowledge is relativistic and contextual, but with qualifications. They may reserve dualistic ideas of right and wrong as subordinate principles for special cases in specific contexts. Thus, even in a relativistic world, they may permit certain instances where facts are truly facts and only one plausible truth exists.

At some point, however, students can no longer accommodate all the internal inconsistencies and ambiguities inherent in position 5. They may want to make choices but often lack clear standards for doing so. So they begin to feel the need to orient themselves in their relativistic world by making some sort of personal commitment. As this need grows, they pass through position 6 and into the more general cognitive stage of *commitment*. When they actually make an initial, tentative commitment to a particular view in some area, they attain position 7. Next, at position 8, they experience and examine the impacts and implications of their choice of commitment. That is, they learn what commitment means and what trade-offs it carries.

Finally, at position 9, students realize that trying on a commitment and either embracing or modifying it in the hindsight of experience is a major part of personal and intellectual growth. This process is, in fact, a life-long activity that paves the road toward wisdom and requires an ever open mind.

Encouraging Cognitive Growth

Nelson (1993), a leading authority on developing thinking skills, contends that we can facilitate students' progress through these stages by familiarizing them with *uncertainty* and *standards of comparison* in our disciplines. He and many others have achieved excellent results by implementing his ideas. (Kloss, 1994, offers a somewhat different approach tailored to literature instructors.)

Exposure to uncertainties in our knowledge bases helps students realize that often there is no one superior truth, nor can there be, given the nature of rational knowledge. This realization helps lead them out of dualistic thinking (position 1) and through multiplistic conceptions of knowledge (positions 2 and 3). Once they can understand uncertainty as legitimate and inherent in the nature of knowledge, they can mature into relativists (positions 4 and 5).

Instructive examples of such uncertainties include the following: 1) the range of viable interpretations that can be made of certain works of literature and art; 2) the different conclusions that can be legitimately drawn from the same historical evidence and scientific data; 3) a discipline's history of scientific revolutions and paradigm shifts; 4) unresolved issues on which a discipline is currently conducting research; and 5) historical and scientific unknowns that may or may not ever be resolved.

Our next step is to help students advance beyond relativism through positions 6 and 7, at which point they can make tentative commitments and progress towards cognitive maturity. To do so, students need to understand that, among all the possible answers and interpretations, some, in fact, may be more valid than others. They must also learn *why* some are better than others—that is, what criteria exist to discriminate among the options, to distinguish the wheat from the chaff.

Disciplines vary on their criteria for evaluating validity. Each one has its own "metacognitive model"—that is, a set of accepted conventions about what makes a sound argument and what constitutes appropriate evidence. Most students have trouble acquiring these conventions on their own; they tend to assume that the rules are invariable across fields. So Nelson advises us to make our concepts of evidence and our standards for comparison explicit to our students.

By the time students reach position 5, they are uncomfortable with their relativism, and by position 6, they are hungry for criteria on which to rank options and base choices. So they should be very receptive to a discipline's evaluative framework.

To encourage students to reach positions 7 and 8, we can provide writing and discussion opportunities for them to deduce and examine what their initial commitments imply in other contexts. They might apply their currently preferred framework to a new or different ethical case, historical event, social phenomenon, political issue, scientific problem, or piece of literature. They may even apply it to a real situation in their own lives. Through this process, they begin to realize that a commitment focuses options, closing some doors while opening others.

We should remind students that they are always free to reassess their commitments, to modify them, and even to make new ones, but with an intellectual and ethical caveat: They should have sound reason to do so, such as new experience or data or a more logical organization of the evidence—not just personal convenience. With a clear understanding of this final point, students achieve position 9.

Bringing Perry's and Nelson's insights into our courses presents a genuine challenge in that students in any one class may be at different stages, even if they are in the same graduating class. Most freshmen are likely to fall in the first few positions, but juniors and seniors may be anywhere on the hierarchy. It may be wisest, then, to help students at the lower positions catch up with those at the higher ones by including knowledge uncertainties, disciplinary criteria for comparison, and opportunities for students to make and justify choices in as many courses as possible.

Keep your students' cognitive growth in mind as you read other chapters in this book. If you try out the objective-centered approach to designing a course, which is outlined in the next chapter, you may want to select a certain level of cognitive maturity as a learning objective for your students.

You will find more strategies for teaching uncertainty and alternative explanations in Chapter 13 on the discovery method. Chapter 21 on teaching your students to think and write revisits the notion of metacognitive models in greater detail and examines some crucial differences in argumentation and evidence across major disciplinary groups.

For further reading:

Aslanian, C.B. 2001. *Adult Students Today.* New York: The College Board.

Featherstone, B.J. 1999. *The Millennial Generation: Leading Today's Youth into the Future.* Salt Lake City: Deseret Books.

Hersch, P. 1998. *A Tribe Apart: A Journey into the Heart of American Adolescence.* New York: Ballantine.

Howe, N. and W. Strauss. 2000. *Millennials Rising: The Next Generation.* New York: Vintage.

In the Beginning:
Course Design by Objectives

Teaching has only one purpose, and that is to facilitate learning (Cross, 1988). Learning can occur without teaching at no loss to anyone, but teaching can and unfortunately often does occur without learning. In the latter case, the students obviously lose time, money, potential gains in knowledge and cognitive development, and perhaps confidence in themselves and/or the educational system. But less obviously, instructors lose faith in their students and in themselves. For our own mental health as well as our students', we need to make teaching and learning synonymous sides of the same coin.

This is easy to do if you design a course wisely. Whether you are teaching an established course for the first time, developing a brand new course, or revising a course you currently teach, you should ask yourself what you are trying to accomplish. No doubt, you want your students to learn certain things, to master a body of material. But you can't assess how well you've met this goal, nor can you assess your students' learning, unless you have them *do* something with that material that demonstrates their learning. What they do may involve writing, discussing, acting, creating a visual work, conducting an experiment, making an oral presentation, designing a web page, teaching a lesson, or any other "display" of learning, as long as you can perceive it though your senses. How else can you determine their internal state—what they know, realize, and understand?

Why Course Design by Objectives?

This chapter proposes starting the course design process with what you want your students to be able to do by the end of the course. But other approaches exist. You can organize a course around your favorite textbook, or the one you've been told to use. You can also develop a course around a list of content topics you consider important to cover. However, these approaches will not ensure that your course is student-active, which we know is essential for learning, or acceptable to your institution's or your school's accrediting agency.

"Course design by objectives" guarantees a high level of student engagement because the process steers you towards student-active teaching strategies. It also conforms to the accountability requirements of an increasing number of accrediting agencies. These agencies hold a unit accountable for meeting certain student learning outcomes and for conducting performance assessments of its success in meeting them. In other words, they require departments and schools to determine what they want their students to be able to do, at least upon graduation, and to produce materials that show what the students can do. Some agencies even take it upon themselves to specify exactly what graduates of a certain area should be able to do.

What Is an Objective?

Before 1990, the term "course objective" or "course goal" described the range of content that a course was supposed to cover, such as "a comprehensive survey of vertebrate animals including their taxonomy, morphology, evolution, and defining facets of their natural history and behavior" or "an introduction to the process of literary criticism." Students could find this type of objective for any course in the course catalog, and they still can. These objectives, as well as similar ones we may write ourselves for the first section of our syllabi, are more *for* ourselves, however. They specify what *we* want to do in the course, especially in terms of content. These are called *general objectives* (Gronlund, 1985; Pregent, 1994).

A course is best designed around another type of objective. It is most commonly known as a *student learning objective, instructional objective*, or *student outcome*, but it's also been called a *specific objective* (Gronlund, 1985; Pregent, 1994). It describes what students must be able to *do* if we are to meet our own general objectives. Thus they are written from a student's point of view—e.g., "After studying the processes of photosynthesis and respiration, the student should be able to trace the carbon cycle in a given ecosystem."

In brief, a general objective reflects the major themes and content of a course, while learning objectives, as we will call them from

here on, detail the behavioral means to the general objectives.

Both types belong in your syllabus (see Chapter 4). If you don't share them, students may justifiably wonder what they are supposed to gain from your course, and they may wander aimlessly looking for it.

Before Writing Learning Objectives

First, find out from your dean or department chair if the learning objectives for your course have already been mandated by an accrediting agency. For instance, the National Council for the Accreditation of Teacher Education (NCATE) specifies objectives for many education courses. The Accreditation Board for Engineering and Technology (ABET) provides program objectives, some of which may be useful and even essential for your course.

If you, like most instructors, are free to develop your own learning objectives, you might first want to research the history of the course. Why was it proposed and approved in the first place, and by whom? What special purposes does it serve? Often new courses emerge to meet the needs of a changing labor market, to update curriculum content, to ensure accreditation, or to give an institution a competitive edge. Knowing the underlying influences can help you orient a course to its intended purposes for student learning (Pregent, 1994) .

Second, get to know who your students are so you can aim your course to their needs and level. Refer to the first part of Chapter 2 for the type of student data you will need—all of which should be available from your institution's admissions office, student affairs office, and career center—to determine the abilities, background knowledge, interests, and course expectations of your likely student population. Ask colleagues who have taught the course before about what topics, books, teaching methods, activities, assignments, etc. worked and didn't work well for them. The more relevant you can make the material to the target group, the more effective your course will be.

If you cannot gather much information in advance, plan to keep your initial learning objectives and course design somewhat flexible. On the first day of class, use index cards and ice breakers to find out more about your students and their expectations (see Chapter 7), then adjust and tighten the design accordingly.

Writing Learning Objectives

A learning objective is a statement of exactly what your students should be able *to do* after completing your course or at specified points during the course. Technically, it has three parts to it, though usually only the first part appears in the learning-objectives section of a syllabus. Sooner or later, however, you will probably have to define the second and third parts as well.

Part 1. A statement of a measurable performance.
Learning objectives center on action verbs (e.g., define, classify, construct, compute; see Table I) rather than nebulous verbs reflecting internal states that cannot be observed (e.g., know, learn, understand, realize, appreciate). For example: "The student will be able to *classify* given rocks as igneous or metamorphic." "The student will be able to *describe* the most important

differences between sedimentary and metamorphic rocks." See Table II for many more examples.

Part 2. A statement of conditions for the performance.
These conditions define the circumstances under which the student's performance will be assessed. Will she have to demonstrate that she knows the differences among igneous, metamorphic, and sedimentary rocks *in writing*, in *an oral presentation*, or *in a visual medium* (drawings, photographs)? Will he be able to identify the parts of a computer system *on a diagram* or *in an actual computer*?

Part 3. Criteria and standards for assessing the performance.
By what criteria and standards will you evaluate and ultimately grade a student's performance? What will constitute just barely meeting the learning objective (C work) versus giving an excellent performance (A work)? For example: "For an A on essay #3, the student will be able to identify in writing at least three differences between igneous and metamorphic rocks, at least three between igneous and sedimentary rocks, and at least three between metamorphic and sedimentary—for a total of *at least nine differences*. For a B, the student will be able to identify *at least six differences*. For a C, the student will be able to identify *at least four differences*, etc.

Types of Learning Objectives

Virtually every college level course has *cognitive* learning objectives, those pertaining to thinking. But there are other types worth mentioning as well. *Affective* objectives specify emotional abilities you may want your students to

19

Course Design by Objectives

Table I

Student Performance Verbs by Level of Cognitive Operation Based on Bloom's Taxonomy

1. Knowledge

arrange	order
define	recall
duplicate	recite
label	recognize
list	relate
memorize	repeat
name	reproduce

2. Comprehension

classify	locate
describe	recognize
discuss	report
explain	restate
express	review
identify	select
indicate	translate

3. Application

apply	interpret
choose	operate
compose examples	practice
demonstrate	schedule
dramatize	sketch
employ	solve
illustrate	use

4. Analysis

analyze	differentiate
appraise	discriminate
calculate	distinguish
categorize	examine
compare	experiment
contrast	question
criticize	test

5. Synthesis

arrange	integrate
assemble	manage
collect	organize
compose	plan
construct	predict
create	prepare
design	propose
formulate	set up

6. Evaluation

appraise	evaluate
argue	judge
assess	rate
challenge	score
choose	select
defend	support
dispute	value

*Depending on the use, some verbs may apply to more than one level.

Table II

Models of Specific Objectives Based on Bloom's Taxonomy

Level	The student should be able to...
Knowledge	define iambic pentameter state Newton's Laws of Motion identify the major surrealist painters
Comprehension	describe the trends in the graph in her own words summarize the passage from Socrates' *Apology* properly translate into English the paragraph from Voltaire's *Candide*

Application	describe an experiment to test the influence of
	    light and light quality on the Hill reaction of
	    photosynthesis
	scan a poem for metric foot and rhyme scheme
	use the Archimedes Principle to determine the volume
	    of an irregularly shaped object

Analysis	list arguments for and against human cloning
	determine the variables to be controlled for an
	    experiment
	discuss the rationale and efficacy of isolationism
	    in the global economy

Synthesis	write a short story in Hemingway's style compose a logical argument on assisted suicide in opposition to your personal opinion construct a helium-neon laser

Evaluation	assess the validity of certain conclusions based on the
	    data and statistical analysis
	give a critical analysis of a novel with evidence to
	    support the analysis
	recommend stock investments based on recent
	    company performance and projected value

Course Design by Objectives

develop—to receive, to respond, and to value (Krathwolh, 1999). In nursing, counseling, and the ministry, for example, it is important that students learn to show empathy and open-mindedness towards patients and clients, even if their performance can be assessed only in a role play or in a case analysis. Such abilities are also very useful in management, medicine, human resources, marketing, and architecture.

Psychomotor skills—the ability to manipulate specific objects correctly and efficiently to accomplish a specific purpose—constitute another type of learning objective that is important in art, architecture, drama, linguistics, some engineering fields, all laboratory sciences, nursing and other health-related fields, and foreign languages.

A wide range of disciplines have added *social* learning objectives to their courses, since the workplace has come to rely on teamwork and cooperative learning has been widely accepted. Many instructors want their students to be able to work effectively in a small group, and they consider both the group product and peer performance evaluations in assessing students' progress in meeting this objective.

Ethical learning objectives are now coming to the fore with new ethics-across-the-curriculum programs. Some institutions and schools are working to ensure that their students take into account the moral considerations and implications in making professional, scientific, technical, and business decisions. The case method, simulations, role plays, service learning, field work, and internships provide both learning and assessment contexts for ethical objectives.

For the purpose of brevity, the rest of this chapter will focus on writing and designing a course around *cognitive* learning objectives, since they are universal.

A Cognitive Hierarchy of Objectives

Bloom (1956) developed a useful taxonomy for constructing cognitive learning objectives. His framework posits a hierarchy of six cognitive processes, moving from the most concrete, lowest-level process of recalling stored knowledge through several intermediate cognitive modes to the most abstract, highest level of evaluation. (Depending upon your field, you may prefer to place *application* at a higher level.) Each level is defined:

Knowledge: the ability to remember and state previously learned material

Comprehension: the ability to grasp the meaning of material and to restate it in one's own words

Application: the ability to use learned material in new and concrete situations

Analysis: the ability to break down material into its component parts so as to understand its organizational structure

Synthesis: the ability to put parts together to form a new whole

Evaluation: the ability to judge the value of material for a given purpose.

To make these terms more concrete, refer to Table I, which lists common student performance verbs for each cognitive operation. You may find it helpful to start developing specific objects from this listing. Simply check the cognitive operations that you'd like your students to be able to perform. Table II gives examples of specific objectives in various disciplines.

Bear in mind that the true cognitive level of a specific objective depends upon the material students are given in a course. If they are handed a formal definition of iambic pentameter, then their defining it is a simple recall or, at most, comprehension operation. If, however, they are only provided with examples of poems and plays written in it and are asked to abstract a definition from the examples, they are then engaging in the much higher-order process of synthesis.

As you check key verbs and construct learning objectives, think about what cognitive operations you are emphasizing. We can foster critical thinking only by setting objectives above the knowledge and comprehension levels. While these lower levels furnish foundations for learning, they are not the end of education. Therefore, it is wise to include some higher-order objectives to challenge students to higher levels of thinking. We will revisit Bloom's taxonomy in Chapter 16 as it is also very useful for framing questions.

Course Design by Objectives

Your learning objectives serve as a scaffolding for your course design. The process of developing an entire course around these objectives is quite simple.

First, formulate your *ultimate* or end-of-the-course learning objectives. These will probably be your most complex and cognitively advanced learning outcomes for your students. No doubt they will require application, analysis, synthesis, and/or evaluation.

Then work backwards, asking what your students will have to be able to do *before* they can accomplish each ultimate learning objective. These are your *mediating* ob-

jectives. Probably your students will have to be able to do several things before they can do well in your ultimate objectives. Very likely these mediating objectives have a logical internal order of their own—that is, students will have to master one type of task *early* in the semester before they can take on a more complex one. So keep working backwards, sorting out which mediating objectives must precede others.

Eventually you work your way back to the beginning of your course, when your learning objectives involve one or more of the following:

1) Your students will master the lowest-level cognitive operations on the subject, recalling and paraphrasing basic facts, processes, and definitions of essential terms and concepts.

2) They will release their dualistic thinking as they discover uncertainties in the field.

3) They will identify and question misconceptions about the subject matter that they first bring into the classroom.

These are perhaps the most basic learning objectives we can set for our students. After all, they can't apply, analyze, synthesize, or evaluate knowledge that they can't summarize or paraphrase. They can't truly explore a knowledge base if they don't grasp its basic uncertainties and the field's standards for evaluating competing interpretations. And they cannot accurately map new, valid knowledge onto existing knowledge that is riddled with misconceptions and misinformation (Nelson, 1993).

To visualize the process of designing a course by working backwards, picture a branching-tree diagram that "grows" from three or more main "trunks" (ultimate learning objectives) on the far right and branches out to the left. These branches represent the basic and mediating objectives that your students must meet before they can attempt the more advanced objectives to the right.

Course Development by Objectives

Course content. Now that you have clear and comprehensive learning objectives, you can select the content that will provide your student the best background for meeting them. The challenge is to limit the content to *only* this purpose. If you specialize in the content area, it will be difficult to narrow it.

Pregent advises brainstorming as many topics and themes as possible. For help, you can consult tables of contents of reputable texts, course catalogs and syllabi from other institutions, and colleagues. Then rank-order the topics according to their relevance to your learning objectives.

Do not hesitate to eliminate topics entirely. Instructors, especially new ones, tend to pack too much material into a course. It is better to teach a few topics well than merely to "cover the material" with a steamroller and wind up teaching very little of anything.

Book selections. Choose books in line with your learning objectives and content. If you are looking specifically for a textbook, you will be fortunate to find one that reflects your general philosophy and preferences. If you're not so lucky, consider selecting the best available option for some of your reading assignments and supplementing it with handouts, reserve readings, web sites, and/or a class packet.

Try to avoid making students purchase more than one expensive text.

Class activities, assignments, and tests. Your learning objectives should direct all the other elements of your course. First, look at your ultimate learning objectives. They should suggest questions or at least foci, themes, or formats for your final exam, final paper assignment, or capstone student project. After all, these objectives delineate what you want your students to be able to do by the end of the course.

Then move backwards through your mediating objectives. Consider how they suggest questions, formats, and themes for quizzes and tests, graded and ungraded homework assignments, and in-class activities. In fact, your objectives can provide a scaffolding for planning every class meeting. If you want your students to be able to write a certain type of analysis by a certain week of the term, then structure assignments and in-class activities that will give them practice in writing that type of analysis. If you want them to be able to solve certain kinds of problems, then design assignments and activities that will give them practice in solving such problems. If you want them to research and develop a point of view, then argue it orally, then give in-class and homework assignments involving research, rhetoric, and oral presentation.

Put simply, move backwards from your learning objectives to plan how to move your students forward. Then fill in your classes and assignments with instruction, guidance, and plenty of practice in how to meet your objectives.

Figure I gives an example of how one instructor moved backwards (or

Figure I.

**Flowchart of Learning Objectives
—Basic, Mediating, and Ultimate—
For a Cross-Disciplinary Course,
"Free Will and Determinism"**

<u>Ultimate Learning Objective</u>

To develop and explain in writing a well-reasoned personal position on the
role of free will, determinism, compatibilism, fatalism, and spiritual destiny in your own and others' lives, and to defend it while acknowledging
its weaknesses and limitations (capstone paper, #3)

<u>Mediating Learning Objectives</u>

To assess how research
and research-based writings
support or refute each
position. (readings &
in-class discussions weeks
6-12, paper #2 due week 12)

To assess how one's
own life experiences
support or refute each
position (journaling
& online discussions
weeks 6-14)

To refute positions from the viewpoints of other positions
(simulation/mock trial week 6, based on paper #1)

To apply the positions to interpret and assess a situation
(paper #1 on criminal case due week 6)

<u>Basic Learning Objectives</u>
To express accurate orally and in writing the free willist,
determinist, compatibilist, fatalist, and spiritual destiny
positions, along with their assumptions and justifications
(readings, study questions, in-class writing exercises,
in-class and online discussions weeks 1-5)

downward in this example) from one ultimate learning objective to mediating and basic objectives that support it. In parentheses after each objective are the activities selected to help the students meet it, followed by the week(s) in the semester that the activities occur. The activities include three papers, readings, in-class and online discussions, journaling, a simulation, study questions, and in-class writing exercises. This flowchart serves as a general outline for developing a class-by-class schedule and detailed descriptions of the activities and assignments.

Other tasks. You may or may not have to tend to other course preparation tasks as well. If you are teaching in a relatively unfamiliar area, you will have to research the subject matter. If you haven't taught the course for a while, you may have to update it. Of course, you'll have to write the syllabus (see Chapter 4) as well as orient and train any support staff you may manage, such as TAs (see Chapter 5).

What if your objectives are soundly written (e.g., begin with action verbs) but don't suggest to you appropriate activities, assignments, and test questions? It may be that you aren't yet familiar with the wide range of effective options to choose from. Explore the many dozens of teaching techniques, classroom formats, and assignment ideas in the later chapters of this book. You will find the class-by-class bricks and mortar for building a successful learning experience onto your course design scaffolding. They will help ensure that your teaching translates into learning.

Once you have a sound course design, your syllabus almost writes itself. The next chapter presents a concise checklist of all the information that can and usually should be included in this important course document.

The Complete
Syllabus

A syllabus is most simply defined as a concise outline of a course of study. But it is also the students' introduction to the course, the subject matter, and *you*. In addition to providing a schedule of class assignments, readings, and activities, it should give students insight into and appreciation for the material. In a sense, then, it is not only the road map for the term's foray into knowledge but also a travelogue to pique students' interest in the expedition.

While syllabi of just a couple of pages are common, students always have many more questions than a brief syllabus can answer. In addition, some courses call for a great deal of first-day information. So here is a suggested checklist for developing a comprehensive syllabus (Nilson, 1990; Altman and Cashin, 1992; Grunert, 1997). It applies to both printed and online syllabi. If you doubt that your students will read such a lengthy syllabus, you will be interested in the last section on inducing your students to read your syllabus.

Appropriate Syllabus Items

1) Complete course information: the course number and title; days, hours, and location of class meetings; credit hours; any required or recommended prerequisites, including permission of the instructor for enrollment; any required review sessions; and any required laboratories or recitation/ discussion sections, with the same information as given for the course. If any course materials, exercises, assignments, exams, etc. are on the web, be sure to furnish the URLs of the course and any supplementary resources.

2) Information about yourself: your full name and title (so students know how to address you), your office hours, your office location, your office phone number, your e-mail address, your home page URL (if you have one), and your department's phone number (for messages). If you decide to give students your home phone number, you may wish to limit calls to emergencies and to certain hours.

3) The same information about other course personnel, such as TAs, technicians, assistants, etc. You might encourage your section and lab TAs to develop their own syllabi.

4) An annotated list of reading materials (textbooks, journal articles, class packs, web materials, etc.) with full citations (including edition), price, location (bookstore, library, reserve status, URL, etc.), identified as required or recommended, and your reasons for selecting them. If you do not plan to give regular assignments from the text, consider making it a recommended, supplementary source. If commercially prepared notes are available, say how helpful they might be.

5) Any other materials required for the course, including cost estimates and where to find them at a good price. For example, some science labs require students to have a personal stock of cleaning supplies and safety equipment. Art and photography classes usually expect students to furnish their own equipment, supplies, and expendable materials. If special types of calculators, computers, or software are called for, these too should be described in detail. If the materials won't be used immediately, specify when in the semester they will be.

6) A complete course description, including the organization or "flow" of the course, your rationale for it, and the major topics it will address. You may even want to list topics it will *not* cover, especially if your course has too much popular appeal and tends to attract less-than-serious students.

7) Your general and student learning objectives for the course, especially your ultimate learning objectives (what students should be able to do or do better at the end of the term). Mediating and basic learning objectives are optional but helpful. Chapter 3 gives guidance on developing learning objectives and designing a course around them.

To encourage students to take responsibility for their own learning as well as to protect yourself legally, you might add these caveats/disclaimers after the objectives:
1) Students may vary in their competency levels on these abilities.

2) Students can expect to acquire these abilities *only if* they honor all course policies, attend class regularly, complete all assigned work on time and in good faith, and meet all other course requirements and expectations.

8) All graded course requirements and a complete breakdown of your grading scale, preferably buttressed by a rationale. Nothing is so annoying as hearing half of your students bargain for points or ask for a curve after an exam. Detail the point values of all graded work: in-class and homework assignments, peer group evaluations, class participation, discussion, electronic communication, tests, papers, projects, etc. Also comment on the expected number and types of tests and quizzes, homework assignments, and papers. Specify whether lowest-scoring work can be thrown out. Finally, state the grading system you will use (criterion-referenced or a curve), along with percentage breakdowns.

9) The criteria on which each written assignment, project, and oral presentation will be evaluated, including your grading system (atomistic or holistic) and your policies regarding revisions and extra credit. As with post-exam grade protests, the choral call for extra credit can be a nuisance unless your position is firmly established from the start.

10) Other course "requirements" aside from those computed in the grade. If you expect students to participate in class discussions, you must tell them. If you plan to give unannounced, ungraded quizzes to monitor comprehension, then let it be known from the beginning. It is better to ensure that all students understand your expectations from the start than to spring new rules on them later in the term.

11) Your policies on attendance and tardiness.
Instructors occasionally debate whether to grade on attendance or not. As one side puts it, how can students learn and contribute to the class without being there? (As Woody Allen once put it, over 90 percent of success is just showing up.) No question, taking and grading on attendance does increase class attendance (Friedman, Rodriguez, and McComb, 2001). But others argue that students should be free to learn as much or as little as they choose by whatever means they choose. However *you* decide, your syllabus should state your policy.

Including attendance and even tardiness in the final grade (some instructors incorporate it under class participation) is not unusual anymore. Absences are a problem at many institutions, especially in required courses (Friedman, Rodriguez, and McComb, 2001). However, most instructors do not count certain absences, such as those for documented medical reasons, documented court obligations, and athletic team commitments.

Some colleges and universities *require* instructors to report students who are excessively absent, so you may have to keep attendance even if you don't intend to grade on it. Check the section on academic regulations in your institution's catalog.

12) Your policies on missed or late exams and assignments.
Students do occasionally have good reasons for missing a deadline or a test, and you may want to ask for documentation for the reason given. State whether students can drop one quiz/grade during the term or if a make-up is possible. If you assess penalties for late work, describe them precisely to put to rest any later disputes. Find out how you may and may not penalize students by reading the section on academic regulations in your institution's catalog.

13) A statement of your and your institution's policies on academic dishonesty, as well as their applications to your course.
Cheating and plagiarism are all too common on today's college campuses, as Chapter 10 documents. Unless you make a strong statement about your intolerance of them, your students may assume that you are naive or will look the other way. This statement may include a summary of the official procedures you will follow in prosecuting violations and the sanctions a student may suffer. (See your institution's catalog, student handbook, or faculty handbook for details.) If your institution has an honor code, state that you will strictly adhere to and enforce it.

Another reason to address academic honesty policies is to spell out how you will apply them to cooperative learning activities and products. Instructors have to devise their own rules on small-group work. If you don't detail your rules, one of two things are likely to happen: Your students may inadvertently violate your and your institution's policies, or they may not work as cooperatively as you'd like.

14) Proper safety procedures and conduct for laboratories.
While you would hope that students

would have the common sense to apply good safety habits to their work, you cannot assume that these habits are intuitive. Specify strict rules for lab dress and procedures. If you threaten to exact penalties for safety violations, then stand ready to make good on your word. Remember, it is better to take away a few lab points than to risk the safety of the entire section.

15) Relevant campus support services and their locations for assistance in mastering course software, doing computer assignments, writing papers or lab reports, learning study skills, solving homework problems, etc. Chapter 1 gives tips on identifying such resources on your campus.

16) Other available study or assignment aids. If you plan to distribute study guides, review questions, practice problems, or practice essay questions, students find it helpful to know about them from the start. If you assign papers, you may wish to suggest possible topics and give specific guidelines for writing papers in your discipline.

17) A weekly or class-by-class course schedule with as much of the following as possible: topics to be covered; class activities and formats (lecture, guest speaker, class discussion, cooperative group work, demonstration, field trip, role play, simulation, game, debate, panel discussion, film or video, slide show, computer exercise, case study, review session, etc.); dates of announced quizzes and exams; and due dates of all reading assignments, handed-in homework assignments, papers, and projects. Be sure to accommodate holidays and breaks.

18) A concluding legal caveat or disclaimer. In our litigious society, a few students have sued professors for failing to follow to the syllabus schedule and policies. Although you may not intend your syllabus to be a legally binding contract, students may think they are not getting their dollar's worth if the syllabus is significantly changed or isn't completed by the end of the term. Therefore, for your own protection, you might append a brief message to the effect: The above schedule, policies, and assignments in this course are subject to change in the event of extenuating circumstances or by mutual agreement between the instructor and the students.

Two other optional syllabus components are recommended:

19) Requirements your course satisfies, such as general education, writing-, speaking-, or ethics-across-the-curriculum, various majors, and any other graduation requirements that your institution or department maintains.

20) Background information about yourself, such as your degrees, universities you have attended, other universities where you have taught and/or conducted research, and your areas of research. Students appreciate knowing something about you as a professional and a person. A little knowledge about you can also help inspire their sense of personal loyalty to you.

Graphics to Append for Clarity

More often than not, students can make more sense of a chart, diagram, or picture than lists and paragraphs of even well-written text. The current generation of young students is particularly visually oriented.

Two parts of a syllabus can especially benefit from adding a graphic: the section on student learning objectives and the weekly or class-by-class schedule of topics and activities. The best type of graphic for these elements is a flowchart because they both represent a *process* that flows through time.

For an example, see page 25 in Chapter 3. The figure is a simple flowchart of how one learning objective precedes and prepares the student for another more advanced one in a particular course. The arrows imply a process in which the basic objectives provide a foundation for a series of mediating objectives, which provide a foundation for the ultimate objectives. Lists cannot portray such relationships among objectives. Using a flowchart, you can lay out *all* your learning objectives for your students without confusing them.

Another type of visual aid is the graphic syllabus, which is a flowchart, graphic organizer, or diagram of the schedule and organization of course topics, sometimes with tests, assignments, and major activities included. It is meant to supplement, not replace, the regular text syllabus (Nilson, 2002).

A graphic syllabus has many advantages. First, it reveals the method to your madness—that is, why you organized the course the way you did. No doubt you put substantial time and mental effort into your course design and topical structure, but without any background in the field, students can't possibly follow your sophisticated logic. They don't know what many of the words mean nor how one concept or topic may relate to another.

In a graphic, you can show such relationships using spatial arrangements and arrows.

Still another advantage is its redundancy. The students are both reading and seeing your course organization, so they are much more likely to remember it than if they only read it. In fact, people's memories of what they see are much stronger than their memories of what they read (Woods, 1989; Gedalof, 1998).

Graphics also appeal to learning styles that reading material and lectures don't reach effectively—those known as "visual," "concrete," "holistic," "global," "divergent," and "intuitive-feeling," depending upon the learning-style framework used. (See Chapter 12 for details on some of these frameworks.) These learning styles are increasingly common, perhaps dominant, in today's student population, while higher-education faculty tend to have quite different styles (Schroeder, 1993). So it's easy for us to overlook our students' needs for visuals. Graphic materials also showcase alternative ways of taking notes, outlining papers, and organizing concepts that students who favor the learning styles above can really use.

Finally, composing a graphic syllabus benefits *you*. It provides a creative outlet, and it helps you identify any problems in your course organization, such as topics that are misplaced or don't fit at all.

Bear in mind that a graphic syllabus shows the structure of your *course*, not the field, its history, or a theoretical model. These may make fine graphics, but under a different name. In addition, a graphic syllabus should "flow" in only one direction, as a course does through time. A final warning: Don't make it too complex, cluttered, or detailed. Its

32

intent is strictly to *clarify*. And *do* refer to it during the course as you would to a map during a trip.

Figure I shows a graphic syllabus of a hypothetical undergraduate Social Stratification course. It helps students *see* the complex interrelationships among the weekly topics. For instance, it makes clear that the first three weeks address theory and the rest of the course, empirical research. It illustrates that one of the two major theories has spawned research on two types of inequality (which support *this* theory), while the other major theory has generated research on two other types of inequality (which support *that* theory). During the last few weeks on how stratification persists, the graphic shows that one explanation derives only from one theory and its research, while the second one integrates both theories and their findings, as well as psychology. The flow of course topics takes on a logic and internal cohesion that a list cannot capture.

The "Learning-Centered Syllabus"

At this point you may be concerned that following this chapter's advice will yield too long a syllabus. In fact, a comprehensive, well-constructed syllabus may easily run five, six, or even ten pages, and this isn't necessarily too long. The more information you include, the less you have to improvise or decide on the run, and the fewer student questions you will have to answer.

A "learning-centered syllabus" can go on for 20, 30, even 50 pages or more and grow into a course handbook. Developed by Grunert (1997), it includes not only the "appropriate syllabus items" listed on pages 27-30, but also the content of course handouts, such as instruc-

tions for assignments, that most instructors distribute during the term. It can include much more as well: a letter from the instructor; reading, studying, note-taking, writing-style, and exam-taking tips and aids; a learning styles inventory and interpretation key; a learning contract; team-building suggestions; and detailed directions for projects, papers, presentations, portfolios, etc. This type of syllabus deserves a title page and table of contents (Grunert, 1997). With a learner-centered syllabus, the students have all the tools to succeed in the course up front, and you have all the elements of the course in place.

Getting Students to Read Your Syllabus

A solid syllabus says good things about you to your class. Among them, it says that you understand students, how they abhor surprises and last-minute assignments, and how they appreciate a tightly organized, explicit course structure around which they can plan the next few months. It says that you respect *them*, as well as the subject matter of the course.

Even so, you can't expect students to really study your carefully constructed document. During the entire term instructors field student questions that are answered in the syllabus. So the challenge is getting students to focus in on the document. While they may not remember every aspect of the course, they should remember where they can look up information.

Reviewing the syllabus during the your first class meeting isn't enough, and besides, you have other matters to tend to during that class period (see Chapter 7). Here are three more effective options.

Teaching at Its Best

Figure I.

Graphic Syllabus of a Hypothetical
Social Stratification Course

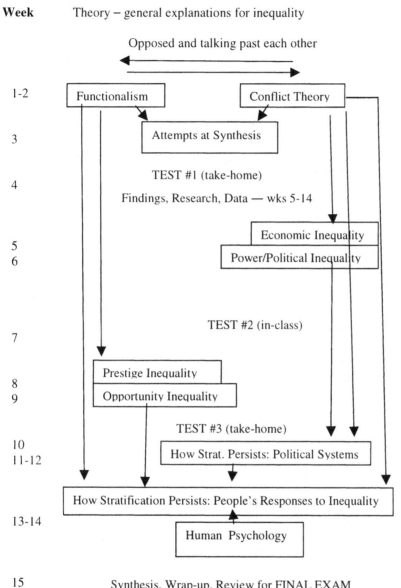

Week   Theory – general explanations for inequality

Opposed and talking past each other

1-2   Functionalism   Conflict Theory

3   Attempts at Synthesis

4   TEST #1 (take-home)

Findings, Research, Data — wks 5-14

5   Economic Inequality
6   Power/Political Inequality

TEST #2 (in-class)

7

8   Prestige Inequality
9   Opportunity Inequality

TEST #3 (take-home)

10
11-12   How Strat. Persists: Political Systems

How Stratification Persists: People's Responses to Inequality

13-14   Human Psychology

15   Synthesis, Wrap-up, Review for FINAL EXAM

33

The Complete Syllabus

34

First, if your syllabus is not too long, you have students read it in class, then break into small groups to discuss it and answer each other's questions. You may want to structure the discussion around some question, such as: Compared to the other courses you've taken in college, do you expect this one to be more or less difficult (or require more or less time), and why?

Another option is to assign the syllabus as homework, answer questions about it the second day of class, then have each student sign a contract with statements like these: I have thoroughly read the course syllabus and understand its contents. I understand the course requirements and the grading and attendance policies stated in the syllabus (Campbell, 2001).

A third option, especially for a long syllabus, is to assign it as homework and give a graded test on it the second day of class. The test items need not be all factual questions on the number of tests, the point value of assignments, and the like. You can ask interesting and thought-provoking short-answer and short essay questions, such as: Which of the student learning objectives for this course are most important to you personally, and why? Of the four papers assigned, which are you least (or most) looking forward to writing, and why? Which of the grading criteria for your oral presentation plays most to your strengths as a learner or a speaker?

Answers to these questions will give you insights into your students' aspirations, interests, insecurities, and self-assessments. Such questions will also motivate your students to think about the value of your course to them personally and professionally.

For further reading:

Grunert, J. 1997. *The Course Syllabus: A Learning-Centered Approach.* Bolton, MA: Anker Publishing.

Nilson, L.B. 2001. The graphic syllabus: Shedding a visual light on course organization. In *2001 To Improve the Academy,* edited by D. Lieberman and C. Wehlburg. Bolton, MA: Anker Publishing.

Course Coordination
Between Faculty and TAs

On the surface, the faculty-TA relationship seems simple and clear-cut. The professor receives an invaluable staff member in return for supervising a graduate student's apprenticeship in college teaching. The TA in turn performs an array of vital support services, under the professor's direction, while preparing for his or her future career. Through the TA, the students benefit from the opportunity for personalized consultation and additional, often more participatory instruction than is possible in a large class with a single faculty member. It is an all-around win-win arrangement.

But often the faculty-TA relationship isn't as productive and mutually rewarding as it can be. Few professors are trained in supervisory techniques, and TAs may be afraid to reveal their ignorance by asking too many questions.

Like all professional relationships, the successful TA-faculty team thrives on respect, trust, cooperation, and communication. This chapter suggests specific ways for both parties to foster these qualities in their working relationship.

Before the Term: Course Review and Role Specifications

First, TA assignments should be made as early as possible, preferably well before the start of the term. Early assignments allow time for the faculty and TAs to discuss the course and their mutual responsibilities, as well as to prepare to meet them. This extra time is crucial for first-time TAs and for experienced TAs taking on new assignments. TAs also need the assurance that they will have support and guidance when the need arises.

If you are faculty, hold an introductory staff meeting at least a few days before classes begin. Hand out your syllabus and present your course objectives, organization, and schedule. Review general mechanics, such as grading policies and grade complaint procedures, even if TAs will not be conducting sections. Students' opinions of the course are influenced greatly by the efficiency and proficiency of the instructional staff.

Next, firmly establish the roles that you and your TAs will play. TAs must know what is expected of them, as well as what they can expect of their faculty supervisors. To ensure clarity, issue a written statement of mutual responsibilities, and make sure everyone understands and agrees.

When allocating course duties, try to divide tasks fairly, equitably, and efficiently. TA responsibilities may include assisting in course preparation, preparing and/or instructing in laboratories, leading discussions, conducting help/review sessions, attending lectures, guest lecturing, taking roll, assisting in assignment and test preparation, being available during tests, grading, calculating grades, and holding office hours. Faculty responsibilities typically involve supervising and participating in test construction, advising TAs on discussion section or laboratory content and methods, coaching them in presentation and teaching skills, providing them with feedback on their teaching effectiveness, scheduling and directing TA staff meetings, and ensuring TAs have whatever supplies they need.

Depending on the size of the class and the number of TAs involved, you may wish to assign an experienced TA to act as a "head TA" in charge of facilitating communication among all course TAs. Strong interpersonal skills are essential here as the head TA must maintain a good rapport with both you and his fellow TAs.

Finally, try to give realistic estimates of the expected time and effort required of the TAs to perform their job well. While these estimates will vary from person to person and from week to week, they will allow TAs to plan their schedules more efficiently. Be sure you know the number of hours per week that each TA assignment involves.

During the Term: Regular Meetings and Teaching Feedback

Once you and your TAs reach a clear understanding on duties and expectations, all parties must first and foremost maintain open lines of communication. If a TA cannot approach you or the head TA with a problem, it may very well worsen and sour the students' learning experience. You and the head TA should actively invite TAs to seek your problem-solving advice.

Of course, communication is a two-way street. If you are a TA, and you fail to seek and/or follow good counsel, openly disagree with your supervising faculty in front of your students, or otherwise are insubordinate, you are liable to get in trouble with the class and eventually your faculty. Clear, open communication is *everyone's* responsibility and is vital to the success of the course.

The easiest and most reliable means of maintaining good communication is the regular, usually weekly staff meeting. (A chat-room meeting is a high-tech alternative to face-to-face.) Scheduling these meetings is the faculty's or head TA's charge. They are essential to the smooth coordination of multisection courses, which are so common at the introductory levels of the laboratory sciences, mathematics, English, and the foreign languages. These meetings should follow a fairly standard agenda of reviewing current and upcoming material, discussing the TAs' lesson plans, and assessing students' learning. Let us take each major topic in turn.

Agenda item #1: Course content. If you are faculty, you must ensure that your TAs have enough background in the upcoming course material to teach or tutor it. If you don't require them to attend your lectures, you might give them copies of your lecture notes. Some TAs may benefit from supplementary readings as well. You should also provide your TAs with leads on the student trouble spots they can anticipate and should address in section and office hours. Especially in the lab sciences, TAs must be well versed in the principles, procedures, hazards, and typical pitfalls of the next laboratory. In addition to your TAs' reputation with students, safety may be at stake here.

If you are a TA, you are in turn responsible for coming to these weekly meetings having read the upcoming readings, including the lab manual section, where applicable. Raise *all* your questions; reserve the "dumb" one for your fellow TAs, if you prefer. You too should anticipate student stumbling blocks and ask for help in leading your students over them. Whether or not your supervising faculty requires it, do attend all lectures. Students often complain on their teaching evaluation forms about TAs who do not. *Always* rehearse a lab you've never done before, preferably with a TA who has.

Agenda item #2: TAs' lesson plans. The second major item is what the TAs should do with the upcoming material in their discussion sections, labs, or help sessions. What teaching techniques and formats will give students the most productive chance to actively *work with* and *play with* the material? Should the TAs start off with a warm-up writing exercise on the major points of the reading, the lab procedures, or the last lecture? If discussion is appropriate, what questions should the TAs pose, and in what order? Should they be written on the board, on an overhead transparency, or in a handout? Or should they be handed out in advance and serve as a study guide? If reviewing homework problems is scheduled, should the TAs have students present their solutions on the board? Should the

TAs have new problems for the students to solve in small groups? How about a short simulation, a case study, or role playing to actively engage students in the material? If a pre-exam review session is planned, would review questions be helpful? How should the students cover them? By writing practice answers individually, or by outlining them in small groups? In any case, the TAs should not be giving the answers themselves.

The options are more numerous than the techniques and formats covered in this book, and appropriate ones deserve discussion. This way, the weekly meetings can function as a teaching methods seminar for the TA staff.

The purpose that supplementary sections and help sessions should *not* serve is to introduce new material. As this book emphasizes throughout, few students can master material only through passive activities like reading and listening, even when supplemented with note-taking (see especially Chapters 12, 13, and 14). Students must also talk about it, write about it, apply it to problems, use it in experiments, act it out, see it demonstrated or demonstrate it themselves—in essence, *do* something with it. The TA's most important role is to design and facilitate opportunities for students to work *actively* with material already introduced.

In addition to covering teaching techniques and formats for the coming week, these TA meetings should review what did and didn't work last time. TAs need not repeat one another's mistakes, and they can help each other solve their problems. Occasionally, too, a classroom failure may call for some damage control, while a genuine success merits recognition, even imitation.

Agenda item #3: Students' learning. The final item of business, assessing students' learning, has two parts. The first part is openly discussing how well students are learning the material. This information may come from homework assignments, quizzes and tests, classroom participation, classroom assessment exercises, consultations with students, and general impressions. By identifying areas of student weakness, all parties know what to review before proceeding to new material.

If you're a TA, you probably have an inside track on how the students are doing. Generally students talk more often and more candidly with you than with faculty. So you have a clearer picture of their involvement and difficulties with the material. You are also probably better positioned to identify individual students who are having academic or emotional trouble. When such cases arise, advise your supervising faculty. But for the students' sake, tell them about the campus units that can help them (see Chapters 1 and 10).

The second part of assessing students' learning is planning the next stage of assessment and testing. Whether you are faculty or a TA, have other members of the course staff review a draft of any assignment, quiz, or test you've written. It is amazing what another set of eyes can pick up—not just typos but also double-barreled multiple choice items, ambiguous essay questions, awkward sentence structure, confusing word usage, and all the other verbal land mines that are so hard to avoid. Sometimes, too, instructors forget to model their test questions on the homework and in-class exercises to which they accustomed their students. It is also easy to overlook important material covered just a few weeks ago. Assignments, quizzes, and exams are important enough to ask others to review.

If you are a supervising faculty member fortunate enough to have all experienced TAs for a particular course, you may be tempted to shorten or forego the weekly staff meetings. But resist the temptation. Your holding these meetings demonstrates your commitment to teaching excellence and staff morale.

One more faculty responsibility—an essential facet of supervision—is to observe and give constructive feedback to each of your TAs who ever appears before a class. The fact that you care enough to do so reinforces your TAs' loyalty and morale, along with the value of teaching in general. It is best to follow up each observation with a one-on-one consultation focusing on strategies for professional growth and improvement. For obvious reasons, do not delegate this task to a head TA.

Extending Managing to Mentoring

Beyond supervising TAs, you will no doubt become a mentor to certain graduate students. The mentoring relationship is complex enough to deserve discussion.

The role of the mentor is a multi-faceted one that extends beyond the "role model" (Murray, 1991). For example, the mentor serves as a source of information about the profession, and she tutors the protégé (or mentee) in specific professional skills. During times of personal turmoil, the mentee seeks advice and a sympathetic ear, casting the mentor in a confidant role. The mentor also helps the protégé plot a suitable career path.

However, the mentoring relationship is a two-way street. As such, the protégé must accept responsibility for and be willing to actively advance his own growth and development. Additionally, he must test his abilities against new challenges and honestly evaluate them in view of career options. Finally, he must be receptive to the mentor's instruction, coaching, and constructive criticism.

Faculty who lament the quality of graduate students entering their disciplines or departments can take heart in knowing that, in both industry and education, mentoring can improve the quality of recruits. For example, General Electric's Power Generation Division uses its mentoring program to impress on potential employees that they are carefully prepared for their jobs, not thrown into a sink-or-swim situation. Universities with alumni mentoring programs, such as Trinity College, have raised their students' academic achievement by arranging opportunities for them to explore career options with successful alumni (Kirby, 1989).

Studies of the public service professions and industry indicate that mentoring can also be an effective staff development tool. Police officers who participate in a formal mentoring program show greater productivity and discipline during their careers (Fagan, 1986).

The mentoring relationship reaps returns for the mentor as well. According to some mentors, it heightens their motivation. While some senior personnel face burn-out, mentors are constantly reminded of what they first found interesting and exciting about their profession. They become more inspired leaders, enhancing overall group and organizational productivity.

Here are some practical guidelines for both faculty and graduate students (Cameron, 1993; Blandford, 2000; Nicholls, 2002):

- *Mentors*, reasonably pace your training and advising. Remember that you didn't learn everything at once or the first time through.
- *Protégés*, regard your relationship as a college teaching tutorial, and budget time for it. If you feel overwhelmed, let your mentor know.
- *Mentors*, be aware that your protégé is probably unfamiliar with various university and department regulations, office procedures, routine deadlines, and endless other professional protocols that are now second nature to you. Do convey this information explicitly.
- *Protégés*, take what your mentor tells you seriously, even if some of it sounds silly or strange.
- *Mentors*, give fair, encouraging, and caring feedback on your protégés' job performance on a regular basis. They may not know when they've done well and when they haven't, and they need to know, for both your and their sakes. Critical remarks can evoke a defensive, even fearful reaction. So couch them in terms of ways to improve and expectations for future success.
- *Protégés*, ask for regular feedback, and don't expect to hear you're doing a perfect job. There is always a lot to learn and plenty of room for improvement. If you find it hard to believe, just trust for now that your mentor's constructive criticism has nothing to do with her not liking you as a person or not believing in

40

you as a junior professional. In fact, it's a compliment; it means she considers you strong enough to hear the truth and to make improvements. If your mentor's counsel sounds inappropriate, ask for clarification, ponder it for while, and pass judgment later.

- *Mentors*, cultivate an environment where temporary lapses and setbacks, fears, and failures can be shared, forgiven, overcome, and filed away as learning experiences. Give your protégés as many chances as your course can afford. Whenever appropriate, counsel them on how to avoid or conquer the problem. For instance, advise an anxious protégé to visualize a worst-case classroom scenario, and together brainstorm ways to defuse the situation. (Your institution's teaching center can help.)
- *Protégés*, bring your performance fears out in the open. Your mentor can help you calm your adequacy anxieties, control your stage fright, and feel capable of handling your worst-case teaching nightmare. Remember, your mentor faced similar fears at one time. She hasn't forgotten and she wants to help you.
- *Mentors*, resist the natural temptation to mold your protégés into your clones. Each must find and explore his own potential.
- *Protégés*, "try on" and borrow elements of your mentor's teaching and testing style that fit you, but shop around. Great teaching takes many forms. Developing your own unique excellence is a creative, long-term process.
- *Mentors*, expect to feel occasionally that your time and wisdom are going unappreciated. Your

protégés probably lack the experience to put your good counsel and training into perspective at the moment. Know that they will acquire that perspective and gratitude over time.
- *Protégés*, thank your mentor for her time, advice, instruction, and caring. Credit her when appropriate. Don't forget that while supervising a course is an assigned task, the more personal attention your mentor is giving you is purely voluntary and its own reward.
- *Mentors* and *Protégés*, review your relationship periodically. Bear in mind that, if it should endure, it is designed to self-destruct over the long run as the protégé evolves into a colleague. In the meantime, expect occasional tensions and imbalances. Mentors can find it hard both to accept and to relinquish their superior role; protégés can vacillate between dependency and the desire to break away. Talking about these stresses informally can resolve them.

These same principles apply to mentoring relationships between faculty and undergraduates and between senior faculty and junior colleagues. At any level, the positive effects of the relationship are mutually substantial and the material costs minimal. An active mentoring program then can greatly enhance a course, a department, and an entire institution.

COPYRIGHT GUIDELINES FOR INSTRUCTORS

As you prepare to teach a course—be it classroom, online, or hybrid—you will likely bump into the issue of copyright. No doubt you will want to assign, play, or show works of other people beyond the required books and CD-ROMs you expect your students to buy.

If so, you have just entered the through-the-looking-glass world of "fair use," "educational purposes," and other such Cheshire categories that make most of us instructors think twice before we press the start button on our copying machine or even consider showing a videotape in class. This is the unwieldy wonderland in which the only legally correct answer to your simplest query may be "probably," "unlikely," and "it depends upon the specific case." For example, Q: Is a classroom a public place? (This issue may affect the legality of showing a videotape in class.) A: Experts disagree and the courts have not yet settled the issue.

In the absence of simple, clear rules of thumb, it is little wonder that we tend to pick up copyright law by word of mouth—and wind up swapping myths and misconceptions. The legal ambiguities only feed our fears of what might happen to us if we were actually caught by the copyright enforcers (whoever they may be) violating their law, even unknowingly.

The laws, guidelines, and enforcement policies are not well publicized in the academic world and may surprise you. Many of them are highly technical, make questionable sense, and are frankly difficult to absorb and remember.

All the legal information in this chapter comes ultimately from title 17 of the United States Code, which includes the Copyright Act of 1976 and its subsequent amendments—literally dozens of them. The Conference on Fair Use (CONFU, 1995-97) and the Digital Millennium Copyright Act of 1998 (one of the amendments to the 1976 law) set the guidelines for multimedia use and distance learning, some of which have an ambiguous legal status. Of course, we will focus on the "fair use" exemptions that are granted by "educational purposes."

Laws, statutes, and guidelines are written to obfuscate, so credit is due those who interpreted them and served as invaluable factual sources for this chapter: Jordan, 1996; Brinson and Radcliffe, 1996; Emett and New, 1997; Orlans, 1999; and especially Harper, 2001.

Free Use: Fair Use, Facts, and Public Domain

"Free use" means no formal permission to reprint or license from the copyright holder is required to copy, distribute, or electronically disseminate the work. However, whether a given case qualifies depends on three rather gray criteria: 1) your use is "fair use"; 2) the material you wish to use is factual or an idea; or 3) the work you wish to use is in the public domain.

CHAPTER 6

In general, fair use means use for noncommercial purposes and specifically for purposes of teaching, scholarship, research, criticism, comment, and news reporting. The courts are most likely to find fair use where the copied work is a factual as opposed to a creative work, as well as where the new work does not pose market or readership competition for the copyrighted work. The amount and the significance of the protected work used also figures into the determination. Use of a tiny amount of the work should not raise concerns unless it is substantial in terms of importance—for instance, the heart of the copied work.

To illustrate, a magazine article that used 300 words from a 200,000-word autobiography written by President Gerald Ford was found to infringe the copyright on the autobiography. Even though the copied material comprised only a small part of the autobiography, it included some of the most powerful passages in the work.

No legal guidelines are given to distinguish factual material or an idea from something else. Determinations are made on a case-by-case basis.

Public domain is a clearer legal concept but is often redefined. A work is now in the public domain if: 1) it was published on or before December 31, 1922; 2) 95 years have elapsed since its publication date *if* it was published between January 1, 1923 and December 31, 1978; 3) 70 years have elapsed since the author's death *if* it was published after 1978. However, if a work was published between 1923 and 1963 and the copyright owner did *not renew* the copyright after the 28-year term that once applied, the work has come into public domain.

The fair-use exemption does *not* permit unlimited copying and distribution. The "privilege" is highly restricted by "guidelines" with legal force, though they are often ambiguous and arcane, and they do not cover all situations. They were negotiated among educators, authors, and publishers. By the way, no copyright exemption excuses you from citing and crediting your sources.

Copying Print Media

Single copying. As an instructor, you may make single copies, including a transparency, of the following for teaching purposes: a chapter of a book; an article from a periodical or newspaper; a short story, essay, or poem; a diagram, graph, chart, drawing, cartoon, or picture from a book, periodical, or newspaper.

Multiple copying. You may make multiple copies—that is, one copy per student in a course—if the work meets the criteria of brevity, spontaneity, and cumulative effect and if each copy contains a copyright notice.

The guidelines define the "brevity" criterion in this way: 1) an entire poem printed on no more than two pages or an excerpt from a longer poem, not to exceed 250 words copied in either case; 2) an entire article, story, or essay of less than 2,500 words or an excerpt of fewer than 1,000 words or less than 10% of the work, whichever is less, but in either event a minimum of 500 words to be copied; 3) one chart, graph, diagram, drawing, cartoon, or picture per book or periodical issue. Multiple copying meets the "spontaneity" criterion when you do not have a reasonable length of time to request and receive permission to copy. (What "a reasonable length of time" may be is not specified.)

The "cumulative effect" is considered acceptably small when your copying is only for one course, and you do not make multiple copies in more than nine instances per term per course. Furthermore, you may not make multiple copies of more than one short poem, article, story, essay, or two excerpts from the same author, or more than three from the same collective work or periodical volume in one term.

Copying short works. Short works such as children's books are often less than 2,500 words, and you may not copy them as a whole. All you may reproduce is an excerpt of no more than two published pages containing not more than 10% of the total words in the text.

Prohibitions to single or multiple copying. Notwithstanding the guidelines above, your intentions and the specific work also come into play. You may not make copies under these conditions: to create, replace, or substitute for anthologies, compilations, or collective works; to substitute for replacement or purchase; of "consumable" works such as workbooks, exercises, standardized tests, or answer sheets; of the same item term after term; if you charge students beyond the copying cost; or on direction of a higher authority.

Course packets and electronic reserves (all types of materials). Limit the materials to single chapters, single articles from a journal issue, and small parts of a work, such as several illustrations, charts, or graphs. Also limit access to students enrolled in the course for that term. Cite and put copyright notices on originals.

Copying and Recording Music

You may record student performances only for evaluation or portfolio purposes. Other sound recordings are limited to one copy for the classroom or reserve room. Copying sheet music is restricted out-of print music and performances "in an emergency."

Videotaping Broadcast Programming

These guidelines specify what educational institutions (e.g., campus media units) can videotape off-the-air for educational purposes without obtaining a permission or license from the copyright holder.

1) These guidelines apply only to off-the-air recording by non-profit educational institutions.
2) Videotapes may be kept for only 45 calendar days after the recording date. After this time the tapes must be erased.
3) The videotape may be shown to students only during the first ten class days after the recording date and may be repeated only once for reinforcement. (Points 2 and 3 are called the "45-10 rule.")
4) Off-air recordings may be made only at the request of an individual instructor and not in anticipation of an instructor's request. The same instructor can request the program be recorded only once.
5) Duplicate copies may be made if several instructors request the recording of the same program.
6) After the first ten classes allowed for showing, the recording may only be used only for evaluation (e.g., an exam).
7) Off-the-air recordings may not be edited or combined with

other recordings to create a new work or an anthology.

8) All videotapes, including copies, must contain a copyright notice when broadcast.

9) Educational institutions are responsible for ensuring compliance with these guidelines.

No guidelines or laws have been written for instructors who wish to videotape a program off-the-air at home, then show it in class. But legal experts recommend that they demonstrate compliance with the spirit of the law by following the same guidelines.

Public broadcast programs. The Public Broadcasting Service, the Public Television Library, the Great Plains National Instructional Television Library, and the Agency for Instructional Television have somewhat less restrictive rules for off-the-air videotaping for educational purposes:

1) Recordings may be made by instructors or students in accredited, nonprofit educational institutions.

2) Recordings may be used only for instruction in a classroom, lab, or auditorium but are not restricted to one classroom or one instructor.

3) The use of recordings is, however, restricted to one institution and may not be shared outside of it.

4) Recordings may be used as often as needed for seven days. Then they must be erased.

Commercially rented videotapes. If a videotape carries the warning "For Home Use Only," the law is unclear on whether you may show it in your classroom. If the classroom is considered a "public place," you may not, but the courts have not resolved this issue. Legal experts reason that you probably can because instructors are clearly permitted to display or perform works in face-to-face teaching situations. However, the videotape must serve a purely instructional objective. Even the hint of entertainment purposes, such as the presence of non-students in the classroom, can raise a legal flag. (Of course, you may show any rented videotape that has been cleared for public presentation.)

Movie studios have built the home video industry into a multibillion-dollar business, in part by strictly enforcing the distinction between instruction and entertainment. To illustrate, in early 1996 the Motion Picture Licensing Corporation, a Los Angeles copyright policing agency representing the studios, sent threat letters to 50,000 day-care centers across the nation. The letters demanded up to $325 per year for what they termed "a public-performance video license" for showing children's videos (e.g., Pooh and Scrooge) to their "public" of toddlers. Apparently Hollywood does not regard its standard products as educational and therefore exempt from licensing fees under the fair use (Bourland, 1996).

Multimedia and the Internet

Images. If an image is not designated for sale or license, you may digitize and use it if you limit access (password-protect) to enrolled students and administrative staff. You may also use the image at a peer conference. Further, your students may download, print out, and transmit it for personal academic use, including course assignments and portfolios, for up to two years.

Performances. This category includes performances and displays of dramatic, literary, audiovisual, and musical works. In the traditional, face-to-face classroom, you and your students may listen to a piece of music, read a poem aloud, act out a play, display a slide, or play a videotape (if lawfully obtained), as long as the purpose is educational. For some years, you and your students could not do *any* of these electronically under fair use protection. The CONFU guidelines required you to obtain a license. Finally, Congress closed this odd legal gap in mid-2002 when it passed the Technology Harmonization and Education Act without debate, after a year-long stall in the House Judiciary Committee.

Despite this good news, electronic copyright is still a volatile area, so stay tuned to the news media, especially the *Chronicle of Higher Education,* to keep abreast of the latest legal developments. Also keep in mind that you may not need to incorporate a web-based image or performance into your course materials. You can simply refer your students to a URL where it is located.

Permissions to Reprint and Licenses

What if you wish to reproduce or show a work or portion of a work in a manner that violates the guidelines above?

1) You can request in writing (email okay) the permission of the copyright holder to reprint, in which case you must identify the exact portion of the work, the number of copies you wish to make and distribute, and the purpose or planned use of the copies (e.g., instruction in a given course for specific term at a given institution). You may or may not be charged a fee, depending mostly on the number of copies you wish to make. A permission granted for classroom use applies only to one course during one term.

The Copyright Clearance Center at http://www.copyright.com/ offers an electronic permission service that usually gets your permission in a day or two. Your library or copy center probably works with the CCC already and can help you.

2) You can request a license of the copyright holder in writing, giving the same precise information. Licenses are usually required to show a work or portion of a work, or to include some non-trivial portion of it in your own work, including your own multimedia production. Licenses always entail fees and may be negotiable.

Common Copyright Misconceptions

Let us dispel some popular misconceptions. First, giving credit to the author(s) of a work is not a way around or substitute for copyright law compliance. All a citation exempts you from is plagiarism. Second, the absence of a copyright notice does *not* mean the work is not protected. While most works have a notice, those published on or after March 1, 1989 are protected even without one. Third, changing someone else's copyrighted work here and there will *not* make it legally yours. In fact, such action may make you *doubly* liable—for infringement of copying right *and* of the copyright holder's modification right.

Finally, flattering or showcasing a work is *not* likely to allay the copyright owner's objections to your free use of the work. This is especially true of multimedia works; their producers view licenses as a new source of income. Freelance writers, music publishers, and musical performers have successfully sued major companies like *The New York Times* and CompuServe for the unauthorized publication and/or distribution of their work on online computer services.

How Copyright Violations Are Actually Handled

So what if you forget to insert an important article in your course packet, and you're tempted to make copies and hand them out to your students in class? What penalties might you face?

The laws state that you face a judgment of up to $100,000 for each willful infringement, and ignorance of the law won't get you off. What may get you off is a convincing argument that you were acting in good faith, believing on reasonable grounds that that your case qualified as fair use. Your institution will probably defend you if you follow its fair use policies.

However, the law doesn't always operate by the law. In the educational arena, only educational institutions, not individuals, have ever been sued, and very few over the past 30 years. Obviously, colleges, universities, school systems, and private schools have much deeper pockets than their teaching staff. So copyright enforcers send them threatening letters every once in a while to remind them of the law and potential penalties. Sometimes a threat is based on a tip that violations have occurred. (Some enforcement agencies maintain tip hotlines.) But even in this case, the designated agent-for-service receives not a summons but a cease-and-desist order. Educational institutions have generally induced its violators to cease and desist immediately and have avoided

further legal action.

Historically, the most aggressive copyright enforcer has been the Software Publishers Association, which patrols software pirating (installation or reproduction without site licenses), and *even it* confines its efforts to organizations and stays out of people's at-home offices.

Corporations, which can rarely claim fair use protection, have never enjoyed such gentle treatment. But then they have the most to gain financially by copyright violations. The copyright cops have ensured that they also have the most to lose. So be aware that publishing houses, which are corporations no matter how academic they may be, interpret fair use very conservatively (Orlans, 1999).

For further reading:

U.S. Copyright Office
Web: http://www.loc.gov/copyright
Address: Library of Congress,
   Washington, D.C. 20559
Public information phone services:
   (202) 707-2100 (leave message)
   (202) 479-0700 (contact to person,
   but line often busy)
Phone ordering of circulars & forms
   (202) 707-9100.
Some circulars are free, such as Circular #2: "Publications on Copyright," an excellent place to start.

PART II.

GOOD

BEGINNINGS

Your FIRST DAY of CLASS

Whether you are teaching for the first time or are a seasoned classroom veteran, the first day of class can evoke anxiety as well as excitement. Like no other day, it affects the tenor of the entire term. It may also represent innovations and experiments in course content, organization, and design, teaching formats and techniques, and assessment methods. Not to mention all those new student faces. This chapter suggests ways to reduce the anxiety, heighten the excitement, and start off the course on a positive, professional, and participatory note. It should be particularly useful to newer instructors. With some adaptation, these strategies apply to online courses as well.

First Impressions

What you do and do not do the first day of class will affect your students' and maybe even your own expectations and behavior for the rest of the term. So think in advance what expectations and behaviors you want to establish in your classroom for the next ten to 15 weeks. Plan to set these expectations and organize class activities that model the level of student involvement you have in mind for the rest of the course. For example, if you hope for considerable discussion, engage your students in discussion, perhaps about their expectations of the course or their current conceptions of the subject matter. If you intend to have a number of in-class writing exercises, start with a short one that first class. If you plan on using cooperative learning, have a small-group activity the first day.

No doubt you want to establish a serious, professional classroom atmosphere, and you communicate this tenor in several ways. First, have a comprehensive, well structured syllabus ready to distribute (see Chapter 4). It tells your class that you are careful, well organized, conscientious, and serious about teaching. Make extra copies for last-minute enrollees, and bring some with you during the first two weeks of class.

Second, say a few words to market the course and the material. Enthusiasm is contagious. Your showing some of yours for the subject matter and the opportunity to teach it will motivate your students' interest in learning it and inspire their respect for you as a scholar.

Third, dress a little more formally than you normally would, at least if you're inclined to more casual attire. A touch of formality conveys professionalism and seriousness. It also gives instructors who are female, youthful-looking, and/or physically small an aura of authority and a psychological edge that help separate them from their students (Roach, 1997). No doubt with time and experience, these benefits fade.

Since you expect students to be prompt, you might set a good example from the start. Arrive in the classroom early and set a welcoming tone by chatting with students informally as they arrive. Make students feel comfortable with you as a person as well as an instructor, but don't confuse your roles; remember the difference between being friendly and being friends.

Finally, make productive use of the entire class period. The rest of this chapter suggests several social and content-oriented activities that you can organize, even if the students have no background in the subject matter. The most important point is not to "waste" the first class—not to treat it as a throw-away day or to dismiss it early. Only if you treat class time like a precious commodity will your students do likewise.

If you are new to teaching, prepare to combat any sudden case of stage fright by practicing your first-day presentation in advance. As you begin class, take a few long, slow, deep breaths—extra oxygen works wonders for shaky nerves—and try to focus on some spot on the wall or an inanimate object to balance yourself. Or try looking just over the heads of your students for the first few minutes. Or try visualizing the situation as conducting a one-to-one tutorial instead of talking to a class. Always feel free to take a moment to collect your thoughts. Remember that many students are impressed by anyone with the courage to speak in public and are forgiving of the occasional lapse of continuity.

Exchanging Information

Information flow should be a two-way street, even (perhaps especially) on the first day. But you as the instructor initiate the exchange, first by displaying the following information before class convenes: the name and number of your course, the section number (if appropriate), the meeting days and times, your name, your office location, and your office hours. This information assures students that they are in the right place.

The next several activities need not come in the order presented, but they are strongly recommended for setting an open and participatory as well as professional tone for the rest of the term.

Student information index cards. Get to know your students, and let them know that you are interested in them personally, by passing out blank index cards and asking them to write down this information for you: their full name, any preferred nickname, their year in school, their major, and their previous coursework in the field. Additional information such as hometown, outside interests, and career aspirations may help you relate class material to your students on a more personal level. Consider also asking them to write out what they expect from this course, why they are taking it (aside from breadth requirements), and/or what topics they would like to see addressed. You may be able to orient the material towards some of their interests and to advise those with erroneous expectations to take a more suitable course.

Your background. Since you're asking students about themselves, it's only fair to tell them something about yourself. (They *are* interested.) You needn't divulge your life history, but giving them a brief summary of your educational and professional background helps reinforce your credibility as an instructor and your "humanness" as a person. A bit of openness also enhances your students' personal loyalty to you.

Include some information about your own research and interests, what attracted you to the field, why you love teaching it, and the implications and applications of the subject in the world. See this as an opportunity to make the material more relevant to your students.

Course information. Mark on your copy of the syllabus the points you want to elaborate, clarify, and emphasize. But rather than reading through the whole document, consider making it an homework assignment, or breaking the class into small groups to discuss it and raise questions (see Chapter 4). Don't otherwise expect students to read the syllabus carefully. Do mention your office hours and urge students to seek your help outside of class (see Chapter 10).

Explain why you've chosen the teaching techniques you plan to use and what benefits they have over other reasonable options, especially if your methods are innovative and/ or collaborative. Your explanation will not only reassure students of your commitment to teaching effectiveness but also help overcome any resistance they may have to unusual formats.

Also explicitly state your expectations of them and their responsibilities for preparing for class and participating. For example, if your course calls for considerable discussion, emphasize the importance of their preparation, your rules for

calling on students, your procedure of asking students to summarize at the end, etc. Also, offer them some advice on how to take notes on discussion; this remains a mystery even to the most verbal students (see Chapter 15). If you plan to lecture at all, give students some pointers on your lecture organization and good note-taking strategies (see Chapter 14). You might also share some helpful reading/study skills and/or problem-solving strategies appropriate to your particular subject matter.

You cannot possibly anticipate all the questions that students will have, especially about your testing and grading procedures. But here are some likely ones that you should be prepared to field: How will you make up the tests? What types of questions will they have? What kinds of thinking will you be testing? How should students best prepare for them? Will you distribute review questions? Will you hold review sessions? On what dimensions will you evaluate papers and other written assignments? How many A's, B's, C's, etc. do you usually give? How possible is it for all students to get a good grade?

Learning students' names. Most students expect their instructors to learn their names, unless the class is very large (near or over 100). This is especially the case at smaller and private colleges and universities. To borrow an old cliche, learning your students' names shows you care. So begin learning and using them to call on students early. If you have trouble remembering names, the strategies below may help you.

You can seat students in specific places and make a seating chart. Students may not prefer a seating chart, but they will tolerate it graciously if you say the reason is to learn their names. Seating them alphabetically before launching into small-group work is also a way to ensure randomly mixed groups.

Some instructors learn names by taking notes about each students' physical appearance on the class roster—information such as body shape and size, hair color and length, dress style, age, and any distinguishing physical traits. It is best to keep such notes concealed from your students' view.

Taking roll in every class helps you learn the names as well as take attendance. While learning names, you can also use the roll to call on students more or less randomly, as long as you tell your class what you'll be doing. Or you may use the index cards to call on students.

Still another strategy is to have students wear name tags or display name cards or tents on their desks. To avoid the hassle of making new name tags or cards for every class, print up permanent, convention-style tags or name cards, distribute them at the start of each class, and collect them at the end of each session for the next one. This is also a subtle way to take attendance.

To impress a large class, take a quick-developing photograph of each student (or have your TAs do so) with his or her name printed below the face. Then use the photos to call on students. You can master the names of over 100 students within a few weeks using this technique. A simpler alternative is to have students bring you a copy of their driver's license or picture ID.

Social Icebreakers: "Getting to Know You"

If your class size allows it, try to incorporate one or two icebreaker activities on the first day. There are two types: the social or "getting-to-know-you" variety, which gets students acquainted, and subject-matter icebreakers, which motivate students to start thinking about the material. Feel free to move beyond the popular examples given here and devise your own.

If you plan on discussion or group work, social icebreakers smooth the way for broad participation and cooperative group interaction. Freshmen, in particular, appreciate the opportunity to meet their fellow students, including more senior ones, who can serve as role models.

Simple self-introductions. Perhaps the simplest version is to have students take turns introducing themselves to the class by giving their name, major, and perhaps a reason for their taking the course (once again, aside from fulfilling breadth requirements).

This activity may work best in a smaller class, however, as the prospect of speaking in front of a large group of strangers can mildly terrify some students. On the other hand, if you will have your students make speeches or oral presentations in front the class later on, this first-day exercise can help them get used to the assignments to come.

Three-step interviews. Alternatively, students can share the same type of information with a neighbor. Then, without knowing beforehand the second part of the task, each partner can introduce his or her counterpart to another pair or to the class. This exercise has the added benefit of teaching careful listening skills (Kagan, 1988).

Class survey. In taking this informal survey of the class, you moderate a brief questioning period. Begin by asking your students to raise their hands in response to some general questions: How many students are from [various regions of the country]? East/west of the Mississippi? Freshmen, sophomores, etc.? How many work full-time? How many are married? How many have children? How many like golf? Tennis? How many have traveled abroad? To Europe? To Asia? Then you may venture into opinion questions, perhaps some relevant to the course material.

Students soon begin to form a broad picture of their class and to see what they have in common. They will find it far easier to interact with classmates who share their interests and backgrounds.

Scavenger Hunt/People Search. In this more structured activity, give students a list of requirements and tell them to move about the classroom seeking fellow students who meet each one. Some possible requirements are "has been to France," "prefers cats to dogs," "has a birthday in the same month you do," "can speak two or more languages," and "cries at movies." The "found" students sign their name next to the requirement they meet. You might give prizes to the three fastest students.

A variation of this icebreaker is Human Bingo. Make a page-size 4x4 table, and write each requirement in a box. Be sure your class as a whole can meet all the requirements. When a student has all the boxes signed by fellow students who meet the requirements, she shouts out, "Bingo!"

"The Circles of _____." Give each student a sheet of paper with a large central circle and other smaller circles radiating from it.

Students write their names in the central circle and the names of groups with which they identify (such as gender, age group, religious, ethnic, racial, social, political, ideological, athletic) in the satellite circles. Then ask students to move around the room to find three classmates who are most and/ or least similar to themselves.

Like Scavenger Hunt/People Search, this exercise makes students appreciate the diversity in the class, as well as meet their fellow students. The Circles icebreaker also produces homogeneous or heterogeneous groups of four if you need them for the next activity.

Subject-Matter Icebreakers

Chapter 27, "Assessing Students' Learning in Progress," describes several classroom assessment techniques that are designed for the first day of class or the day you introduce a new topic.

Background Knowledge Probe, ***Focused Listing***, and ***Self Confidence Surveys*** are particularly useful and appropriate for the first class. The products are not to be graded. They are meant to inform you about your students' level of cognitive and psychological preparation for your course and to orient them to the subject matter.

Problem-posting. To whet students' appetites for the material, one particularly useful first-day activity is problem-posting (McKeachie et al, 1994). First, ask students to think about and jot down either: 1) problems they expect to encounter with the course or 2) issues they think the course should address. Then act as the facilitator, recording student responses on the board or an overhead transparency. To build trust with your class, check your understanding by restating the comments and requesting approval, and avoid seeming judgmental or dominating.

As the frequency of student suggestions begins to decline, propose stopping. Make sure, however, that all students have had a chance to contribute, even if you have to coax the quiet ones. If some wish to speculate on how to address any of the points listed, keep a close rein on the discussion, not letting it stray too far afield. Tell students which of their questions the course will address; this gives them something to look forward to. But also be honest about the ones your course will not cover.

Problem-posting is useful not only at the beginning of the course, but also later on when broaching a particularly difficult topic. The exercise accomplishes several purposes. First, it opens lines of communication between you and your students as well as among students. Second, it lends validity to their concerns and assures them they're not alone. Third, it reaffirms that you are approachable and as capable of listening as you are of talking. Finally, it encourages students to devise solutions to problems themselves, reducing their reliance on you for the definitive answers.

Common sense inventory.
Another way to break students into the subject matter, as well as to help them grasp its relevance, is to have them respond to a brief inventory or pretest (Nilson, 1981). Assemble five to 15 "common sense" statements directly related to the course material, some (or all) of which run counter to popular belief or prejudice—for example: "Suicide is more likely among women than men." "Over half of all marriages occur between persons who live within 20 blocks of each other." Then have students individually mark each statement as true or false and share their answers in pairs or small groups.

Let students debate their differences among themselves, or thicken the plot by assigning each pair or group one or more statements, instructing members to reach consensus. Have a presenter from each group defend its position. After the presentations, you can give the "correct" answers, which may spark even more debate, or take the cliff-hanger approach and let the class wait for them to unfold during the term.

Drawing Class to a Close

At the end of the class, you may want to ask students to write down their anonymous reactions (McKeachie et al, 1994). Pose general questions such as: What is the most important thing you learned during this first day? How did your expectations of this course change? What questions or concerns do you still have about the course or the subject matter? You can address remaining concerns as a warm-up activity to open the next class.

Finally, and it's worth repeating, do not dismiss the first class early. If you conduct some of the activities in this chapter, the time will be more than adequately filled and productively spent. Not only will your students enjoy an introduction to the course and its subject matter; they will also have a chance to get acquainted with you and their classmates.

PREVENTING AND RESPONDING TO
CLASSROOM INCIVILITY

Classroom management has only recently received attention as classroom incivility has become a national problem in higher education. The topic includes preventing and sanctioning disciplinary problems and maintaining a controlled, orderly environment that is conducive to learning. Knowing preventative measures and constructive responses to disruption can greatly enhance your relationship with your classes because even minor minor incivilities can mar the atmosphere, break your concentration, and really get under your skin. And losing your temper is not an option.

What Is Incivility?

Students surveyed at Wright State University cited six common classroom behaviors that *they* found annoying (Ballantine and Risacher, 1993):
1) talking in class
2) noisily packing up early
3) arriving late and/or leaving early
4) cheating
5) wasting class time — a general category including being unprepared for class, dominating discussion, repeating questions, and asking for a review of the last class meeting.

6) showing general disrespect and poor manners toward the instructor and other students.

Instructors surveyed also identified these student behaviors as unacceptable (Royce, 2000):
7) eating in class
8) acting bored or apathetic
9) making disapproving groans
10) making sarcastic remarks or gestures
11) sleeping in class
12) not paying attention
13) not answering a direct question
14) using a computer in class for non-class purposes
15) having cell phones and pagers that go off in class
16) cutting class
17) dominating discussion
18) demanding make-up exams, extensions, grade changes, or special favors
19) taunting or belittling other students
20) challenging the instructor's knowledge or credibility in class
21) making harassing, hostile, or vulgar comments to the instructor in class
22) making harassing, hostile, or vulgar comments or physical gestures to the instructor *outside* of class
23) sending the instructor inappropriate emails

24) making threats of physical harm to the instructor.

While the most extreme forms of incivility are rather rare, all the other behaviors listed above have in fact occurred at least "sometimes" at Indiana University, Bloomington, according to faculty reports (Royce, 2000). These students behaviors were almost unheard of up through the mid 1980s.

Why the Increase?

The academy has changed in many ways over the past 20-plus years that have probably exacerbated behavioral and disciplinary problems. Increasing student diversity has brought in many students who don't share the traditional academic values, norms, and communication styles. The student-instructor chasm has also widened as faculty have become increasingly specialized. In addition, as universities have grown in size, they have become more transient and impersonal, generating an atmosphere of distrust and indifference (Leatherman, 1996; Baldwin, 1997-98).

No doubt, other changes have contributed as well. Universities are working harder than ever to retain students, so they sanction only the most seriously offensive student behaviors.

In addition, the factors that are associated with classroom incivility have become more common in the academy—namely, large classes and instructors who are young, female, and low status (adjuncts, lecturers, and TAs) (Royce, 2000). Another high-incivility context is the required course. Also male students are more likely perpetrators than females.

The rest of this chapter suggests strategies for minimizing and responding to specific types of incivilities in and outside of the classroom. Of course, prevention is the preferred outcome, but this behavior is not always in your control. So acceptable ways to stop the behaviors are also covered. Unfortunately, none of these strategies are absolutely foolproof.

Preventing Incivility: Balancing Authority and Approachability

Most students accept your authority without question, whether you are a tenure-track faculty member, an adjunct, or a TA. But some students may be reluctant to accord the same respect to an instructor who violates the traditional "professorial stereotype" of the mature, white male with an imposing stance and a low, deep voice. Clearly, if you look young, are physically small, have a relatively high voice, are non-white, and/or are female, you *may* encounter some unspoken student resistance. A few of these simple strategies may help you take control of your class look more authoritative (Nilson, 1981):

1) Stand up in front of your class instead of sitting, move around the room, and use broad gestures. The dramatic effect is to make you appear "larger than life." Interestingly, increasing one's apparent size is a common aggressive/defensive posture throughout the animal kingdom.

2) Try to deepen your voice slightly and to project it further by speaking from your diaphragm. Also try to avoid ending a declarative sentence with a questioning rise in pitch.

3) Favor more formal dress to convey that you are serious and business-minded (Roach, 1997).

4) Add an air of formality and dignity to your classroom. For instance, address students by their last names, and ask that they address you by your title (Dr. or Professor) and last name.

5) Refer in class to your own research, where appropriate. This establishes you as an authority on the subject and elevates you in your students' eyes.

Female instructors, in particular, must take measures to reinforce their legitimacy and authority. While research shows that female gender does not depress student evaluations of teaching in any consistent or significant way (Feldman, 1992, 1993; Nilson and Lysacker, 1996), students do tend to underestimate the educational attainment of female instructors, even controlling for many other instructor characteristics (Miller and Chamberlain, 2000).

Other instructors face the opposite problem of intimidating students. They can do so either by too perfectly matching the somewhat chilly professorial stereotype or by violating it in the other, more imposing direction. From your students' viewpoint, you may fall in this category if you are male and are some combination of very tall, physically large, deep-voiced, rugged-looking, serious and reserved, or have an aggressive or curt social style. Some behaviors can make you seem more approachable and likable (Nilson, 1981):

1) Assume a relaxed posture in the classroom. Sit down or perch casually on the corner of a desk.

2) Speak more softly in class, as long as everyone can still hear you. Also toss out more questions for students to address.

3) Dress down slightly (e.g., a loosened tie and a sports jacket or a two-piece suit vs. a three-piece suit).

4) Chat casually with students before and after class so they can see you as friendly and personable. Address students by their first names. (If you are a TA, consider asking them to call you by your first name.)

5) Smile whenever appropriate.

6) If you are a TA, mention that you, too, are a student and that you can identify with the academic demands they are facing.

Preventing Incivility: Setting Ground Rules

All the literature on classroom management considers setting ground rules essential (Nilson, 1981; Brooks, 1987; Ballantine and Risacher, 1993; Sorcinelli, 1994; Boice, 1996; Baldwin, 1997-98; Gonzalez and Lopez, 2001; Feldmann, 2001). So announce on the first day, especially in a large class, exactly what disruptive behaviors you will not tolerate in your course—and why. Your most convincing reason—and one that is research-based— is that such behaviors annoy the other students in the class. (Reiterate this reason when handling a noisy disruption.)

Some rules also belong in your syllabus, especially your expectations and any grading issues regarding attendance, tardiness, class participation, extension requests, missed assignment deadlines, and make-up exams (see Chapter 4). You may want to add statements forbidding sleeping in class, eating in class, side conversations, cell phones and pagers, and showing respect for fellow students. Then be prepared to ask any offenders to stop the behavior immediately or leave the room.

You may prefer to emphasize

appropriate behaviors rather than disruptive ones. If so, express your rules in a positive way—for example, "Students are expected to hand in assignments on time" rather than "Students will be penalized for late assignments."

Some instructors have reduced classroom incivilities by having their students collectively draw up and a "contract" or set of rules for behavior to which they will agree. Here's the procedure. On the first day of class, lead a discussion on the student behaviors that genuinely bother the members of the class. Then from the notes you take, type up a contract for all students to sign at the next class meeting in which they promise not to engage in the disruptive behaviors listed. Instructors who use contracts claim that, for the rest of the semester, students pretty much police themselves, keeping even minor violations to a minimum (Ballantine and Risacher, 1993; Baldwin, 1997-98). Some institutions publish a student code of conduct, but students often don't buy into what they don't feel they own.

Preventing Incivility: Modeling Correct Behavior

Sometimes, classroom incivility starts with the instructor's behavior towards the students, such as being rude, sarcastic, condescending, indifferent, insensitive, or inflexible (Boice, 1996; Gonzalez and Lopez, 2001). Your efforts to model good manners do not guarantee that students will *always* imitate you. But they will consider your standards and requirements more fair if *your* behavior reflects them, and no doubt more students will honor them.

For instance, if you don't want students to interrupt one another during discussions, judiciously try not to interrupt students yourself. If you value punctuality, come to class ahead of the bell and complete your board work before class begins. If you want assignments turned in on time, return papers promptly. If you expect students to come to your office hours, keep to your schedule faithfully.

Preventing Incivility: Commanding Class Attention

Sometimes students become restless, apathetic, and potentially disruptive simply because their attention is wandering or they're bored. Your practicing good platform skills enables you to command their attention and interest for longer periods of time.

These skills come up briefly again in Chapter 14 because they strongly influence the motivational and teaching effectiveness of a lecture. They also affect how easily you can keep students awake, quiet, orderly, and on task for all or part of a class period. Aristotle had good reason then for evaluating rhetorical oratory on not only invention (content) and arrangement (organization) but also style (sentence structure and word usage), delivery (vocal and physical performance), and memory (freedom from notes).

Excellence in public speaking involves many different behaviors. As Chapter 14 addresses invention and arrangement, and since you are probably gifted with respect to style, let us proceed directly to delivery. It, too, is comprised of many different behaviors, most of them "small," so to speak. But they add up to a tremendous difference in the way the speaker and the message are received and regarded.

Below is a simple listing of

major platform skills (adapted from Toastmasters International speech manuals and other materials):

Effective use of voice: volume adjusted to be audible for the room and audience; words enunciated clearly; rich, resonant quality, projected from chest and diaphragm; vocal variety (changes in intonation to complement content and for emphasis); volume variety (either extreme for emphasis); varied and appropriate speaking pace (never hurried and dramatically slower for most important content); "pregnant" pauses (for emphasis before and after major points); imagery plays on words (e. g., drawing out "slow" and "long," saying "icy" in an icy tone, saying "soft" softly, saying "strong" with especially deep resonance).

Effective use of body: solid, natural stance (unless moving, legs comfortably apart, knees slightly bent, arms hanging at sides, shoulders relaxed, and back straight); natural movement around lectern/ stage and out towards audience (for emphasis and to complement content); abundant gestures to complement content (especially broad ones before large audiences); word dramatization (e.g., momentarily acting out "timid," "angry," "anxious," "huge," etc.); varied facial expressions (more dramatic in a large room), including smiles where appropriate; only occasional glances, if any, at notes; steady eye contact with the audience (at least three seconds per audience sector or quadrant recommended).

Effective use of visual aids and props: In addition to rehearsing their use to avoid awkwardness, see Chapter 21 for pointers.

Emotions to project: relaxed confidence, conviction; enthusiasm, excitement, passion, dramatic interest; sincerity, concern, honesty, openness, warmth; a sense of humor, curiosity, suspense, surprise.

Minimization/elimination of distracting behaviors: um, uh, you know, sort of, kind of, and-and, that-that, etc.; mispronunciations; false sentence starts; mid-sentence switches to start of a new sentence; volume fade-outs at end of sentences; pacing, swaying, or other repetitive movements; leaning on lectern, against wall, against chalkboard, etc.; lengthy checks of notes; ritual apologies to audience (e.g., "I hoped to have prepared this lecture more carefully").

Of course, all these skills assembled together seem impossibly numerous and precise to master. But you probably have inadvertently learned most of them already and may only need to polish a few. If your institution has a teaching center, it probably will videotape you teaching a class and offer you the chance to view your tape with a trained specialist. This service can help you assess your current platform skills and identify ways to enhance your public speaking effectiveness.

For now, the most important skill you should check is your eye contact with your students. In large classes, it is easy to forget the far half of the class, and that is exactly the half you usually need to control the most. Your eye contact is a powerful control tool. Eye contact also personalizes your comments, encourages students to return your attentiveness to them in kind, and enables you to "read their faces" to gauge their interest

60

and understanding.

Another key skill to monitor is your voice. Accurately or inaccurately, its tonal variety and pace reflect your level of engagement in the material and your enjoyment of teaching. A voice can sound monotone because the person speaks at the same *pitch* or at the same *pace* for long periods of time. If you find yourself droning this way through a dry section of your lecture, try consciously to modulate your voice and vary your speaking pace to keep student interest.

Not speaking for too long. Finally, as you will read in Chapter 14, students have a rather short attention span for lecture. Unless you're a truly charismatic speaker, you're inviting disruptions if you lecture beyond 10 to 15 minutes at a time. Whenever you spot a bored expression or glazed eyes while you are lecturing, pause and change the pace. Pose a question, open the floor for questions, or use any of the student-active breaks suggested in Chapter 14. If you don't shift your students' attention to a learning activity, they will shift their attention to a non-learning activity.

Responding to Incivility

If you encounter a discipline problem in your classroom, the first thing to do is to **stay calm and in control**. Count to ten, breathe deeply, visualize a peaceful scene—anything to keep you from losing your temper. No matter how much an offensive student tries to bait you, you lose credibility if you lower yourself to his level. If you keep your composure, you win the sympathy and support of other students. They may even start using social pressure to discipline the offenders themselves.

Keeping your composure, however, does not mean accepting and tolerating the abuse. It is critical that you do *not* ignore or otherwise tolerate the behavior. You must ***respond immediately***. The longer you let the incivility continue, the higher the level of response you will have to take later on (Gonzalez and Lopez, 2001; Feldmann, 2001). Here are some specific, appropriate measures you can take in response to disruptive behaviors (Nilson, 1981; Watkins, 1982; Ballantine and Risacher, 1993; Sorcinelli, 1994; Boice, 1996; Baldwin, 1997-98; Gonzalez and Lopez, 2001; Feldmann, 2001). Always be extra strict in enforcing the rules early in the semester.

Talking in class. Occasional comments or questions from one student to another are to be expected. However, chronic talkers bother other students and interfere with your train of thought. To stop them, try a long, dramatic pause. Then, if necessary, accompany your pause with an equally dramatic stare at the offenders. Another option is to walk over to them while you continue to teach. If still necessary, refer to the contract or rule for behavior that the class authored and signed. If you don't have a contract, say something general such as, "I really think you should pay attention to this; it will be on the test" or "You are disturbing your classmates." If the problem persists, get stern with the offenders outside of class. Direct intervention and public embarrassment are strictly last resorts.

Packing up early. Routinely reserve some important points or classroom activities (e.g., quizzes, writing exercises, clarification of the upcoming readings, study guide

Teaching at Its Best

distribution) until the end of class. Or have students turn in assignments at the end of class. Paper-rustling and other disruptive noise-making during class can be stopped the same way as is talking in class.

Arriving late and/or leaving early. State your policies clearly on these offenses in your syllabus and on the first day of class. You can insist that students inform you, preferably in advance, of any special circumstances that will require them to be late to class. You can even subtract course points for coming late and leaving early, as long as you set this policy at the start. You might draw attention to offenders by pausing as they walk in and out. Alternatively, you can set aside an area near the door for latecomers and early leavers. Finally, as you can do to discourage packing up early, you can routinely schedule important class activities at the beginning and the end of class.

Cheating. Academic dishonesty is such a serious and wide-spread problem in higher education today that the entire next chapter is devoted to preventing and responding to it.

Being unprepared for class. This problem, too, is so widespread that an entire chapter addresses "getting students to do the readings."

Dominating discussion. If students habitually try to monopolize class time, tell them to speak with you after class to clarify their questions and discuss more of the issues. You can also broaden the discussion and call attention away from the disruptive student by asking the rest of the class for the answers.

If the student is rambling around or off the subject, take control by seizing the chance to interrupt the student and para-phrase whatever meaning you can salvage. Then supply an answer and move along. Alternatively, you can defer answering it for the sake of saving class time by advising the student to raise it outside of class.

Asking questions you've already answered. A student asks you about the procedure for doing an assignment that you've already explained. Rather than putting down the student ("Where were you when I gave the assignment?"), just answer the question civilly and quickly, or say that you already answered the questions and repeat the answer only outside of class. Another option is to refer that student to the written instructions you've provided and ask exactly which aspect of the assignment needs clarification.

Asking wheedling questions. Occasionally students try to wheedle answers out of you to avoid having to work out the answer for themselves. In class, you can invite other students to suggest leads and possibly get a discussion going. But one-on-one, the best way to avoid giving in is to answer each of the student's questions with another question that should help him think through the answer. In fact, this occasion provides the perfect opportunity to use the Socratic method (see Chapter 13). A student who is asking questions solely to pry answers out of you will soon tire of your questions and go away.

Asking argumentative questions. A student who tries to entrap you in an argument just for

62

the sake of arguing either wants attention or has an authority problem. Just acknowledge the student's input and quickly move on. To lower oneself to the bait jeopardizes your credibility with the class. If another incident occurs, tell the student you will discuss the issue outside of class. After class, invite the student to make an appointment and inform the student that you do not appreciate such disruptive behavior in your classroom.

Another strategy is to handle questions through a different media. You can collect written questions in a box and briefly address some of them at the next class meeting. You can also encourage students to e-mail their questions to you or to put them on the course listserv or newsgroup. While less personal, these options offer a less confrontational format.

Asking loaded questions. The rare nefarious student may design a question just to embarrass you and put you on the defensive. Like the argumentative student, this type is also probably seeking attention and respect from their peers. You can often turn the loaded question back on the student asking it:

Student: You're not really saying...?

Instructor: What I'm saying is....Now, what is your perspective on this topic?

Demanding a grade change. To discourage this situation from happening very often, set a policy in your syllabus that if a student wants to protest a grade, either 1) you will regrade the entire test or assignment, or better yet, 2) you will not accept a grade protest unless it is in writing.

If a student still comes to you demanding a grade change, try to

neutralize her emotion and delay dealing with the issue until she calms down. Schedule an appointment with her in your office at least a day or two later. Then open with a positive, empathetic statement: "I understand your frustration. Let's take a look at your paper (or test) and talk about the grading." Maintain eye contact and try to agree with the student wherever possible. If necessary, explicitly disassociate the grade from the student's worth as a person. Even if you can't turn the student's opinion around, you can reduce both your anxiety levels by showing yourself to be an ally (at least partially). Finally, try to give the student a graceful way to retreat from the situation. Just don't be intimidated into changing the grade.

It is very rare that an instructor feels physically threatened by a hostile student, and it invariably happens when others are not around. While verbal hostility calls for a private approach, the physical version requires quite the opposite: Try to move yourself and the student into as public a place as possible, even if just the hallway.

Using a computer in class for non-class purposes. Some students claim they are facile at "multitasking," so they can read and respond to their email, "messenger" with a friend, participate in a chat room, make purchases, or surf the web, *and* pay attention in class at the same time. But if this were true, people could talk on their cell phones and drive safely (a low-concentration cognitive task) at the same time, and we know that even young people can't.

Unfortunately, few computer labs allow instructors to monitor student computer screens. You may or may not be able to roam around the room to see what the students are doing. With more and more universities mandating laptops, the problem can only get worse.

But you can take measures to reduce the behavior drastically. When you assign an in-class computer task, keep your students extra busy by giving them minimal time to complete it. Also have them work in small groups, each group with one terminal. Chances are, three or four students won't be able to agree on a renegade site. Between computer tasks, have students turn off their computers or close their laptops.

If your institution will install it in its computer classrooms, there are a few rather expensive hardware-controlled systems (e.g., Robotel®) that allow the instructor to monitor and control the students' screens. A few less costly software-controlled systems have recently been developed (e.g.,Netop® and Synchroneyes®), but they tax the network, and you or the institution must require the students to install the sofware on their computers. Some of these products even allow an instructor to project a student's screen to the entire class.

Showing disrespect in general. If your prevention measures fail, talk to offenders privately and explain that their behavior is affecting their fellow students' ability to learn. Be aware that sometimes students show disrespect to get the attention they believe they can't get through any other means. They want to vent their anger towards authority or express some other deep-seated emotional problem. Leave such cases to the professionals and refer them to your institution's psychological or counseling center.

Cutting classes. These are the top three reasons students give for cutting class: 1) Attendance is not taken or does not affect the grade. 2) The instructor does not see or care if a student is missing. 3) The class content is available elsewhere. We also know that attendance drops off in required, large, and more lecture-oriented classes (Friedman, Rodriguez, and McComb, 2001).

From these findings, the best ways to increase attendance, especially when used in combination, suggest themselves: basing part of the course grade on attendance; taking attendance regularly (even if you don't calculate it in the grade); basing part of the course grade on participation in discussion (see Chapter 15); making the class more interactive and participatory; giving frequent, graded quizzes; regularly taking up homework to be graded; covering in class a great deal of material that isn't in the readings; not allowing commercial production of your lecture notes; not putting your lecture notes on the web (outlines are okay); putting students on their own to catch up with any classes they've missed; conducting cooperative learning group activities in class and grading students in part on peer performance evaluations (see Chapter 18); and conducting other frequent, graded in-class activities (see Part III).

Asking for extensions and missing assignment deadlines. In your syllabus, specify penalties for late work (e.g., docking a portion of the grade), with or without an "approved" extension. Some instructors feel comfortable strictly enforcing this policy. But if you prefer to be flexible, you probably realize that students occasionally

64 have good reasons for not meeting deadlines. But they also occasionally lie. You must assess each extension request and excuse on a case-by-case, student-by-student basis, perhaps allowing a single, documented incident but drawing the line at the second.

A student with a habitual problem deserves a private talk and the full penalties as described. You might ask other instructors in your department for the names of any chronic cases that they have encountered.

Seek Assistance

Ask your more respected colleagues how they handle given incivilities. Requesting their advice will *not* lead them to believe you are an ineffective teacher. Another source of strategies is the student affairs staff. These officers usually understand students, their worlds, and how to communicate with them better than most faculty. Also speak outside of class with your best behaved students, enlisting them to help you keep an orderly learning environment.

With serious incivilities, your turning to others is essential. You should refer students with ego, authority, or anger-management problems to your institution's psychological or counseling center and even mildly violent incivilities to Student Judicial Affairs, if not the campus police.

For further reading:

Richardson, S.M. 1999. *Promoting Civility: A Teaching Challenge.* New Directions in Teaching and Learning 77. San Francisco: Jossey-Bass.

PRESERVING
ACADEMIC HONESTY

The term "cheating" refers to a variety of behaviors generally considered unethical (Barnett and Dalton, 1981). In its basic form, it is theft of intellectual property. Plagiarism, a type of cheating, is claiming the ideas or words of others to be one's own, if just passively by not citing their true source. Whether a student plagiarizes a report, copies an answer on a test, or pays another student to write a term paper, she has dishonestly obtained information and lied in passing off the work as original and her own.

How Prevalent Is Cheating?

In the early 1990s, research found that cheating was a way of life for students at American colleges and universities. In a national survey of undergraduates, 45 percent reported having cheated at some time in college, while an additional 33 percent copped to being habitual or "hardcore" cheaters—i.e., cheating in eight or more classes while in college (Collison, 1990a). The figures were comparable at 31 highly selective American universities, where 67 percent of the students admitted to cheating (Kibler, 1992). Nationally, plagiarizers numbered about ten percent (Collison, 1990b).

Fast forward a decade or so and 75 percent of American college students reported having cheated, the major difference being use of the internet for purchased papers and stolen sources (Altschuler, 2001). The incidence of plagiarism soared.

A quarter of the students said that they at least sometimes copied and pasted text from the web without attribution, and 28 percent admitted lifting text from printed material (Kellogg, 2002). As shocking as these figures may be, other sources have reported even higher ones (Kleiner and Lord, 1999).

Who Cheats and Why?

According to many college administrators, student cheating only reflects the ethics and behavior of the broader society. An overall decline of public morality started in the self-centered era of the 1970s and 1980s and has just gotten worse. Media depictions of "the good life" whet students' appetites for something that they are not sure they will be able to afford. Moreover, the now commonplace, scandalous antics of business and political leaders make amoral and immoral behavior seem normal, and the small price these leaders pay makes it look profitable (Collison 1990a). In fact, 90 percent of the college students don't think that cheaters ever pay the price (Kleiner and Lord, 1999). As one student put it, "Cheating is a very common practice in our country. Everyone wants to make a lot of money, and cheating is a way to beat out other people" (Collison, 1990b).

When asked why the cheat, student cite grade competition and peer pressure from fellow fraternity and sorority members rather than future money (Collison, 1990b).

They also cheat in specific courses because they are not interesting in learning the material (Kleiner and Lord, 1999).

The prevalence of cheating varies by major. Half the economics majors self-report hardcore cheating behavior, followed by communications and psychology majors with 42 percent hardcore, then English and history majors with 18 percent hardcore, and finally science majors only five percent (Collison, 1990b).

Religious affiliation is unrelated to cheating (Nowell and Laufer, 1997), and studies are mixed on the effects of gender and GPA (Barnett and Dalton, 1981; Kerkvliet, 1994; Nowell and Laufer, 1997). But cheating does seem to be associated with fraternity or sorority membership, heavy drinking behavior (Kervliet, 1994), being employed (Nowell and Laufer, 1997), and students' perception of the prevalence of routine cheating (Barnett and Dalton,1981; Bunn, Caudill, and Gropper, 1992; Mixon, 1996).

Still, the single most important determinant of cheating is opportunity. The lower the chances of getting caught (low supervision) and the lower the sanctions for getting caught (low threat)—as students size up the situation—the more prevalent cheating is. So not surprisingly, cheating is related to class size and the use of multiple-choice tests (Barnett and Dalton,1981; Mixon, 1996; Nowell and Laufer, 1997; Kerkvliet and Sigmund, 1999). It is also more common in classes taught by nontenure-track and graduate student instructors (Nowell and Laufer, 1997; Kerkvliet and Sigmund, 1999).

Detecting Cheating

Catching incidences of cheating is not rocket science. In exams you can often *see* wandering eyes and students passing notes, cheat sheets, and even bluebooks to one another. Sometimes you can spot a ringer in a face you've never seen before. Other tip-offs are a heavily erased exam, suspicious behavior (e.g., leaving the room during the exam, rustling through one's things, repeatedly looking at one's hands and arms), and, of course, a considerable number of identical answers, even incorrect ones, across exams. Be concerned, too, if a student improves his exam performance meteorically without having seen you or your TA for extra help.

Plagiarism is possible when a student hands in a paper 1) without quotations or references, 2) with references that don't fit with the text, 3) with odd, esoteric, or inaccessible references, 4) on a topic other than the one(s) assigned, 5) with a format different from your requirements, 6) with a cover-page type face different from the text's, 7) late, 8) on a recently changed topic, 9) with a shifting writing style, 10) with familiar-sounding sections, 11) heavy on facts not tied together, 12) that is photocopied, or 13) that is just too perfect and mature for the student in question.

Realize that you may not be able to trace all purchased papers to their source, and there are dozens of "paper mills" on the web. However, you can uncover most cases of plagiarism by using one of several web-based text-matching services (for a fee) or by typing, in quotations marks, a distinctive suspect phrase or sentence into one or more web search engines (for free).

Preventing Cheating

Except for your instructor status, the crucial determinants of cheating are within your control.

So you can stop or at least drastically reduce academic dishonesty in your classes with proven prevention measures. Most of these heighten students' perceived chances of getting caught and of facing dire consequences, thereby reducing their temptation to cheat (Barnett and Dalton, 1981; Office of Educational Development, UC Berkeley, 1985; Wilhoit, 1994; Johnson and Ury, 1998; Kleiner and Lord, 1999; Johnson and Ury, 1999; Brauchle, 2000):

1) Motivate your students' interest in your subject so they will *want* to learn it (see Chapter 11).

2) Define cheating and plagiarism to your students, and give examples and hypothetical cases. Your students may not understand these terms. Also teach them how to cite sources correctly.

3) State verbally and in writing your own and your institution's policies on academic dishonesty and their applications to each assignment and exam you give. State that you strictly enforce these policies and will check for plagiarism electronically. Include statements in your syllabus (see Chapter 4).

4) If you're a graduate student or adjunct instructor, be especially assertive. Students may think they can get away with more in your class since you're supposedly less savvy than regular faculty.

5) Though even good students don't want to "squeal," appeal to their social ethics and their desire to protect their own intellectual property to report cheating.

6) Make your exams as original as possible to reduce student reliance on old tests for study. Solicit potential new test questions from TAs and students.

7) Ensure equal access to study aids by placing a file of old tests and assignments on reserve in the library for all students to use.

Fraternities and sororities often keep test files for their members.

8) Proctor tests judiciously, enlisting the aid of your TAs and colleagues. Don't allow yourself or your assistants to work on any other project while proctoring. Charge only one proctor (perhaps yourself) with answering any questions during the test.

9) Make different forms of tests, especially multiple-choice tests, by varying the order of the questions.

10) During tests, if the room permits, seat students with space between them and place their personal belongings far away from them (e.g., at the front of the room).

11) In large lecture halls, have assigned test seats and keep a chart of students' names.

12) Supply scratch paper if needed.

13) Clear all calculators before passing out a test..

14) If bluebooks are used, have students turn them in just before the test, then redistribute them randomly.

15) Check for cheat notes in nearby restrooms, on the underside of baseball cap bills, on students' skin (perhaps visible only through a hole in their jeans), and in other highly imaginative places.

16) Collect tests from students individually to avoid a chaotic rush at the end of class.

17) When grading tests, clearly mark incorrect answers with an "X" or a slash. Also place a mark at the end of each answer to discourage additions after you return the tests.

18) Return exams, papers, and assignments to students in person.

19) Collect your exam questions after you review the tests.

20) Assign paper topics that are unique and specific and that require original critical thinking and/or critical self-examination.

21) Give explicit collaboration rules.

68

22) Change your writing assignments as often as possible to discourage paper "recycling."

23) Take class time to discuss difficulties in the assignments and how to overcome them.

24) Make specific format requirements, and grade in part on adherence to them.

25) Require a certain combination of sources—so many from the web, so many from print material in the campus library, so many from videos in the campus collection, etc.

26) Require a personal interview as a source, preferably taped or conducted over email, with the documentation to be turned in.

27) Meet with students early and often to monitor their progress on a major assignment and to gauge the development of their ideas.

28) Guide and monitor students through the process of researching and writing. Have them complete assignments in stages and turn in progress reports.

29) Require students to submit first drafts. This ensures you see a work in progress and allows you to provide early feedback.

30) Require students to turn in photocopies of the print and web material they use, at least the first page.

31) Require students to turn in the original of their paper and a copy for your files. You can refer to the file copy if you suspect piracy later.

If you suspect any form of academic dishonesty, take swift, decisive action. Know your institution's policies and the person to whom to report the violation. (Ask your dean or chair, or refer to your institution's faculty handbook, student handbook, or course catalog.) Hopefully, the prosecution process won't be discouragingly time-consuming, laborious, and biased in the students' favor. Some instructors don't take the official route and handle cases quietly on their own—e.g., giving an F to papers and tests where plagiarism or cheating is evident (Schneider, 1999). Ask senior colleagues how much *de facto* discretion you have and should take.

We don't know the incidence of cheating in online classes. Their typically small size may counteract their anonymity. But it's almost impossible to know who is taking an online exam unless the instructor and the students have still or video cameras on their computers.

Honor Codes

Campuses with a well established and well enforced honor code have a somewhat lower incidence of cheating, by as much as 25 percent, than those that do not (Collison, 1990a; Gordon, 1990; McCabe and Trevino, 1996). However, these codes only reflect the *real* reason for the difference, which lies in the campus culture's high regard for academic integrity and honor (McCabe and Trevino, 1996).

In the hopes of changing the culture, several large, public institutions are testing the efficacy of "modified honor codes." While instructors still take precautions such as proctoring exams, students take an honor pledge and to an extent police themselves. For example, a student-dominated judicial board is set up to "try" alleged violators and decide their fate. Thus far, various forms of cheating have dropped—to rates about midway between those of honor-code campuses and those of no-code campuses—on the campuses that have adopted modified codes (McCabe and Pavela, 2000).

While modest, the success of traditional and modified honor codes shows that the student culture has an impact independent of the larger societal culture.

Teaching at Its Best

Making the Most of
Office Hours

When you think of your role as an instructor, you normally picture yourself lecturing, facilitating discussion, answering questions, and the like in front of a classroom or laboratory—in any case, interacting with a *group* of students. During office hours, however, you interact with and tutor individual students as well. This is a golden teaching opportunity because one-on-one tutoring yields more learning by far than does group instruction (Bloom, 1984). Yet we rarely discuss or conduct research on holding effective office hours.

Face-to-face in private, students share their confusions, misunderstandings, and questions more candidly and completely than they do in class, and you are in the best position to give them the individual attention they need. The problem is getting them in your office.

Find out the number of office hours per week that your institution or department requires or expects of instructors. You may want to add another hour when you have a relatively large class or an intensive writing course, or if you are a professor without a TA.

Getting Students to See You

Students see TAs during their office hours with little hesitation. But most of them, freshmen in particular, are intimidated by the prospect of visiting even the kindest, most hospitable faculty member. If you're a TA who teaches your own course, you may be mistaken for faculty and face the same problem. Spending your office hours alone with your research and writing may seem attractive at first, but it won't after you see those disappointing first papers, lab reports, or quizzes. So it is best to make efforts to induce the students to see you. These efforts include finding the right place, setting the right times, and giving a lot of encouragement.

The right place. Office hours need not always be in your office. Howard Gogel (1985) of the University of New Mexico School of Medicine conducted an informal experiment that broadened the location possibilities. During a three-year observation period, he scheduled his office hours in a remote office building for the first and third years and in a common study area in the medical library the second year. In the first and third years, only one student showed up each year, predictably just prior to an exam. In the second year, however, a full 20 percent of his students paid him visits at various times during the semester to discuss the material and to ask questions.

Could it be that students are more intimidated by your office than by you? Or perhaps the issue is the convenience of your office location. Does this mean you should move your office hours out of your office? If your office is out of the way for your students, the idea is worth considering, especially before exams and paper deadlines.

You might even split your office hours between two locations—some in your office and some in the student union or an appropriate library.

The right times. Be careful and considerate in scheduling your office hours. If you are available only briefly during prime class time—that is, when students are attending their other classes—then you immediately reduce your students' ability to see you. If you teach a discussion, recitation, or laboratory section, make sure that your office hours do not overlap with the lecture portion of the course. If there aren't enough hours in the day, consider scheduling an early evening office hour, perhaps in the student union, an appropriate library, or another student-friendly location.

During the term, remind your classes periodically that you also meet by appointment.

The right encouragement. Start out by publicizing your office hours, first in your syllabus, then on the board during the first day of class, and intermittently during the term before "high traffic" weeks, such as before exams and paper deadlines. You might have your students write your office hours and location(s) on the front of their course notebooks. In addition, post your hours prominently outside your office door.

It also helps to establish a friendly classroom atmosphere on the first day of class by having students fill out index cards on themselves, by conducting ice-breaker activities, and by sharing highlights of your own background (see Chapter 7). On that day and throughout the term, warmly invite students to stop by your office to talk about the course as well as the material.

But even the warmest series of invitations may not provide enough encouragement. You may have to require the pleasure of their company. Here are several acceptable ways:

- Make it a regular course requirement for each student to schedule a time to meet with you as early in the term as possible. The first meeting will pave the way for future voluntary visits.
- Have students schedule individual meetings while they are writing the first paper. You can use this opportunity to review their first draft and to clarify your expectations for the paper.
- Have students turn in papers, problem sets, lab reports, extra credit work, etc. *not* in class but in your office during certain hours of a non-class day.
- Have students schedule meetings with you to get their grades on their papers or written assignments. You can return their marked papers or assignments in class for them to review before meeting with you, but hold the grades "hostage."
- If you divide your class into cooperative learning groups or assign group projects, you might have each group schedule at least one appointment with you to give a progress report.

When students arrive, especially the first time, try to make them feel welcome and at ease. After all, they're on *your* turf, and it takes courage for them to be there. You might spend the first minute or two finding out how they are, how the course is going for them, and what they think of their college experience in general.

In this day and age, however, too warm an approach can be misunderstood. If you are meeting in your office, close the door for privacy but leave it slightly ajar. Also maintain a respectable seating distance.

Should an emergency or illness prevent you from making your office hours, leave a note, or ask your department staff to leave a note, apologizing for your unavoidable absence.

Making the Time Productive

Most students who come to your office hours do so with a definite purpose in mind, often one that you have defined in class. So it is worth a little class time, if not a section in your syllabus, to advise students on how to prepare for meetings with you. You cannot be expected to read their minds.

For instance, you might instruct them to come with appropriate materials: their journals and/or lecture notes, their lab books, their homework problems, drafts of their papers, and/or the readings with troublesome passages marked. You might even tell them to write out their questions or points of confusion as clearly as they can. If the issue is a homework problem, insist that they work it out as far as they can, even if they know their approach is faulty. If the issue is a grade, tell them to bring in a written justification—with citations to the readings, lectures, discussions, labs, etc.—for changing their grade.

Reserve the right to terminate and reschedule a meeting if a student is not adequately prepared. Why waste both your time? In addition, counsel students that they are not to use your office hours to get a condensed version of the classes they've missed nor to get you to write their papers or do their homework problems for them. See Chapter 8 for suggestions on handling problematic student demands and questions.

When a student does come properly prepared, try to give her your undivided attention. If you cannot prevent intrusive phone calls, do keep them brief. If other students are waiting outside your door, work efficiently without letting their presence distract you.

Student-Active Tutoring

To maximize the value of your consultation, make it as student-active as possible. Refer to Chapter 13 on the discovery method, especially the section on the Socratic method, and Chapter 16 on questioning techniques for recommendations on how to help students work through their confusions as much on their own as possible. While some students resent this strategy, you can often be most helpful by respond to their questions with other questions that will lead them to answers. After all, they won't really learn what *you* tell them— only what they themselves realize (Bonwell and Eison, 1991).

Usually, the single most informative (to you) and helpful (to them) question that you can pose to students you are tutoring is *why* they chose the answer or problem-solving approach that they did (especially if it's an incorrect one), *why* they came to the conclusion they did (have them reason it through), or *why* they stopped solving the problem, researching, reasoning, writing, etc. where they did. This question should lead *both* of you to the key misconception, misunderstanding, missing step, or error in reasoning.

Sometimes students want to see you to give them a sense of security. For instance, they have revised

72

their paper according to your or their peer group's specifications, but they lack confidence in their writing. Or they have done their homework problems, but they want you to check them over. Rather than giving just perfunctory affirmations, you can help them acquire their own sense of security by having them explain and justify to you their revisions or problem solutions. If they can "teach" their rationales, they've earned the right to feel confident.

Identifying student errors calls for extra gentleness. Students who come to you for extra help are probably feeling somewhat insecure and self-conscious. So it is a good idea to praise their smallest breakthroughs generously, and let them know you appreciate their coming to see you. You want them to feel welcome to come back.

If a student fails to show up on time for an appointment, call to remind her and reschedule if necessary. If she simply forgot, counsel her that your time is too valuable a commodity to be forgotten.

Students in Academic or Emotional Trouble

Dealing with students in serious trouble is beyond the scope of an instructor's responsibility. Students who seem overwhelmed by the material or who lack basic writing, reasoning, and mathematical skills should be referred the learning skills or academic assistance center on your campus. As described in Chapter 1, a unit of this type usually offers individual tutoring and workshops on a range of academic skills, such as textbook reading, writing, studying, problem solving, note-taking, critical thinking, test preparation, and general learning.

Emotionally distressed students usually need professional help. For your own peace of mind, it is important to remember that you are neither the cause of nor the solution to their problems, even if they try to attribute them to a grade you've assigned. You can be most helpful by knowing how to identify such students, promptly referring them to your institution's psychological or counseling center, and informing the center about the encounter. Here are some warning signs:
- angry challenges to your authority
- physical aggression, either real or threatened
- complaints of rejection or persecution
- distorted perceptions of reality
- unjustified demands on your time
- expressions of hopelessness or extreme isolation
- apparent drug or alcohol abuse
- dramatic mood swings or erratic behavioral changes
- continual depression or listlessness

The most immediate proper responses to aggressive behaviors are simple and easy to remember: When dealing with *verbal* aggression, make arrangements to meet with the student later in a *private* place to allow the emotions to defuse (verbal, private). If you sense the situation may elevate to *physical* abuse, move yourself and the student into a *public* area (physical, public).

It is impossible to anticipate all the different kinds of help that your students may need. Chapter 1 will help you refer them to the right office.

MOTIVATING
YOUR STUDENTS

In the academy, the term "motivating" means stimulating interest in a subject and, therefore, the desire to learn it. Let us begin with some basic principles about motivation (Frymier, 1970). First, the motivation to learn is neither fixed nor easily modified in the short term. Second, motivational incentives work most effectively in optimal rather than maximum doses. In other words, they reach a point of diminishing returns, as do many other investments. Third, highly motivated students have better self-images than the less motivated. Fourth, these students also make better, more informed judgments about careers, courses of study, and their futures in general. They take the past, present, and future into account, while less motivated students tend to avoid decision-making altogether. This last principle suggests that instructors must use a variety of motivational strategies to reach different segments of the student population.

Extrinsic and Intrinsic Motivators

Motivation may derive from either extrinsic or intrinsic factors. Among the most powerful extrinsic forces are the expectations of significant others, such as parents, spouses, and employers. Teachers, other relatives, and family associates can also shape a student's aspirations.

Other extrinsic motivators are more material in nature. Returning students often have their eye on a promotion or a favorable career change. Many of today's younger students pursue a major because of its earning potential. For them, high achievement in the form of top grades may mean entrance into a professional school and ultimately a high-paying occupation. Other students may care about grades just so they can stay in school or have someone else pay for it. In the 1960s, some male students were motivated to excel in part to stay out of the Vietnam War. To them, their lives depended on decent grades.

Intrinsic factors are of the purer sort and pertain more to the subject matter itself. These include a genuine fascination with the subject, a sense of its relevance and applicability to life and the world, a sense of accomplishment (for its own sake) in mastering it, and a sense of calling to it. While instructors can't always affect extrinsic forces, they *can* enhance their subject matter's intrinsic appeal to students, and intrinsic motivators are usually far more powerful than extrinsic (Hobson, 2001; Levin, 2001).

Strategies for Motivating Students

Happily, effective motivational techniques and effective teaching techniques greatly overlap. Of course, by definition, more moti-

74

vated students want to learn more, so they achieve more. But it is also true that better teaching generates more rewarding learning experiences, which beget more motivation to learn. It is not surprising, then, that you motivate students using the same methods and formats that you do to teach them effectively. To reach as many students as possible, use as many of the following strategies as you can (Owens, 1972; Ericksen, 1974; Gigliotti and Fitzpatrick, 1977; Cashin, 1979; Marsh, 1984; Watson and Stockert, 1987; Theall and Franklin, 1999; Hobson, 2001; Levin, 2001).

Your Persona

1) Deliver your presentations with enthusiasm and energy. Strive for vocal variety and constant eye contact. Vary your speaking pace, and add dramatic pauses after major points. Gesture and move around the class. Be expressive. To your students, be they right or wrong, your dynamism signifies your passion for the material and for teaching it. As a display of *your* motivation, it motivates *them* (see Chapters 8 and 14).

2) Make the course personal. Give reasons why you are so interested in the material, and make it relevant to your students' concerns. Show how your field fits into the big picture and how its contributions are important to society. In so doing, you also become a role model for student interest and involvement.

3) Get to know your students. Ask them about their majors, interests, and backgrounds. This information will help you tailor the material to their concerns, and your personal interest in them will inspire their personal

loyalty to you. (See Chapter 7.)

4) Foster good lines of communication in both directions. Convey *your* expectations and assessments, but also invite your students' feedback in the form of classroom assessment exercises (see Chapter 27) and some form of midterm evaluation (e.g., your own questionnaire or some type of class interview conducted by your institution's teaching center).

5) Use humor where appropriate. A joke or humorous anecdote lightens the mood and can enhance learning. In fact, according to Norden (1994), the cerebrum's learning center is adjacent to the emotional center. Given this proximity, positive emotions such as humor indirectly stimulate learning. Just be sensitive to context, setting, and audience.

6) Maintain classroom order and civility to earn your students' respect as well as to create a positive learning environment.

Your Course

7) Design, structure, and develop your course with care, and explain its organization and your rationale for it to your students (see Chapter 3).

8) Give students some voice in determining what the course will cover. If they have input, they will feel more invested and responsible for their learning.

9) Appeal to extrinsic motivators as well. Inform students about what jobs and careers are available in your discipline, what attractions they hold, and how your course prepares students for these opportunities. Whenever possible, link new knowledge to its usefulness in some occupation.

Your Teaching

10) Explain to your student why you are using the teaching methods that you are.

11) Use examples and realistic case studies freely. Many students learn inductively.

12) Use a variety of presentation methods to accommodate various learning styles (see Chapter 12).

13) Teach by discovery whenever possible. Students find nothing so satisfying and intrinsically motivating as reasoning through a problem and discovering the underlying principle on their own (see Chapter 13).

14) Use a variety of student-active teaching formats and methods, such as discussion, debates, press conferences, symposia, role playing, simulations, problem-based learning, the case method, problem solving, writing exercises, etc.—all covered in later chapters. These activities directly engage students in the material and give them opportunities to achieve a level of mastery for achievement's sake.

15) Use cooperative learning formats. They are student-active, and they add the motivational factor of positive social pressure (see Chapter 18). Give students choices in forming their groups.

16) Give students plenty of opportunity to practice meeting your learning objectives for them.

17) Teach with the arts to stir student emotions. This is a standard culture-learning strategy in the foreign languages, but it has far broader application. In math courses, show the utility of concepts and equations in visual design and musical composition. In history,
anthropology, literature, and comparative politics courses, show students the art of the age or place. If possible, have them read native literature and listen to native music. Such experiences give students an intuitive feel for the times and places (Burns, 1993).

18) Make the material accessible. Explain it in common language, avoiding jargon where possible.

Assignments and Tests

19) While students must acquire some facts to master the basics of any discipline, stress conceptual understanding above rote memorization. Facts are only tools with which to construct broader concepts, thus means to a goal, not goals in themselves.

20) Set realistic performance goals and help students achieve them by encouraging them to set their own reasonable goals. Striving to exceed a personal best is a mighty motivator.

21) Design assignments that are appropriately challenging given the experience and aptitude of the class. Those that are either too easy or stressfully difficult are counterproductive.

22) Allow students options for demonstrating their learning, such as choices in projects and other major assignments.

23) Design assignments that give students practice in their future occupational activities.

24) Evaluate work by an explicit rubric (set of criteria) that students understand before they tackle the assignment.

25) Place appropriate emphasis on testing and grading. Make tests fair, which means consonant with your student learning objectives, topical emphases, and previous quizzes and as-

signments. Tests should be a means of showing students what they have mastered, not what they haven't.

26) Give students prompt and constant feedback on their performance, as well as early feedback on stages and drafts of major assignments.

27) Accentuate the positive in grading. Be free with praise and constructive in criticism and suggestions for improvement. Acknowledge improvement made. Confine negative comments to the particular performance, not the performer.

28) Let students assess themselves.

Equity in the Classroom

Equity and its opposite powerfully impact student motivation, thus achievement. Not that instructors purposely show favoritism, but research documents that some do so unconsciously.

Studies have uncovered gender inequity in classrooms from primary school through college, with males being favored over females (e.g., Hall and Sandler, 1982; Krupnick, 1985). K-12 teachers often praise (or at least fail to punish) boys for being aggressive but discourage girls from acting similarly. Many college instructors express this same bias by allowing males more time to respond to discussion questions and giving disproportionate approval to males' marginal answers. Females, as well as minority and disabled students, are more likely to be ignored or interrupted, and their correct answers, merely accepted.

Equity in the classroom begins with instructor awareness of these unconscious dynamics. The following guidelines translate this awareness into behavior:

1) Give attention to all students as equally as possible. If a white male tries to answer every question, wait until other students raise their hands and spread the participation around.

2) Praise students equally for equal quality responses.

3) Use non-stereotypical examples in presentations. If you use a female in an example, make her a scientist, an accountant, or a surgeon rather than a nurse, a teacher, or a secretary.

4) Use gender-neutral language. Try to avoid using the pronouns "he" and "him" exclusively when discussing people in general.

5) Resist falling into reverse discrimination. Do not give inordinate attention to minority and disabled students, as this may appear to reflect your expectation of their failure.

6) Be sensitive to difficulties your students may have in understanding you. International, ESL, and hearing-impaired students may have trouble with idiomatic expressions and accents. Ask such students privately if they do, and urge them to request clarification.

Chapter 15 on discussion has many more suggestions for ensuring equity in the classroom. Equity is really about increasing and broadening student participation, not only in discussion, but in higher education and beyond.

For further reading:

Theall, M. 1999. *Motivation from Within: Approaches for Encouraging Faculty and Students to Excel.* New Directions for Teaching and Learning 78. San Francisco: Jossey-Bass.

PART III.

VARIETIES OF LEARNING

AND TEACHING STRATEGIES

TEACHING TO DIFFERENT LEARNING STYLES

People learn, or more precisely *prefer* to learn, in different ways. Many favor learning by doing hands-on activities, some by reading and writing about a topic, others by watching demonstrations and videos, and still others by listening to a lecture. All of these preferences key into the different ways people learn most easily, commonly known as learning or processing styles.

Should instructors then teach their material in different ways to cater to these different styles? Maybe they should prepare students for life in the real world by *not* giving them special treatment. On the other hand, their knowing and being able to take advantage of their learning-style strengths also prepares them for the real world. Particularly now when our society is concerned with fairness and equality for those of different genders, races, ethnicities, and abilities, teaching to different learning styles is a major facet of equity.

The approaches, frameworks, models, and typologies of learning styles that are in academic currency number well over a dozen. Kolb's model of the learning cycle and learning styles (1984) is experiential, Fleming and Mills' (1992) is sense-based, and Krause's (2000) is one of several derivatives from the Jungian-based Myers-Briggs psy-chological (or temperament) typology. Still other frameworks identify individual differences in information processing, orientations to learning, perceived locus of control, types of intelligence, hemispheric dominance, and personality on other than Jungian dimensions (Sarasin, 1998; Theall, 2000).

Of the many models of learning styles, the three mentioned by author(s) above are particularly popular, accessible, and relevant to college students and those of us who teach them.

Kolb's Cycle of Learning Modes

Kolb portrays the process of meaningful learning as a series of events that integrates the functions of feeling, perceiving, thinking, and acting. The learner moves through a cycle comprised of four different phases: concrete experience (CE), reflective observation (RO), abstract conceptualization (AC), and active experimentation (AE).

Let us take experiential learners as an illustration. By directly involving themselves in new experiences, these learners enter the first phase of the cycle, designated concrete experience (CE). As they observe others and reflect on their own and others' experiences, they proceed to the reflective observation (RO) phase. Next, they attempt to assimilate their observations and perceptions into logical theories, thus moving into the third phase of abstract conceptualization (AC). When they use concepts to make decisions and solve problems, learners exhibit the final phase of the learning cycle, that of active experimentation (AE).

Individual learners enter the cycle at different points, typically because they prefer the activities associated with a particular part of the cycle. Thus, the various phases of the learning cycle form the basis for categories of learning modes.

The *concrete experience* mode is characterized by a reliance more on feeling than on thinking to solve problems. In this mode, people interpret human situations in a very personal way and focus on the tangible here and now. Intuitive, open-minded, social, and artistic in their information processing, these learners center on knowledge that demonstrates the complex and the unique as opposed to systematic, scientifically derived theories and generalizations.

The *reflective observation* mode is similarly marked by intuitive thinking, but as applied to observing and understanding situations, not solving and manipulating them. Using this mode, a learner is quick to grasp the meanings and implications of ideas and situations and can examine situations and phenomena empathetically from different points of view. Patience, objectivity, and good judgment flourish in this mode.

Reliance on logical thinking and conceptual reasoning characterizes the *abstract conceptualization* mode. It focuses on theory building, systematic planning, manipulation of abstract symbols, and quantitative analysis. This mode can generate personality traits such as precision, discipline, rigor, and an appreciation for elegant, parsimonious models.

Finally, the *active experimentation* mode is directed towards the practical and concrete (like the CE) and rational thinking (like the AC). But its orientation is towards results: influencing people's opinions, changing situations, and getting things accomplished—purely pragmatic applications. This mode fosters strong organizational skills, goal-direction, and considerable tolerance for risk.

Now visualize a graph with two axes: the x-axis from active (on left) to reflective (on right), and the y-axis from abstract (at bottom) to concrete (at top). This arrangement places the concrete experience mode at 12 o'clock, the reflective observation at 3 o'clock, abstract conceptualization at 6 o'clock, and active experimentation at 9 o'clock. Connecting the modes by arrows going clockwise, you can see Kolb's theoretical learning cycle.

Kolb's Derived Learning Styles

Kolb went a step further to define a "learning style" and a "learning type" in each quadrant. *Accommodators* rely heavily on concrete experience and active experimentation. They enjoy engaging in new and challenging experiences, particularly those requiring hands-on involvement. They attack problems intuitively with a trial-and-error methodology and quite effectively teach themselves through an inquiry-based discovery process. They tend to gravitate towards action-oriented careers, such as marketing and sales.

Divergers, on the other hand, utilize concrete experience as well as reflective observation. They examine situations from different angles and like to be personally, even emotionally involved with their work. They crave to know why things happen as they do. Their major motivator is personal meaning, never competition. They tend to move toward service fields, the arts, and the social sciences.

Convergers rely primarily on their skills of abstract conceptualization and active experimentation in their learning. They are often characterized as asocial and unemotional, preferring to work with things rather than people. What grabs their attention is how things work. They enjoy assignments that require practical applications, experimentation, and, in the end, precise, concrete answers. In general, many engineers and computer scientists fall into this category.

Assimilators combine abstract conceptualization and reflective observation into a style that excels at organization and synthesis. They specialize in integrating large quantities of data into a concise, logical framework, from which they extrapolate theories and generalizations. These individuals focus on abstract ideas and concepts rather than people or practical applications. Many scientists and academicians are assimilators.

In reality, people's learning styles may shift from situation to situation, encompassing an area that spans two and even three quadrants. So take care not to categorize yourself or others too rigidly. Still, when designing a course, try to build in various opportunities for students to board the learning cycle: some lessons that are experiential and tangible, some reflective and intuitive, some logical and conceptual, and others applied and practical.

Teaching to Kolb's Types

These teaching recommendations were developed by Smith and Kolb (1986) and Harb et al. (1995).

Accommodators benefit most from these learning activities:
- group work: brainstorming, discussions, projects, problem solving
- open-ended problems, essays
- inquiry-based discovery learning
- making presentations
- experiential methods such as field trips, role plays, simulations, the case method, problem-based learning, and service learning.

Divergers respond best to:
- discussions of all types—whole-class, small-group, and one-on-one
- group projects
- subjective tests
- emotionally moving lectures and stories, and interactive lectures
- experiential methods such as field trips, role plays, simulations, the case method, problem-based learning, and service learning.

Convergers are most successful when taught by:
- demonstrations and guided labs
- objective homework problems and exams
- computer-aided instruction and simulations
- assignments involving defining and justifying a model
- field trips and cases studies.

Finally, *assimilators* prefer:
- logical, factual lectures
- instructor demonstrations and modeling of problem-solving methods (live or video)
- textbook reading assignments
- independent or library research, including data gathering.

Three of these four types rely on student-active teaching to learn the material. Assimilators do not only because they read and listen so actively on their own.

Fleming and Mills' Sensory-Based Learning Style Typology

Australian scholars Fleming and Mills (1992) advanced another learning-styles framework that uses a more descriptive classification nomenclature. Here, the terminology reflects the preferred physical sense involved in learning, as reflected in the four categories of digital ("read-write"), auditory ("aural"), visual, and kinesthetic. Using the first letter of each type (R for "read-write"), Fleming and Mills dubbed their typology "VARK." The model presumes that individuals rely on more than one style.

Digital. Students with a digital learning style excel when asked to read and write about a topic. They rely heavily on recognizing logical, deductive relationships, such as the classic outline form, and can easily find pattern and flow in a well constructed lecture or textbook. Their memory structure is more abstract than that of any other style. They store information as organized sets of symbols, such as outlines, equations, diagrams, and typologies. As you can imagine, digital learners do well in the traditional educational setting; the reading and lecture format so common in classrooms is tailor-made for them. They need no special instructional considerations.

Auditory. Students with an auditory learning style perform well when they are given information in a form they can hear, such as a discussion, a lecture, a debate, or another type of verbal presentation. In fact, they learn best when they can hear themselves express an idea. Consequently, they benefit from most standard teaching methods, especially those that require student participation. As they process and store information in

chronological relationships, they thrive in fields that base data and analysis on stories, cases, and events, such as history, political science, law, business administration, and literature. Many also have musical talent. Strong auditory learners can retrieve knowledge in "memory tapes" and are aided by mnemonic devices.

Students who rely more on the next two styles face difficulties in the traditional college classroom. Unless they also have a digital or auditory processing style on which to rely, visual and kinesthetic learners are often left behind in lecture-based courses, through no fault of their own. So additional forms of stimuli may be necessary in order to optimize their learning experience.

Visual. Individuals with a primarily visual learning style rely on their sight to take in information. They work well with maps and rarely forget a face, a scene, or a place. Some gravitate to artistic fields where they can express their flair for design and color. Consistent with their visual nature, these individuals organize knowledge in terms of spatial interrelationships among ideas and store it graphically as static or moving snapshots, flowcharts, pictures, or diagrams. Some even have photographic memories.

With little additional preparation, you can easily supplement your teaching presentations with aids for visual learners. The object is to portray knowledge in two-dimensional spatial relationships that reflect the logical, chronological, or mechanical links among concepts, processes, and events. The less "space" and more connections between two ideas, the more closely related the visual learner will comprehend and remember them.

Among the visuals that this learning style appreciates is the graphic syllabus (see Chapter 4), as well as illustrations, pictures, diagrams, flow charts, graphs, graphic models and organizers (conceptual "tree" and "bubble" diagrams), and graphic metaphors. This last type of graphic is a drawing of an analogical relationship, such as a sketch of a building to represent a Marxian view of society, with the basement as the "substructure" and the floors above as the "superstructure."

Visual teaching tools are readily available: the chalkboard, overhead transparencies, slides, and handouts. Some instructional computer software and videotapes also feature outstanding graphical depictions of mathematical, physical, and biological relationships (see Chapter 22).

Using only the least expensive options, you can diagram the relationships among major points in your lectures and the readings. You can add visual components like graphs and histograms to the day's lesson. You can chart complex, logical relationships among overlapping concepts with Venn diagrams. You can draw flow charts of multi-stage assignments, such as the essay writing process, problem-solving strategies, and laboratory procedures. You can even flow-chart your student learning objectives from the beginning to the end of the term. Since students have such trouble taking notes on class discussions, you might "spider map" them as they proceed—that is, diagram a discussion with the central theme as the hub and web lines to the related arguments and points the students make. Then "web off" the evidence presented to support each point.

Kinesthetic. This final learning style benefits most by doing. It uses active involvement as the primary learning mode. Those strong in this style demonstrate superb eye-hand-mind coordination and natural-born mechanical ability. In the recent past, however, these learners were often maligned and rarely taught "their way" except in shop or home economics courses. While mechanical skills may seem narrow and unintellectual, kinesthetic individuals make excellent surgeons, dentists, health care professionals, musicians, technicians, engineers, and architects. In processing information, they easily grasp physical interrelationships and store knowledge as experiences with both physical and emotional components.

You can reach strongly kinesthetic students using the same techniques as you do for strongly visually oriented students, as both types relate well to graphic representations of themes and concepts. But since kinesthetic processors rely heavily on inductive reasoning, they especially benefit from multiple examples and hands-on experiences from which they can formulate general hypotheses and principles. Thus they learn best from student-active, experiential teaching formats like simulations, case studies, role plays, field trips, independent (but instructor-guided) research projects, laboratories, problem-based learning, service learning, and discovery methods, all of which are explained in later chapters.

Physical models and analogies are also important learning tools to these students. For instance, an English instructor faced a kinesthetic student with little concept of how to organize the assigned

Table I: Intake and Mastery of New Knowledge

Digital	Auditory	Visual	Kinesthetic
list, outline	attend lectures	underline, highlight books, notes	use all senses
study headings	attend study sessions	make symbols, flow charts, graphs, pictures, videos	take advantage of laboratories, field trips, exhibits, tours, films, simulations, role plays, cases, problem-based learning
refer to dictionaries, glossaries	discuss topics with students, instructors	spatially arrange concepts on page	study examples, applications
read handouts, manuals, textbooks, books	explain new concepts to others	study textbook diagrams	do trail-and-error experiments
take lecture notes	use tape recorder	recall instructor's gestures, stance, mannerisms	collect specimens
take lecture notes	recall stories, jokes, mnemonic devices, cases		develop procedural recipes
write essays			study previous exams, assignments, papers

Table II: Study Suggestions

Digital	Auditory	Visual	Kinesthetic
outline text, notes	expand notes through discussion	condense notes into spider map, pictures	recall real things, examples
recopy notes	summarize notes on tape	make tables, charts, graphs, diagrams	use examples in summaries
reread notes	explain topics to others	rearrange images	discuss notes with others
rephrase key ideas, concepts	read notes aloud	redraw pages from memory	review labs, lab manual
organize visuals into statements	make up mnemonic devices to remember lists, principles	replace words with symbols	use pictures to illustrate ideas
turn actions, reactions into words			recall labs, field trips, exhibits, tours, films, simulations, cases, role plays, problem-based learning
imagine lists as multiple choice questions			record and recall reactions to the material

Table III: Output and Applications for Teaching and Evaluation

Digital	Auditory	Visual	Kinesthetic
write exam answers	talk with instructor	recall page layouts	write practice answers
practice multiple choice questions	practice writing answers	make diagrams from memory	role play exam situations alone
write essays	read, practice answers aloud	turn visuals back into words	
arrange words in hierarchies	request oral exam		

literature review, even after being given oral instructions. So the instructor decided to use a mechanical illustration. With paper and pencil in hand, she compared the introduction, which contains the thesis, to the motor that drives the paper. The next paragraph contains the points supporting one view, like a series of pulleys all turning in the same direction. The direction of the paper then shifts to the opposing arguments and evidence, much as a mechanical system changes direction if the drive belts are twisted. Finally, in the conclusion, the writer chooses to endorse one direction or the other.

The three tables on the preceding page list different strategies of knowledge intake, study, and recall for each sense-based learning style. Do share these recommendations with your students.

Krause's Cognitive Profile Model

Krause's (2000) model defines four "pure" learning-style types by crossing two of Jung's (1990) bipolar dimensions, Sensor(S)/Intuitive (N) and Thinker(T)/Feeler(F). Each quadrant represents a type: Sensor Thinker (ST), Sensor Feeler (SF), Intuitive Thinker (NT), and Intuitive Feeler (NF). From a 60-item inventory a person's results are plotted on a graph as fours points, one in each quadrant, reflecting the extent to which she favors each style. Connecting the points yields a "cognitive profile," which typically has one dominant quadrant identifying the primary learning-style type.

Krause (1998) conducted research on 2000 general chemistry students to define and test the most effective study strategies for each type. She found that in general students who followed recommended strategies performed significantly better in the course that did the control group.

The **Sensor Thinker** has an analytical, inductive mind that learns in a methodical, organized, step-by-step way. This ability allows the learner to memorize and retain vast quantities of factual and procedural information, as well as to master very complex tasks and repeat them without error. All of these cognitive strengths equip Sensor Thinkers to be successful as physicians, lawyers, accountants, and airline pilots and in other occupations that involve large bodies of knowledge and complex procedures. This type of learner studies best by listing and organizing material sequentially, building from details to concepts, devising step-by-step approaches to problems, memorizing material, and drilling and practicing with it.

Sensor Feelers also think sequentially, inductively, and concretely, but they learn by verbalizing, through stories, by hands-on experience, and in social interaction. Their gift for relating to people attracts them to the helping professions (e.g., social work, nursing, teaching). Their most beneficial study routines are practice, study groups/buddies, and talking through the material.

Intuitive Thinkers have minds that operate abstractly, complexly, logically, and deductively—quite differently from the way schools usually teach. Unlike the "sensors" above, they learn *not* by building up from details and examples but by first understanding the overarching global principle. Their talents include pattern recognition and visualization, which make them fine researchers, engineers, architects, and project managers. When they study, they should first find the overall pattern or logic, which may mean examining a chapter's graphs, illustrations, flowcharts, and closing summary before reading it. Taking graphical, diagram-type notes is also helpful.

Intuitive Feelers are often brilliant, creative individuals who so loathe routine and organization that they suffer and may fail in the regimentation of school. They think visually, abstractly, globally, and more metaphorically than logically, so they thrive as artists, designers, musicians, and inventors. Their most effective study methods overlap with the Intuitive Thinkers', but they best absorb new knowledge by comparing it to some similar process or concept that they already understand.

Parallels Across Models

Though anchored in different intellectual traditions, Kolb's and Krause's models generate similar, though not exactly the same learning-style types, while the sense-based framework cuts across both of them. Accommodators have traits in common with Sensor-Feelers, including being auditory and kinesthetic in their sensory leanings. Divergers approximate Intuitive Feelers, and they share visual and auditory preferences. Convergers parallel Sensor Thinkers, and both favor digital and kinesthetic processing. Finally, Assimilators are akin to Intuitive Thinkers, both of whom lean towards the digital and visual styles.

Multi-Sensory, Multi-Method Teaching: Most Effective for All

In all the learning-style frameworks, it is important to remember that learners prefer one or two learning styles, but they may also use the other modes to a lesser extent. In fact, *all* students learn more and better from multiple-sense, multiple-method instruction.

Perhaps because of the passive way most students read, they remember only ten percent of what they get out of books alone. With only 50,000 neurons connecting the ear to the brain, people retain only ten percent to 20 percent of what they hear. By contrast, the eye has 1.2 million neural links to the brain, which may be why most students can recall 30 percent of what they see in pictures and graphics—roughly twice as much as what they hear (Woods, 1989; Clute, 1994).

The major benefits derive from multi-sensory, multi-method teaching. Students remember half of what they hear *and* see. Because speaking involves active cognition as well as hearing, they retain 70 percent of what they say. Couple speaking with doing and the recall rate soars to 90 percent (Woods, 1989). But teach in *three* sensory modes—the auditory, the visual, and the experiential—and students remember 97 percent of the material (Clute, 1994).

Teaching to multiple styles and senses can also help revitalize classroom presentations that have become routine through repetition. Adding visual and kinesthetic components, the discovery method, group activities, and experiential learning may take some time and effort, but the change can avert burn-out.

Therefore, to maximize all students' learning and your own professional fulfillment, try to use a rich variety of teaching techniques and learning media in your courses. In addition, acquaint your students with the broad range of learning and studying strategies.

An Introduction to Student-Active Teaching: The Discovery Method

The evidence is overwhelming that at the college level, student-active teaching methods ensure more effective, more enjoyable, and more memorable learning than do passive methods—the most passive being the lecture. Most people neither absorb nor retain material very well simply by reading or hearing it. The best methods permit learning by *doing*, by *acting out*, by *experiencing first-hand*, or by *thinking through to realization* (Woods, 1989; Bonwell and Eison, 1991; McKeachie et al, 1994; Leamnson, 1999)

Student-active teaching methods also build in motivation. As they don't allow for wallflowers, they engage even the most reluctant students in the material, giving it a chance to capture their interest. In addition, they pique natural human curiosity, set up doable, short-term challenges, and leave students with satisfying senses of accomplishment and ownership of the material they learn. Finally, as student-active methods often involve application of knowledge, they may demonstrate to students the practical utility of the material. All of these features motivate learning (Gigliotti and Fitzpatrick, 1977; Bandura, 1977; Cashin, 1979; Nosich, 1993; Theall and Franklin, 1999; Levin, 2001).

This chapter focuses on a subset of student-active teaching tech-niques that fall under a loose classi-fication called "the discovery method." These include four types of activities for in-class discussion or homework assignments for-warded by Nosich (1993), as well as the Socratic method of teaching by questioning. The chapter concludes with a preview of other student-active formats, explained later in detail, that encourage discovery through identification, direct experience, collaboration, writing, open-ended problem-solving, and scientific inquiry.

Recreating Historical Discoveries

Nosich (1993) offers a number of examples that may inspire you to set up historical recreations for your particular courses.

In a physics course, ask students how they could tell whether two flashes of lightning occurred at the same time. They can tackle the problem in small groups or in a general class discussion, if the class is not too large. With a little background, they should be able to restructure Einstein's experiment on simultaneity and rediscover aspects of his theory of relativity.

In chemistry, ask students how an early scientist like Lavoisier could have devised an experiment to discover something as counter-intuitive as the weight of oxygen.

In biology, students can rediscover pecking orders in various species of animals by making observations at a zoo, a wildlife park, or a farm. You can make this an outside assignment or a class field trip.

In nursing, allow students to discover the nursing process on their own by making observations in a medical facility—again as an assignment or a field trip.

In art or art history, set up an arrangement of cubical blocks that lets students discover the principle of perspective and the vanishing point on their own.

In music, rather than telling students about the concept of resolution and how Wagner avoided it in *Tristan and Isolde*, give them the first four chords of the piece, without identifying them as such, and assign them the task of writing 12 more bars of chords that do not reach resolution. Students will discover first-hand how difficult it is to avoid resolution and will then appreciate why Wagner made the chord choices he did.

Discovering Naive Misconceptions

Here the challenge is to lead students to realize that their current thinking on a subject is naïve—and, therefore, that the knowledge your course offers has relevance—*without your telling them.* Your task is to explicitly or implicitly present their misconception as a proposition and to elicit discussion by offering a key counter-example. After the discussion, ask students to reconsider the original proposition (Nosich, 1993).

In physics, students invariably enter an introductory course with an Aristotelian working concept of the world. The problem is, they often leave it the same way. Present a demonstration or devise a laboratory experiment that yields results that run completely counter to their Aristotelian world view. They will then be more open to and appreciative of Newtonian, then Einsteinian concepts.

In chemistry, raise the proposition that putting chemicals in things is bad, and either toss out a counter-example or ask the students if they can think of any.

In biology or paleontology, have students consider the popular evolutionary belief that *Homo sapiens* "progressed" from the "lower" forms of life, or from the dinosaurs, or insects, or chimpanzees. You can direct the discussion to examine the notion of "evolutionary progress" and "lower" forms of life, as well as to introduce cladistics.

In history or political science, invite students to examine the premise that the majority rules in the United States.

In sociology, have them take another look at their private belief that social taboos and restraints don't influence them personally.

Discovering Our Ignorance

One of the most thought-provoking discoveries that people can make is realizing what they *don't know.* We may not fully appreciate the value of our ignorance because we are constantly on the lookout for unknowns in our own field so we can intelligently direct our research agenda. Students, however, tend to think they "know" African history or physical chemistry or nineteenth-century French literature or anthropological linguistics after completing a course by that name. They may never know what they *didn't* learn, let alone what *we* know we don't know.

One way to evoke such discoveries is to ask the class after a reading assignment, "What did the article (or book) *not* tell you?" Nosich (1993) gives an extended example of what a typical book on the revolutionary war doesn't tell students, and what they can discover by an instructor's asking what they didn't learn—for instance: What were children doing during the war? What was it like to be gay or lesbian at the time? What did the troops eat? Or people in general? Suddenly, students become curious about issues that never crossed their minds before.

Another method is to let your entire class or small groups chew on a question the reading and lectures never actually address, such as, "Why doesn't an atom fall together?"

A final thought-provoker: Human beings discovered fire. Let us consider, what have we missed?

Discovering Alternative Explanations

This technique works especially well in the social sciences, history, literary criticism, and psychology, in which a book or article, however scientifically respectable, may reflect a particular theoretical or ideological point of view among several that exist. The method also works in the physical and biological sciences but at somewhat advanced levels of study, where such debates tend to emerge.

First, have your students demonstrate that they understand the explanation, hypothesis, interpretation, or argument in the assigned reading. Second, invite them to develop an alternative explanation, then either to defend it with evidence or to design a research project that would adequately test it against the one in the reading (Browne and Keeley, 1986; Nosich, 1993).

You can simply have your class brainstorm and discuss alternative explanations and the type of evidence or research needed to examine them. Or you can make it an assignment in which students work either individually or in small groups. It can be done in class, as homework, or as an essay question on an exam.

Discovery by the Socratic Method

Socrates himself never wrote a word. But Plato, one of his admiring students, recorded Socrates' teaching strategies in *Dialogues*, particularly in "Symposium," "Meno," and "The Apology," Socrates' defiant, unsuccessful defense at his trial.

Perhaps the strongest proponent of the discovery method, Socrates started with the rather radical learning theory that the human mind contains *all* knowledge within it—quite the opposite of the "clean slate" portrayal. The mind cannot actually "learn" anything in the sense of taking in new knowledge. (It can only take in new information, which is not to be confused with knowledge.) The challenge is to access the knowledge that is already there. The role of teaching then—and the only thing it can hope to accomplish—is to bring this knowledge to consciousness—as Socrates put it, to help the student "remember." How? By asking a series of questions that taps into the knowledge.

"Meno" contains a demonstration of Socratic learning and questioning techniques. By drawing a simple diagram and asking a series of questions, Socrates coaches an uneducated slave boy to reason through and discover some basic geometric principles (the relationship between the lengths of the sides of a square and its area). When the boy makes an error in reasoning and reaches an impasse, Socrates comments to his friend Menon, "Just notice how after this difficulty he will find out by seeking along with me, while I do nothing but ask questions and give no instruction" (Rouse, 1984, p. 48).

Socrates also took on adults and their conceptions of abstract notions such as love and virtue. Here is a sample of his style from "Symposium." In this section he is responding to an informal speech given by an associate, Agathon (Rouse, 1984, pp. 96-97; only dialogue extracted):

S: Come now, let us run over again what has been agreed. Love is . . . of those things which one lacks?

A: Yes.

S: This being granted, then, remember what things you said in your speech were the objects of Love . . . [that] there could not be a love of ugly things. Didn't you say something like that?

A: Yes, I did.

S: And . . . if this is so, would not Love be love of beauty, not of ugliness? . . . Then Love lacks and has not beauty?

A: That must be.

S: Very well: do you say that what lacks beauty and in no wise has beauty is beautiful?

A: Certainly not.

S: Then if that is so, do you still agree that love is beautiful?

A: I fear, Socrates, I knew nothing of what I said!

Couched in conversation, Socrates' questions appear to be spontaneous responses to the answers he receives. But they are also carefully crafted to lead the usually unwitting student down the blind alley of his or her position to an internal contradiction or absurd conclusion.

Being shown in public to have erred in reasoning didn't bother the slave boy nor apparently Agathon. But the affluent and powerful of Athens, many of whom Socrates also challenged, had much less gracious reactions. It took them decades, however, to bring him to trial on the charges of introducing new gods and corrupting the youth. In "The Apology," he argued that all he ever did was to ask people questions, and if their ill-reasoned answers made them look foolish, they could choose to learn. Those who instead were prosecuting him for their being wrong were only proving him to be right all along, he contended. This thoughtful but hardly conciliatory defense did nothing to soften the judges. But Socrates reached the ripe old age of 70 before being condemned to death in 399 B.C.

Socrates' learning theory and version of the discovery method may indeed seem extreme today. It is one thing to reason through basic mathematics and philosophical issues via a series of questions; both fields are reason-based. But questions alone could hardly impart foreign languages, literature, the arts, or data-based fields like history and the sciences.

Still, these fields wouldn't progress far without questions *about* that knowledge. Moreover, at least some of them do have data-independent, reason-based subfields, such as literary analysis, historical methods, statistical analysis, and the scientific method in general. Guided by the right questions, students no doubt can "reinvent" many of the principles in these areas.

A psychology professor who relies on the Socratic approach, Overholser (1992) gives numerous examples of his students' "rediscovering" or "reinventing" basic research and clinical principles in response to a series of questions. They have reasoned through the need for a control group and double blind research controls, successively narrowed down clinical diagnoses, progressively refine definitions, generate hypotheses from theories, and come to understand the effects of experimenter's expectancies and self-fulfilling prophecies.

The questioning style that Socrates employed also contained a fatal (as it turned out) flaw: It alienated people, all but the most humble, eager, and open-minded. The modern university ethos eschews trying to teach students by verbally "backing them up against a wall," cross-examining them for crimes of ignorance, or otherwise publicly humiliating them. (Some of us might admit though to taking vicarious glee in the Professor Kingsfield character in "The Paper Chase.")

Still, you can use the Socratic method with tact and gentleness. When a student ventures a wrong answer to a reasoning question, you can take the focus off that particular student and warn him or her and the entire class where your next question will lead. For instance, you can say, "I imagine that some of you agree with Bob, but I doubt that many of you agree with the implications of his statement. If you have only one group in your design, and you give it the treatment and measure the change, how will you know that the change is due to the treatment?" If Bob still looks blank after a patient wait and extra encouragement, call on another student for an answer.

Chapter 15 offers guidelines and suggestions for managing classroom discussions, including those that incorporate Socratic questioning. Chapter 16 provides an overview of other questioning schema, as well as tips on constructing thought-provoking questions. For a more extensive, cross-disciplinary treatment on framing questions that generate "reinventive" and critical thinking, see Browne and Keeley (2000), aptly entitled *Asking the Right Questions*.

Discovery in Other Student-Active Formats

The next several chapters examine a wide variety of other student-active techniques, many of which contain elements of discovery. Some of the activities are brief enough to sandwich between sections of your lecture (see Chapter 14).

Discussion is a near-universal method for engaging students in the material. Structured around well-crafted questions, it can direct students to discover subtle facets of the material (see Chapters 15 and 16).

Experiential formats, both simulated and real, provide discovery learning opportunities as well (see Chapter 17). In role playing and simulations, for instance, students find out vicariously, by identification, how it "feels" to be in certain positions in lifelike situations. Discovery also grows out of direct experience—for example, field trips, guest speakers from outside the academy, videotapes and films, outside research, and service learning projects.

Collaboration also fosters

discovery. High-functioning cooperative learning groups develop a synergy that generates novel approaches and solutions that none of the members would have conceived on their own (see Chapter 18).

Writing is another discovery tool. In some writing-to-learn exercises—notably free writes and journals—students free-associate, unearthing new ideas, deep-seated feelings, and subconscious assumptions. In learning logs students can discover their own learning processes and styles (see Chapter 20).

Part IV features problem-solving formats that can encourage discovery. The case method (Chapter 23) and problem-based learning (Chapter 24) add the element of identification to a true-to-life application in which students realize what they don't know and must ask about or research. Finally, science and engineering laboratories can reproduce the discovery inherent in the scientific method when the cookbook exercises are replaced by genuine inquiry-based experiments. In such labs, students receive objectives and background but are on their own to collaboratively devise viable data collection and analysis procedures (see Chapter 26).

The Key to Discovery

The key to bringing out the discovery potential in all these teaching formats is to refrain from instructing students what to find and what to infer. Discovery learning depends on students' inductively arriving at *their own* conclusions.

The process takes longer than feeding students so many facts in a lecture, but it becomes a part of each student's life experience. Whatever our learning style, our life experience is one thing we tend to remember pretty well. So students will retain the learning experience—and the knowledge it contains with it. In addition, they will feel like they "own" the knowledge because they "discovered" it.

If discovery learning and the student-active methods that foster it strike you as hit-or-miss, indeed, it's just like real life, which they say is the best teacher. Still, you can significantly reduce students' mindless "hacking" by having them work through questions, cases, problems, simulations, and experiments in small groups.

MAKING THE LECTURE A LEARNING EXPERIENCE

The room funnels downward like the Roman Coliseum. It was full of restless students the first day of class, but now maybe a third show up. The vast majority cram themselves into the back six rows. At first, the students are animated in their own conversations. When the lecture begins, the chatter slowly tapers off, except in a few isolated pockets.

Fifteen minutes later, about the half the students are sleeping, eating, writing personal notes, whispering to their neighbor, browsing through the student newspaper, doing homework from another course, or instant-messaging on their laptops. The other half...it's more difficult to say. Some take notes when the instructor writes on the board, but many never apply their pen to paper. They just sit there, glancing about the room, checking the clock.

This is what many, if not most instructors look out to when they lecture in large classes. Only the percentages of students doing this or that may vary by the selectivity of the institution. This discouraging educational scenario makes perfect sense in view of the extensive research on the learning experiences of college students. But *it does not have to happen.*

The Effectiveness of Lecture: Learning, Motivation, and the Lecturer

Both McKeachie et al (1994) and Bligh (2000) cite numerous studies indicating that the lecture is as effective as any other method in conveying factual knowledge. But on other criteria—attitude change, development of thinking and problem solving skills, transfer of knowledge to new situations, student satisfaction with the course, motivation for further learning, and post-course retention of knowledge—the lecture falls short of more student-active methods such as discussion.

Actually the lecture *can* be highly motivational, but its success depends on the *lecturer.* A very expressive, enthusiastic instructor can ignite students' interest in the material, while a reserved, reticent one can douse it.

To some extent, the platform skills that convey energy and dynamism can be learned. Public speaking courses and clubs help people develop and practice effective verbal pacing and pausing, gestures and movements, facial expressions, eye contact, vocal quality and variety, lectern and microphone use, visual aid display, etc. (see Chapter 8). Those who start out weak in these skills but who work on them diligently can achieve impressive results within a year.

Some scholars may dismiss such presentation techniques as mere acting. In fact, some people seem to have a knack for them, while others indeed acquire them only with concentration and practice. Acting or not, like it or not, these public speaking techniques have a powerful impact on students' motivation and learning, as well as on their course and instructor evaluations (see Chapter 31), *to the extent that an instructor relies on the lecture format.* But with the variety of teaching methods available, no instructor *need* rely on it much at all.

Therefore, instructors have a choice: Those who happen to have an expressive, dynamic public personality, or are willing to acquire the trappings of one, can afford to use the lecture more in their teaching. (For the sake of student learning, however, even the most charismatic instructor should not depend on it exclusively.) Those who do not have such a persona can avoid lecturing whenever possible and appropriate and employ other, more student-active methods. In brief, instructors can play to their natural and acquired strengths. The wide array of effective teaching methods should put to rest the notion that good teachers are born and not made.

The Effectiveness of Lecture: Time and Attention Spans

According to studies cited in Bonwell and Eison (1991) and Bligh (2000), a lecture begins with a five-minute settling-in period during which students are fairly attentive.

This attentiveness extends another five to ten minutes, after which students become increasingly bored, restless, and confused. Focus and note-taking continue to drop—some students effectively fall asleep—until the last several minutes of the period when they revive in anticipation of the end of class. Bligh (2000) reconfirmed this pattern using students' heart rates as a measure of arousal. Even medical students display similar patterns of concentration levels: an increase over about 15 minutes, followed by a sharp decrease.

This should come as unsettling, sobering news to the higher education community. After all, if highly motivated learners like medical students demonstrate such a brief attention span, what can we expect of our undergraduates? If we are realistic, we should expect the scenario described at the beginning of this chapter.

No doubt the enthusiastic, engaging lecturer can modestly extend that narrow time horizon. But students are programmed from far too young an age to override the pattern entirely. So when we must lecture, what can we as instructors do?

In a word, pause. One study supports the practice of pausing at least three times each lecture to allow pairs or small groups of students to discuss and clarify the material (Rowe, 1980). Another recommends pausing for two minutes every 15 to 18 minutes to permit student pairs to compare and rework their notes (Ruhl, Hughes, and Schloss, 1987).

This latter study was designed experimentally with a control group receiving a series of traditional non-stop lectures and a treatment group hearing the same lectures with periodic pauses. Both groups took

1) free-recall quizzes during the last three minutes of each lecture (that is, students individually wrote down everything they could remember from the lecture) and 2) the same 65-item multiple choice test 12 days after the last lecture. In two different courses repeated over two semesters, the treatment group performed much better than the control group on both the quizzes and the test, better enough to make a mean difference of up to two letter grades, depending upon the cut-off points (Ruhl, Hughes, and Schloss, 1987).

Translated into learning terms, sacrificing the least important 12 percent of your lecture content for periodic two-minute pauses can increase the learning of your current "C" students to that of your current "B" and even "A" students.

Graded or not, quizzes at the end of a lecture drastically enhance students' retention of the material. From research dating back to the 1920s, lectures have an infamous reputation for being utterly forgettable. Their much-replicated "forgetting curve" for the average student is 62 percent immediate recall of the material presented, 45 percent three to four days later, and only 24 percent eight weeks later. Giving some kind of test right after a lecture doubles both factual and conceptual recall after eight weeks (Menges, 1988).

To Lecture
or Not to Lecture?

The eminent psychologist Abraham Maslow once said, "If your only tool is a hammer, you're apt to go around treating everything as if it were a nail." For centuries, the lecture has been the primary teaching tool in higher education, and indeed almost all knowledge and college students have been hammered like nails.

Since college-level teaching research came into its own in the early 1970s, we have been learning that the lecture is only one of dozens of devices in a well-stocked instructional tool box. Sometimes a hammer is just the thing, and at other times it isn"t.

The lecture is probably your most effective and efficient option, at least for part of a class period, when your objective is one of the following (McKeachie, et al, 1994; Bligh, 2000):

- To pique student curiosity and motivation to learn *if your style is very expressive*
- To model an approach to problem solving or a style of thinking
- To give a background knowledge summary that is not otherwise available
- To adapt very sophisticated or theoretical knowledge to your students' level and needs in a way that no other available source does
- To present a particular organization of the material, one that clarifies the structure of the textbook or the course or that helps students organize the readings
- To add your personal viewpoint on the material, including your own related research
- To present up-to-date material that is not yet available in printed form.

Under other conditions, however, the lecture only wastes precious class time. The next several chapters suggest many student-active teaching formats and techniques that will convey the material and meet your objectives much more effectively. Demonstrations, films, and videos may also better serve the purpose. Alternatives to the lecture are most appropriate when you want your students to accomplish the following (Bonwell and Eison, 1991; McKeachie et al, 1994; Bligh, 2000):

- To become interested in a topic in which they are not already interested *if your style is not very expressive*
- To examine and possibly change their attitudes
- To explore controversial or ambiguous material with open minds
- To be able to transfer knowledge to new situations
- To develop problem-solving skills (broadly defined)
- To develop higher-order or critical thinking skills
- To learn a performance technique or technical procedure
- To improve their writing
- To continue to pursue the subject beyond the particular course
- To remember particular knowledge for months or years to come.

Two other circumstances call for restraining from lecturing. First, if you are uncertain of your students' level of expertise, preparation, and interest, have them do a classroom assessment exercise (see Chapter 27) before planning your presentation. Otherwise, you risk going over the students' heads or boring them with basics.

Second, it is best not to lecture if the material you plan to cover simply duplicates what is already in assigned readings or other course materials. Not that duplication is necessarily a problem in itself, but student-active exercises can duplicate the material at a higher cognitive level, such as application, analysis, synthesis, and evaluation.

Deleting a redundant lecture frees plenty of class time for other activities. Besides, if a lecture primarily repeats the readings, any rational student will decide *either* to do the readings *or* to attend lecture. No doubt this is *not* what you intend.

Preparing an Effective Lecture

Bligh (2000) lays out several organizational models for lectures, but they share this common ground:

Class objectives. First, determine your student learning objectives for the class period. What precisely do you want your students to learn that day? How will you express your objectives to the class? Perhaps the lecture will serve only one or two of three goals you have for the class. Then the lecture should fill only part of the period.

Overview. Whenever possible, limit one class's lecture to *one major topic.* Some students find it difficult to pick up a lecture from one period to the next, and global thinkers need to see the big picture before any of the details and examples will make sense. Also lay out a time-content schedule, bearing in mind the two most common lecturing errors: trying to include too much material and delivering the material too fast. While you're lecturing, you will have to proceed slowly enough—including pausing after major points—for students to take notes. So if anything, *underbudget content.*

To start planning your lecture, you might begin by *subdividing the major topic into ten to 15 minute chunks.* Then plan *student-active breaks of two to 15 minutes* between these chunks.

The next section suggests a wide variety of timed break activities of different lengths that you can use, but feel free to devise your own. Most of these activities can be (and have been) conducted in large lectures of hundreds of students, as well as smaller classes. So class size need not deter you. Finally, allow *two to five minutes* for some kind of *recap activity* at the end.

Then turn to *internal organization*. The skeleton for any lecture is the introduction, the body, and the conclusion.

Introduction. The ideal introduction has three parts, the order of which is really an aesthetic decision: a statement that frames the lecture in the context of the course objectives; a statement reviewing and transitioning from the material covered in the last class period; and an attention-grabber for the new material. Effective attention-grabbers include an intriguing question the lecture will answer, a story or parable that illustrates the new subject matter of the day, a demonstration of a non-obvious phenomenon, a reference to a current event or movie, a case or a problem that requires the lecture's information to solve, or a strong generalization that contradicts common thought. The idea is to draw in the class with surprise, familiarity, curiosity, or suspense.

Body. The body is your presentation and explication of new material. It is within this section that you subdivide the major topic into *"mini-lectures,"* each of which should revolve around *one and only one major point*. There is no best logic to follow in organizing a mini-lecture, except to keep it simple. You can choose from an array of

options: deduction (theory to phenomena/examples); induction (phenomena/examples to theory); hypothesis testing (theory to hypothesis to evidence); problem to solution(s); cause to effect; concept to application; familiar to unfamiliar; debate to resolution; a chronology of events (a story or process)— to name just some common possibilities. To appeal to different learning styles, try to vary your organization from one mini-lecture to another (see Chapter 12).

Organizational outline. Make whatever organization you select explicit to students. For instance, tell the class, "I am going to describe some common manifestations of dysfunctional family behavior, then give you a definition and general principles that apply to the phenomenon."

It is best to provide an outline of the body of your lecture on the board, on an overhead or slide, or in a handout. An outline will ensure that students are following your logical flow, especially if you occasionally refer to it to point out your location in the lecture. It should also highlight new terms you are introducing. However, keep this outline skeletal so students still have to take notes. Research shows that the process of note-taking has learning and retention benefits (see "Helping Students Take Notes," pp. 100-101.)

In addition, try to integrate as many of these learning aids as you can:

Visuals. As you plan the material, think about how you can convey or repackage it visually—in pictures, photographs, slides, graphic metaphors, diagrams, graphs, and spatial arrangements of concepts or stages linked by arrows. Prepare them for presentation to the class. While such visual aids facilitate almost everyone's learning, they can be critical for students with a visual learning style.

Examples. Also think about illustrating abstract concepts and relationships with examples. Ideally these examples should be striking, vivid, current, common in everyday life, and related to students' experiences (past, present, or future). Making them humorous also helps students remember them. Students who favor a kinesthetic learning style rely on examples to process and retain new material.

Restatements. Consider, too, how you can restate each important point in two or three different ways—in scholarly terms, in layperson's formal language, and in informal language. Restatements not only demystify the material, making it more comprehensible, but they also build students' vocabulary and encourage their own paraphrasing of the material.

Conclusion. For learning purposes, the conclusion should be a two-to-five-minute recap of the most important points in your lecture. It is too important to be rushed after the bell. You should plan and direct the recap activity, but the *students* should do it. The prospect of having to summarize the material helps keep all students on their toes. The recap activity may take the form of a oral summary presented by one or more students, a free-recall writing exercise (see Chapter 20), or a classroom assessment technique, such as a one-minute paper (see Chapter 27).

Lecture notes. Your lecture notes should be easy to read at a glance and as sketchy as you can handle. After all, you know the material; you will even in front of a group. So all you need is a map showing your next conceptual destination. Therefore, consider laying out the lecture *graphically* in flow charts, tree diagrams, Venn diagrams, network models, bubbles and arrows, etc., including any visual aids you plan to put on the board. Some instructors like to color code their notes for quick visual reference. If a graphic organization does not appeal to you, make a sketchy outline of your lecture. But be sure it's very sketchy. In any case, write big and leave a lot of white space.

The habit to avoid is writing out sentences (except direct quotes). Doing so may tempt you to read them in class. Then you'll lose spontaneity, expressiveness, flexibility, eye contact, and most importantly psychological contact with the class, lulling students into a passive, even inattentive state of mind (Day, 1980). Confine the words in your notes to key concepts and phrases, transitions to make explicit to the class, and directions to yourself (e.g., "board," "pause," "overhead," "survey class," "ask class question," "break activity #2 - voltage problem").

Options for Student-Active Breaks

Once you incorporate student-active breaks into your lecture, you are giving an "interactive" lecture, during which your students are in some way interacting with the material for brief, controlled periods of time. The focus is on "controlled." You must carefully time-control the student-active breaks by informing your students that they will have exactly X number of minutes to complete the activity you assign them. Strictly enforced time limits keep students focused on the task. To make managing easier, bring a timer or stopwatch to class.

These breaks work well in any size class. In larger classes, however, having students work with their neighbor(s) (in *ad hoc* pairs or triads) is quicker and easier than having them get into pre-organized small groups.

During any pair or small group activity, circulate around the classroom to let students know you are listening to them and are willing to answer any procedural questions.

Ask students to work and talk as quietly as they can, but expect the classroom to get noisy anyway. After their activity time is up, you can bring even the largest class to silence within seconds by taking this tip from cooperative learning researchers: Set the rule that you will raise your hand when the time is up. Tell your students that, as soon as they see your hand up, they should immediately stop talking and raise their hands. The rest of the class will quickly follow suit.

Below are some commonly used break activities, along with the number of minutes each typically take. They come from Bonwell and Eison (1991), Cross and Angelo (1993), McKeachie et al (1994), and informal collegial exchanges. Let them serve as your inspiration to conceive and experiment with your own innovations.

Pair and compare. Students pair off with their neighbor and compare lecture notes, filling in what they may have missed. This activity makes students review and mentally process your lecture content. Time: 2 minutes.

Pair, compare, and ask. Same as above but with the addition that students jot down questions on your lecture content. You then field questions that students cannot answer between themselves. Time: 3 minutes, plus time to answer students' questions.

Periodic free-recall, with pair-and-compare option. Students put away their lecture notes and write down the most important one, two, or three points of your lecture thus far, as well as any questions they have. The first two times you conduct this, use an overhead or the board to give instructions; then just telling them will do. Again, this activity makes students review and mentally process your lecture content. Students may work individually, but if they work in pairs or triads, they can answer some of each other's questions. Time: 2 minutes, plus time to answer students' questions.

Listen, recall, and ask; then pair, compare, and answer. Students only listen to your mini-lecture—no note-writing allowed—then open their notebooks and write down all the major points they can recall, as well as any questions they have. Instruct students to leave generous space between the major points they write down. Finally, they pair off with their neighbor and compare lecture notes, filling in what they may have missed and answering one another's questions. Again, this activity makes students review and mentally process your lecture content. Time: 3-4 minutes for individual note-writing, 2-4 minutes for pair fill-ins and question answering, plus time to answer any remaining questions.

Solve a problem. Students solve an equational or word problem based on your lecture content. (Chapter 25 describes a problem-solving strategy you can teach them.) They can work individually or, better yet, in *ad hoc* pairs or triads. Put the problem on the board, a slide, or an overhead and, to make class debriefing easier, give four multiple choice options. Ask for a show of hands for each option. You can also ask student pairs to rate their confidence level in their answer. This activity, developed by Mazur (1997), makes students apply your lecture content while it's fresh in their minds, and it immediately informs you how well they have understood your lecture material. You can then clarify misconceptions before proceeding to new material. Time: 1-3 minutes for problem solving, depending upon the problem's complexity, plus 1-3 minutes to debrief and answer questions.

Quick case study. Students debrief a short case study (one to four paragraphs) that has them apply your lecture content to a realistic, problematic situation. (Chapter 23 addresses the case method, including tips on developing your own cases.) Display a very brief case on an overhead or slide; put longer ones in a handout. You may add specific questions for students to answer, or teach your class the standard debriefing formula: What is the problem(s)? What is the remedy(ies)? What is the prevention(s)? Instruct students to jot down their answers. They can work individually or, better yet, in *ad hoc* pairs or small groups. Time: 3-8 minutes, depending upon the case's length and complexity, plus 10-15 minutes for class exchange and discussion.

Pair/group and discuss. Students pair off with their neighbor or get into small groups to discuss an open-ended question that asks them to apply, analyze, or evaluate material in your lecture or to synthesize it with other course material. The question should have multiple possible correct answers. (Refer to Chapter 16 for helpful questioning schema and question framing techniques.) Have students outline their answers in writing. This activity makes students examine and extend as well as process your lecture content and serves as a perfect prelude to a general class discussion. Time: 3-10 minutes, depending upon the question's complexity, plus 5-15 minutes for class exchange and discussion.

Pair/group and review. Same as above but with an essay question designed for pre-exam review. Student pairs/groups present their answers to the class, while you mock-grade them and explain your assessment criteria. You can also have the rest of the class mock-grade pair/group answers to help students learn how to assess their work. Time: 3-10 minutes, depending upon the question's complexity, plus 5-15 minutes for pair/group presentations.

You will find many other options for student-active breaks in Chapter 18 (learning in groups), Chapter 20 (writing-to-learn activities), and Chapter 27 (classroom assessment techniques).

Helping Students Take Notes

Research conducted on lecture note-taking provides several useful insights for both instructors and students (Carrier, 1983; Mc-

Keachie, 1986; Johnstone and Su, 1994; McKeachie et al, 1994; Bligh, 2000). Your classes may even be interested in hearing about them.

First of all, it is well worth recommending that your students take lecture notes, specifically *their own* lecture notes. Students who do take notes learn and remember more than those who just listen. Note-taking fosters deeper cognitive processing—that is, more thoughtful and active listening involving paraphrasing, interpreting, and questioning, as well as integrating new material into one's organized bank of prior knowledge. It also helps students process the knowledge for "far transfer," which means the ability to apply it in new and different situations. Put in terms of students' immediate interests, note-takers perform better on both objective and essay tests.

Second, advise your students to *review* their notes as well. Again, research shows that they will learn more, remember more, and perform better on all kinds of tests if they do. Of course, you can structure break activities during class periods to ensure students review their notes.

Third, instructors can facilitate note-taking by organizing their lectures clearly and simply, making this organization explicit to students, and highlighting the most important material. This chapter has already detailed these methods.

Fourth, instructors can also present material in ways that compensate for students' most common note-taking weaknesses. For instance, students record 90 percent of the information written on the board, slides, and overhead transparencies. But they rarely record detailed sequences of arguments, examples of applications, the meanings of technical terms

and symbols, or information related to demonstrations. When such material is genuinely important, instructors should say so and should display or distribute it in written form. In addition, students tend to make errors in copying diagrams, equations, and numerical figures. Instructors can easily overcome this problem by disseminating such material in handouts (Johnstone and Su, 1994).

Finally, students need to find their own best note-taking strategy, as no one strategy is effective for everyone. Some students benefit most from a formal outline structure, others from graphic diagrams, a few even from practically transcribing a lecture. Note-taking, however, can actually interfere with learning and retrieval for a small subset of students: those with relatively low ability, poor short-term memory, or little prior knowledge of the subject matter. These students are unable to assimilate new material as quickly as a lecture demands. They are dependent on instructional aids, such as lecture outlines you provide and published course notes, and on student-active breaks like "pair and compare" that allow them to draw on their neighbor's notes.

Whatever your students' note-taking styles, you can offer pointers that will help *most* of them. Share with your class the applicable tips in the boxed section, "29 Lecture Note-taking Tips for Students." They come from a wide variety of study skills manuals and handouts (e.g., Ellis, 2000), as well as Bligh (2000). Maybe you can add a few of your own, including some specific to your subject matter. Refer students who need more than pointers to your institution's learning skills/academic assistance center; it may offer a note-taking workshop.

Making the Lecture a Learning Experience

29 LECTURE NOTE-TAKING TIPS FOR STUDENTS

1. You learn better by taking notes actively than by tape-recording a lecture passively. Besides, reviewing written notes takes less time than does listening to a taped lecture.

2. Keep a separate notebook for each course. Date, number, and label your notes from each class period. Also date and label handouts from each class, and attach them securely to your class notes with staples or tape.

3. Complete the reading assignment due the day of the lecture *before* you attend lecture. The material will probably make a lot more sense.

4. Come to the lecture well prepared with your favorite pen, a back-up pen, a pencil or two, your notebook, any applicable handouts, any study guides on the readings assigned for the day, and anything else you think you may need. Unlike when you travel, it's better to overpack for class than to underpack.

5. Sit near the front towards the center. You can see the board and screen better, hear the lecture better, and avoid distractions more easily. In addition, there is some evidence that students who sit front and center perform better on tests.

6. Arrive early to warm up your mind. Review your notes from the previous class and from the readings assigned for the day.

7. Take note of what you don't completely understand from the last class and the assigned readings, and plan to ask for clarification as early in the class period as possible.

8. Avoid cramming your notes or writing them too small. Strive for easy readability. Leave a generous left margin, as you may want to use it later to write in key words and abbreviations for important material.

9. Organize your lecture notes according to the instructor's introductory, transitional, and concluding words and phrases, such as "the following three factors," "the most important consideration," "in addition to," "on the other hand," and "in conclusion." These signal the structure of the lecture: cause and effect, relationships, comparisons and contrasts, exceptions, examples, shifts in topics, debates and controversies, and general conclusions.

10. Identify the most important points by watching for certain instructor cues: deliberate repetition, pausing, a slowdown in speaking pace, a rise in level of interest or intensity, movement toward the class, displaying a slide or overhead transparency, and writing on the board.

11. Pay close attention to the instructor's body language, gestures, and facial expressions, as well as changes in pace, pitch, and intonation. The instructor's subtlest actions punctuate and add meaning to the substance of the lecture.

12. Record your lecture notes in outline or graphic form, whichever works best for you. (If you're not sure, experiment with both for a few weeks.) Outline form involves indenting less important and supporting points below the more important, more general ones. This way, the more important material stands out. Points of equal importance or generality should start at the same distance from the left margin. (Some outlining enthusiasts also number and letter different points.) Graphic form involves clustering closely related concepts, steps, stages, etc. and linking them with arrows representing relationships between them. An arrow pointing to the right means "causes," "leads to," or "implies," while one pointing to the left signifies "is an effect of," "derives from," or "is implied by." When in doubt, label your arrows.

13. Whenever possible, draw a picture or a diagram to organize and abbreviate the relationships in the lecture material. It is easier for most people to recall a picture than it is a written description.

14. Avoid writing complete sentences unless the specific wording is crucial.

15. Develop and use your own shorthand, such as abbreviations and visual symbols for common and/or key words (e.g., btw for between, + for and, b/c for because, rel for relationship, df or = for definition, cnd for condition, nec for necessary or necessitates, hyp for hypothesis, T4 for therefore, + and - for more and less, up and down arrows for increasing and decreasing, two opposing arrows for conflicts with, a delta triangle for change).

16. Take notes sparingly. Drop all unnecessary words from your note-taking vocabulary. Write down only the words and symbols that are essential to make you recall the idea for which they stand.

17. Take notes fast and at opportune times. Use the instructor's pauses, extended examples, repetitions, and lighter moments to record notes. You can't afford to be writing one thing when you need to be listening to another.

18. If the instructor tends to speak or to move from point to point too quickly, politely ask him or her to slow down. You are probably the most courageous student of many who cannot keep up either.

19. To help speed your note-taking, try different pens until you find an instrument that glides smoothly and rapidly for you.

20. Occasionally glance back over the last few lines of notes you've taken, and rewrite any illegible letters, words, or symbols.

21. Make key words, important relationships, and conclusions stand out in your notes. Underline, highlight, box, or circle them, and/or rewrite/abbreviate them in the left margin.

22. Practice keeping your mind on the lecture. Try to understand the value of the content.

23. If you lose focus or listening-writing coordination and miss part of a lecture, leave a space, and ask a classmate, the TA, or the instructor to help you fill in the blanks. Tell whoever is willing to help you exactly what happened. You may even get some sympathy; it happens to everyone.

24. If, on the other hand, you come into the lecture late, leave it early, or spend part of it in private conversation or any other activity, you deserve no sympathy nor back-up assistance. The University community regards such behavior as extremely discourteous. It is distracting and disruptive to both the instructor and your fellow classmates.

25. Postpone debating the instructor. If you fight new material, you won't learn. Note your disagreement and, if it persists, debate the instructor in private.

26. Separate from your lecture notes your own comments and reactions to the material. Write your thoughts in the margin or a corner of the page, perhaps with a box around them, or on a self-stick removable note.

27. Try not to evaluate the worth or validity of the material on the basis of the instructor's lecture style. The two are totally unrelated.

28. Review, edit, clarify, and elaborate your notes within 24 hours of the lecture, again a week later, and again a month later—even if for just a few minutes. When you review your notes, recite, extract, and rewrite the key concepts and relationships. With enough review, the knowledge will become yours forever.

29. When your attention or motivation sags, remember that this course is designed to serve some goal related to your longer-term educational, career, and/or personal aspirations. Flow with it for your own sake. Try to think of ways the material you're learning may be useful, or ask your instructor for insight.

For further reading:

Bligh, D.A. 2000. *What's the Use of Lectures?* San Francisco: Jossey-Bass.

Leading
Effective
Discussions

The last chapter examined the weaknesses of the lengthy lecture and recommended breaking it up with intermittent activities that allow students to work with and test their understanding of the material. In all but very large classes, one of the easiest and most effective student activities to lead is the well-directed discussion. In smaller classes and seminars, discussion may best meet your learning objectives and serve as your primary classtime activity. Certainly a "discussion section" should remain true to its name and rely heavily on this format.

The Times for Discussion

When might discussion be your technique of choice? Early studies on the efficacy of discussion have been replicated over the decades with similar results: While lecture and discussion are roughly equal in helping students acquire factual and conceptual knowledge, discussion is superior in developing their problem-solving skills. (For literature summaries, see Bonwell and Eison, 1991, McKeachie et al, 1994, and Bligh, 2000.)

These skills apply not only to solving math problems but to all kinds of solution-oriented tasks, whether they call for one correct answer, one best answer, or many possible correct answers. Such tasks include designing a research project, explaining deviations from expected results, writing a computer program, solving a case study, evaluating one's own and others' positions on an issue, analyzing a piece of literature, and developing approaches to tackling real-world social, political, and environmental problems.

Discussion also surpasses the lecture in changing students' attitudes, helping them transfer knowledge to new situations, and motivating them to further learning. In addition, students retain material acquired in discussion longer than they do the same material learned from a lecture.

One final benefit of discussion for you as well as your class: Across disciplines, student ratings of instructors vary positively with the amount of time and encouragement an instructor gives to discussion (Cohen, 1981; Cashin, 1988).

So what exactly is a discussion? It is a productive exchange of viewpoints, a collective exploration of issues. To be productive and not degenerate into a free-association, free-for-all bull session, you as the instructor must chart its course and steer it in the right direction. It is your responsiblity to plan and control the content and conduct, to keep hot air from blowing it off course. But it is also your responsibility to go with the breezes at least occasionally, to keep it flexible and fluid. Your challenge is to strike that delicate balance between structure and openness. Finding that balance helps you broaden participation and keep all hands on deck.

A Discussion Primer: Starting Out

Explaining the role of discussion. If you plan to make discussion an integral class activity, even if not a primary one, it is best to inform your students at the beginning of the term. Making an announcement about its role in your course will encourage students to take the activity more seriously. So will telling them your reasons for using discussion (e.g., how the research supports its effectiveness in developing problem-solving skills). Follow up by explaining how class discussions will relate to other assignments such as papers, readings, and tests. It is wise to build quizzes and exams around both reading assignments and the discussions around them.

Grading on participation. You may or may not wish to include the quality and quantity of class participation in your final grading scheme. But doing so will probably increase the likelihood of your students coming to class prepared. If you do, you should make this very clear in your syllabus and your first-day presentation. You might even explain your conception of adequate quality and quantity.

Consider, too, the class level and size in deciding the weight to give participation. Freshmen may feel comfortable with 20 percent in a class of 20-25 but may find it unreasonably stressful in one of 45-50. More advanced students should be able to handle a slightly higher percentage even in a large class. An alternative is to have students vote on the percentage (give them options) and follow the majority rule.

Setting ground rules for participation. To help ensure that all students get involved in discussions, set the ground rules on the first day that everyone's participation is expected; no backbenchers allowed. Describe how you foresee the conduct of class discussions, and explain how you will call on students. You have several options for calling on them: 1) by random selection (e.g., shuffling and drawing index cards or simply finding students who haven't spoken recently); 2) in some predetermined order (e.g., according to seating, alphabetically, or by index card order); and 3) by raised hands.

The first method obviously ensures broad participation and may encourage preparation. But it can engender a stressful class environment. The second method, too, ensures broad participation and preparation, but it creates a stiff, recitation type of atmosphere. In addition, it raises the stress of the student next in line while encouraging others to tune out. Used alone, the raised-hand method keeps the class relaxed but does little to motivate preparation. Most important, participation is bound to be uneven, with a few verbal individuals monopolizing the floor and most students becoming passive wallflowers.

Too often, if you rely on voluntary participation alone, you will inadvertently wind up reinforcing social inequities. According to many gender and ethnic bias studies, female and minority students are unconsciously discriminated against in the discussion dynamic because of the dominant posturing of white male classmates (see Chapters 2 and 11). If anything, you should make special efforts to draw out female and minority students and give them confidence in their answers. Women in particular often preface their discussion contributions with a self-deprecating remark or ritualistic apology, such as "Maybe I'm wrong, but...."

For many reasons, then, you may want to combine methods in your policy for calling on students. For example, when the hands-raised method fails to generate broad enough participation, you might plan to shift to a variant of random selection—perhaps calling on students who have been silent for a while.

If you ever intend to use the random selection or predetermined order methods, another good ground rule to set is the "escape hatch." In other words, you will permit a student to pass on answering a question. It is demoralizing to the class, as well as counterproductive to the discussion, to badger, belittle, or otherwise put a student on the spot for not having a comment when you demand it. A student with nothing to say may simply have nothing new to contribute. While it's possible he isn't prepared, he may simply agree with other recent remarks, or may have no questions at the time, or may be having a bad day and not feel like talking. To cover these instances, inform your class that you will occasionally accept responses such as "I don't want to talk right now" or "Will you please call on me later?"

A final rule to set is a reassurance: "The only stupid question is the one you don't ask." Students are downright terrified by the prospect of looking stupid or foolish to you or their peers. They appreciate being told that you will welcome *all* questions and ensure that they are answered. A similar but modified rule should apply to all *answers* as well: You will welcome all contributions given with good intentions. But this *doesn't* mean that you won't correct faulty answers or allow other students to correct them.

By the same token, you should make it clear that excessive attempts to divert the purpose of the discussion towards a comedy act or to instigate an inappropriate debate will not be tolerated. Being explicit on these issues will help you maintain classroom control (also see Chapter 8).

Creating the social environment. As Chapter 7 recommends, try to create a discussion-friendly setting from the first day. If at all possible, start spatially with arranging the chairs so that students can see one another. It isn't easy to talk to the back of a classmate's head.

Secondly, try to learn your students' names as quickly as possible, and use them regularly in class. More than this, it is important to get to know your students. You might have them fill out index cards to familiarize you with their hobbies, hometown, academic and outside interests, current beliefs about your subject, reasons for their taking the course, etc. Make individual or small-group appointments with them early in the term, and include casual conversation on the agenda.

Your knowledge of your students will help you pitch the course at the right level, as well as to develop a solid rapport with your class quickly. If your students are comfortable with you as a person, and you feel comfortable with them as well, your discussions will flow more evenly and honestly.

Help your students get to know each other, too. They will find it easier to speak out among "friends." So conduct social or subject-oriented ice-breakers on the first day (see Chapter 7). Try to get every student to say something that day. You might draw students out by directing questions to them individually, such as, "Jane, what interested you in this seminar?" or "Matt, what topics would you like to see addressed in this course?" Alternatively, you might invite them to expand on information they offered on their index card.

If your class is especially diverse and/or the subject matter of your course encompasses race, ethnicity, and class, it's best to bring differences out in the open early. Brookfield and Preskill (1999) describe several classroom activities that acknowledge and honor diversity. In one of them, "Naming Ourselves," students first reflect on the cultural, racial, ethnic, or socioeconomic group with which they identify. Then they each introduce themselves as members of their group, stating the label they prefer for this group and what their identification means to them (e.g., how it has affected their values, beliefs, language, behavior, etc.). In another, "Expressing Anger and Grief," students get into groups and exchange personal experiences of cruelty set off by racial, ethnic, or class prejudice. Then the group analyzes the stories for common and disparate themes, emotions, and effects.

To ensure gender equity, Brookfield and Preskill (1999) recommend that instructors model and encourage female ways of interacting, such as disclosing personal information, taking risks that could lead to mistakes, and connecting discussion topics with personal experiences. They also offer several classroom exercises and assignments for acclimating students to both male and female ways of talking. One involves the students making scrapbooks or journals focused on how gender has affected their lives. Another has students write down five or so demographic identities or facts about themselves, including gender, then explain how each has shaped their point of view.

Finally, establish good eye contact and physical proximity with all of your students as equally as possible. A good rule of thumb is to maintain eye contact with one student (or, in a large class, a cluster of students) for at least three seconds. Your very look makes a student feel included. If your class sits in a circle or around a table, varying where you sit can help you equalize your eye contact and physical proximity. If you do not normally sit down in class, move about the classroom as much as you can.

Breaking the class into discussion groups. A time-saving way to guarantee broad participation, especially in larger classes, is to break the class into discussion groups. If you intend to do so only on occasions and/or as a brief warm-up to a general discussion, you may simply want to break the class into informal, *ad hoc* "buzz groups" based on seating proximity.

But if you'd like students to work on a project together for at least a few weeks, then assemble long-term, "formal" groups. This way group members get to know one another well enough to develop a sense of loyalty, group identity, and mutual respect, all of which help to improve performance. Stable groups also provide a context for confidential "peer group evaluations"—that is, having students grade one another on the quality and quantity of their group contributions. If you specify the evaluation criteria and provide multiple evaluation opportunities, you should get a valid and reliable picture of each student's relative leadership, preparation, participation, work share, and cooperative skills. Then you can incorporate these peer assessments into the course grade, as little as 10 percent or as much as 25 percent (see Chapter 18).

Improving Participation Through Skillful Discussion Management

Having covered the mechanics of setting up a discussion format, let us consider how to keep it going with optimal student involvement.

Your roles as instructor. First and foremost, you are the discussion *facilitator*. This may seem a trendy and hackneyed term, but it is a fitting one nonetheless. To faciliate a discussion means to make it easy for students to participate. Doing so can begin even before class. By arriving a little early and casually chatting with students as they arrive, you can loosen them up for dialogue. Facilitating also entails starting off the discussion and adding to it when necessary. But once the discussion takes off, it largely involves directing traffic (see section by that name). Still, at all times, you serve as *manager-on-call* to control the focus and structure of the exchange.

Depending upon the circum-stances, you may briefly assume a wide variety of roles: *coach, moderator, host/hostess, listener, observer, information provider, presenter, counselor, recorder, monitor, instigator, navigator, translator, peacemaker,* and *summarizer.* During particularly animated or agitated student exchanges, you may even find yourself playing *referee*!

Motivating preparation. Chapter 19 gives dozens of way to induce your students to do the readings, and the following are among them as applied to discussion specifically. Include the reading assignments on the topical agenda of the day they are due. Reading-focused discussions can be enriched by having students take notes on the readings, draft answers to study guide questions you've prepared, bring in their own written questions on the readings, or make journal entries about their responses to them. Then allow students to use these notes and questions in the discussion. They will feel more confident and more willing to participate with a written point of reference in front of them. (If you want your students to write notes, study guide answers, or journals on the readings, be sure to collect these regularly or periodically to ensure their keeping up.)

Presenting a road map. Before or at the beginning of class, put an outline on the board, a slide, or an overhead of the day's activities, objectives, topics, or the process through which you will guide them. (A list of discussion questions may justify a handout.) In other words, lay out the territory for the class to cover. Not only will you *look* more organized, you will *be* more organized, and so will the discussion. You will also encourage your students to take notes on the discussion and help them learn how to do it. It is a technique they find hard to master.

To help students put the upcoming discussion into perspective, begin with a brief review of the last class period. But draw the highlights out of the students by posing questions like "What are the major points we covered last time?" Let students refer to, and thus review, their notes.

Igniting the exchange. Several proven strategies can launch a discussion (McKeachie, 1986; McKeachie et al, 1994; Brookfield and Preskill, 1999). One is to start with a common experience, which you can provide with a video, film, demonstration, simulation, or role play. Another sometimes hot ignition switch is to stir up a controversy. You can set up a student debate in advance (see Chapter 17) or play devil's advocate yourself. As students can interpret your representing the devil as manipulative, untrustworthy, and occasionally confusing, it is crucial that you explain what you're doing in advance. While you're assuming the role, you might even wear a hat or a sign with "Devil's Advocate" written prominently on it.

Of course, the most common way to stimulate a discussion is to ask the first in a series of questions you have planned in advance. As we rely on this strategy so extensively, and for good reason, the entire next chapter is devoted to questioning techniques.

Waiting for responses to increase participation. No matter how you launch and direct a discussion, always allow sufficient time for students to respond—at least ten to 15 seconds, depending upon the difficulty of the challenge. While a few students may jump at the chance to say anything, even if it is incorrect, most need time—more time than we might expect—to think through and phrase a response they are willing to announce.

If the question is particularly difficult, lengthy, or involved, you might advise students and give them time to outline their answer first. Again, having a response written in front of them will enhance their confidence and courage. You may also get higher quality answers. This way, too, you can feel free to call on anyone, as all are equally prepared.

Watch for non-verbal cues of students' readiness to respond, especially changes in facial expression. Still, you might refrain from calling on anyone *until you see several raised hands or eager faces.* When you have many possible students from whom to select, you can spread the attention and participation opportunities across students who haven't spoken recently.

Encouraging non-participants. It is a good idea to monitor participation in every class, especially if it's a component of your students' grade. Then actively encourage it where it's lacking. If one side of the room seems too quiet, you can make it a point to say so, and direct a question exclusively to those in that area. If an individual is not contributing, use the same tactic, but be extra gentle; you want to avoid putting that person too much on the spot.

Another icebreaker with quiet students is to call on them to read a passage of text, a question, or a problem aloud. This technique is particularly effective where a narrative or play is involved, but it can be useful in many contexts. You might then follow up by asking the student to comment on the reading.

Persistent non-participation may be a symptom of a deeper problem that calls for a private approach. It is a good idea to have the student see you in your office, and tactfully ask why he has been so quiet in class. Accept any answer as legitimate, then encourage him to become involved. One way to help a student overcome fear is to give him one or more discussion questions in advance of the next class and let him rehearse his answer with you.

Dealing with dead silence. When no one says a word after a generous wait time, you might break the silence and tension with a touch of humor: "Hello, is anybody out there?" But you should definitely find out the reason for the silence. Perhaps your question was ambiguous, or students didn't understand it, or they misunderstood it. For your own benefit, ask them to identify the specific points of contention.

Responding to student responses. Give approval, verbal or non-verbal, to *all* student contributions, but do so with discretion and discrimination. Students want to know how correct and complete their own and their classmates' answers are. But they also want your judgment to be delivered in a diplomatic, encouraging way.

Approval can take the form of a nod, an interested or accepting facial expression, the simple act of recording the response on the board, or appropriate verbal feedback. Here are some verbal response options you may wish to use:

When the answer is correct, praise according to what it deserves.

When the answer is correct but only one of several correct possibilities, ask another student to extend or add to it. Or frame a question that is an extension of the answer. Avoid premature closure.

When the answer is incomplete, follow up with a question that directs the student to include more—e.g., "How might you modify your answer if you took into account the _____ aspect?"

When the answer is unclear, try to rephrase it, then ask the student if this is what she means.

When the answer is seemingly wrong, follow up with one or more gently delivered Socratic questions designed to lead the student to discover his error. For example: "Yes, but if you come to that conclusion, don't you also have to assume ____?" (See Chapter 13, the section on the Socratic method.)

When the answer is incomplete, unclear, or seemingly wrong, invite the student to explain, clarify, or elaborate on it. Or ask other students to comment on or evaluate it. Avoid identifying and correcting errors yourself for as long as possible.

Directing traffic. As some of the above response options suggest, sometimes you best facilitate by doing and saying very little, acting only as the resource of last resort. You should step in only if no student supplies the needed clarification, correction, or knowledge or if the discussion strays off track. In fact, the most successful facilitator's primary task is to direct traffic—that is, signaling students to

112 react to their peers' contributions.

In addition to inviting students to comment on and extend each others' answers, ask them to address their comments to the classmate to whom they are responding, to actually look at that person and address him by name. For the first few weeks, name tags or placards may be essential. The goal is to get the spotlight off you and on the students.

Don't forget to invite your students to help *you* out as well. When you sense that you aren't explaining a point or answering a question effectively, ask them to give their version. Students speak one another's language.

Transitioning and wrapping up. Before moving the discussion on to the next topic, be sure the current one is settled. You might ask if anyone has something to add or qualify. If no one does, ask a student to summarize the main points made during the discussion of the topic. *Then* move on, making a logical transition to the next topic.

Watch the clock and try to reserve time at the end of class to wrap up and summarize the discussion. Again, ask one or more students to give the highlights, and add as necessary. A review at the end encourages students to check their notes and fill in important omissions. It also keeps them on common ground.

An alternative is to close on a classroom assessment technique (see Chapter 27). Probably the most popular and easiest to administer is the one-minute paper. Ask the students to take out a piece of paper and write down the one, two, or three major things they learned during the class and any questions that remain. Collect their responses (without their names) and review them with an eye toward correcting misconceptions and addressing their questions at the beginning of the next class.

Discussion appeals most strongly to the auditory learning style (see Chapter 12), and even discussion can get monotonous after a while. So consider varying your participatory formats to better serve other learning styles, as well as to add spice to life. The various student-active, experiential, and cooperative learning formats described in Chapters 17 and 18 offer stimulating alternatives to the all-class discussion. These include brainstorming, debate, change-your-mind debate, the press conference, the symposium, the panel discussion, role playing, simulations, field and service work, and various small-group activities.

Of course, engaging questions and sound questioning techniques can keep the discussion format lively and challenging for weeks on end. They can also inform your quizzes and exams so you can better assess the level of thinking you're trying to teach. So let us turn now to crafting questions.

For further reading:

Brookfield, S.D. and S. Preskill. 1999. *Discussion as a Way of Teaching: Tools and Techniques for a Democratic Classroom.* San Francisco: Jossey-Bass.

Christensen, C.R., D.A. Garvin, and A. Sweet. (1991). *Education for Judgment: The Artistry of Discussion Leadership.* Boston: Harvard Business School.

QUESTIONING TECHNIQUES FOR DISCUSSION AND ASSESSMENT

Questioning is a central teaching skill and has been for millennia. Socrates honed it to such a fine art that an entire method of questioning is attributed to him. The college teaching literature offers several schema for classifying and organizing questions, the major ones of which will be summarized here.

Sound questioning techniques enhance instruction in four ways:

1) Questions launch and carry discussion, one of the most commonly used student-active teaching techniques (see Chapter 15).

2) They stimulate the exploratory, critical thinking on which the discovery method, including Socratic questioning, is based (see Chapter 13).

3) When used for classroom assessment, questions yield answers that help us gauge what students are learning and whether to review a topic or to proceed to the next (see Chapter 27).

4) Questions are the means by which we evaluate and grade our students' learning; the better our questions reflect what we've been teaching, the fairer and more useful our testing and evaluation procedures (see Chapters 29 and 30).

Questioning schema and techniques fall into two major categories: those that suggest leading students through a more or less orderly *process* of inquiry and those that classify questions into more or less useful *types*. This chapter couches the material in the contexts of discussion and discovery, but later chapters will return to these schema and techniques in assessment contexts.

Questioning as a Process of Inquiry

The Socratic method.
Described in Chapter 13, the Socratic is perhaps the most spontaneous questioning technique. You may begin with a planned question to open a dialogue on a given topic, but you shape your succeeding questions in response to the answers the students give. Of course, with experience, you may be able to anticipate the blind alleys and misdirections your students will take on specific topics and develop a general discussion plan.

Most instructors don't feel comfortable with such a spontaneous, unstructured format for an entire discussion period. Students don't either; they have a hard enough time taking notes on the most structured discussion.

"Working backwards from objectives." A second strategy, one that has gained the status of a "conventional wisdom," is to work backwards from objectives. It involves advance planning. First, jot down your objectives for the day: the one, two, or three points you want your students to understand by the end of class. Then, for each point, develop the key question that the point will answer. (This step resembles the game of Jeopardy.) Finally, for each key question, develop another two or three questions that logically proceed and will prepare students for the key question. In other words, work backwards from the key points you want your students to understand through the questions that will lead them to that understanding. (The next section gives pointers on how to write *good* questions for stimulating a lively discussion.)

When class begins, launch the discussion with one of the last questions you framed. You can lend structure to the discussion by displaying all the questions (key ones last) on the board, a slide, or an overhead or in a handout (preferably with note-taking space below each question). Still, unless you frame too many questions, you can afford to be flexible. You can allow the discussion to wander a bit, then easily redirect it back to your list of questions.

Bloom's taxonomy of questions. A third approach is to follow Bloom's (1956) taxonomy of questions, guiding your students up through his hierarchy of cognitive levels, where *knowledge* (recitation) represents the lowest thinking level and *evaluation* the highest. This schema first appeared in Chapter 3, where it was applied to developing student learning objectives. The lists of verbs associated with each cognitive operation are just as useful here for framing questions.

To structure a discussion as a process of inquiry, you might start off with *knowledge* questions on the highlights of the last lecture or reading assignment. This factual recall exercise serves as a mental warm-up for the students and gives those who did not attend the lecture or do the reading a chance to pick up a few major points and follow along, if not participate later. Avoid questions that call for one- or two-word answers, however; aim for multi-sentence responses.

Fair warning: Do not spend more than several minutes on this level. The boredom potential aside, students will not answer many recitation questions because they fear their classmates seeing them as apple polishers—"bailing you out," so to speak. More important, whatever our field, our educational mission is to develop more sophisticated critical thinking in our students.

Therefore, rapidly move the discussion up the hierarchy through *comprehension* so you can find out whether your students understand the material and can put it in their own words. If they understand it, they should be able to answer *application* questions and use the material to solve problems, devise examples, or correctly classify your examples. If they can do this, they should be ready to progress to *analysis* of the material: pulling apart its elements to draw comparisons and contrasts; identifying assumptions, causes, effects, and implications; and reasoning through explanations and arguments.

Once students have found their way *through* the material, they are prepared to step *outside* of its confines and attempt *synthesis*. This type of question calls for integrating elements of the material in new and creative ways—composing or designing something new with them or combining elements from two different sources. When students can synthesize material, they have mastered it well enough to address *evaluation* questions. They now can make informed judgments about its strengths and shortcomings, its costs and benefits, and its ethical, esthetic, or practical merit.

Bloom's taxonomy helps rein in students from leaping into issues they aren't yet prepared to tackle. Often students are all too eager to jump to judging material without thoroughly understanding it first. In addition, if you teach the taxonomy to your students, they acquire a whole new metacognition on thinking processes and levels. If you label the level of your questions, you maximize your chances of obtaining the level of answers you are seeking. Students also quickly learn to classify and better frame their own questions.

The taxonomy should be used flexibly, however. Some discussion tasks, such as debriefing a case (see Chapter 23), may call for an inextricable combination of application, analysis, and synthesis. Moreover, a comprehension question in one course may be an analysis issue in another. How any question is classified depends on what the students are given as "knowledge" in lectures and readings.

Types of Well Constructed Questions

There is more to constructing questions than turning around a couple of words in a sentence and adding a question mark. Well-crafted ones take thought and creativity and in turn require the same of students. They all have one feature in common: They have *multiple respectable answers*. Therefore, they encourage broad participation and in-depth treatment.

Often, too, multiple-answer questions spark debate. Welcome the conflict and let students argue it out. Before letting the issue rest, ask for possible resolutions and/or analyses of the conflict if they don't evolve on their own.

McKeachie's categories.
McKeachie et al (1994) suggests three types of fruitful, challenging questions. *Comparative* questions ask students to compare and contrast different theories, research studies, literary works, etc. Indirectly, they help students identify the important dimensions for comparison.

Connective questions challenge students to link facts, concepts, relationships, authors, theories, etc. that are not explicitly integrated in assigned materials and might not appear related. These questions are particularly useful in cross-disciplinary courses. They can also ask students to draw and reflect on their personal experiences, connecting these to theories and research findings. When students realize these links, the material becomes more meaningful to them.

Finally, *critical* questions invite students to examine the validity of a particular argument, research claim, or interpretation. If the class has trouble getting started, you can initiate the discussion by presenting an equally plausible alternative argument. This type of question instills in students an appreciation for careful, active reading. When you ask the class to comment on what a student has just said, you are also posing a critical question. Used in this context, it fosters good listening skills.

These three types of questions resemble Bloom's analysis, synthesis, and evaluation questions, but McKeachie does not order his as a process. Use the typology you find most straightforward.

Andrews' "high mileage" types. Andrews not only developed categories of questions but also conducted classroom research to identify their relative "mileage"— that is, the average number of student responses each type evokes (Gale and Andrews, 1989). Using his results, we can learn how to ensure our discussions are lively. Here are his top mileage types, all of which can be pitched at high cognitive levels:

Brainstorm questions, found to yield 4.3 student responses per question, invite students to generate many conceivable ideas on a topic or many possible solutions to a problem. For example: "What issues does Hamlet question in the play?" "What trends starting in the 1960s may have negatively impacted American public education?" "How might the public be made to care about ecological imbalances?"

Typically the instructor, acting as facilitator, records all responses on the board, an overhead, or a flip chart. Only after all brains stop storming do the students begin editing, combining, eliminating, grouping, etc. It is best to let them sort and evaluate options using criteria they generate themselves.

Focal questions elicit an even higher 4.9 responses per question. They ask students to choose a viewpoint or position from several possible ones and to support their choice with reasoning and evidence.

Students may develop and defend their own opinions, adopt those of a particular author, or assume a devil's advocate stance. For example: "Do you think that Marx's theory of capitalism is still relevant in today's post-industrial societies?" "To what extent is Ivan Illich a victim of his own decisions or of society?" "Is the society in *Brave New World* a utopia, a nightmare of moral degeneration, or something between the two?"

A variation on a focal question is for you to play devil's advocate on an issue. Alternatively, you can make a contentious, controversial statement and invite your students to react against it. But as recommended in Chapter 15, be sure to let your class know exactly what you are doing.

Playground questions hold the mileage record with 5.1 responses per question. They challenge students to select or develop their own themes and concepts for exploring, interpreting, and analyzing a piece of material. For example, "What do you think the author is saying in this particular passage?" "What underlying assumptions about human nature must this theorist have?" "What might happen if (present a counterfactual)?" When posing such open-ended questions, however, be aware that this type of question tends to veer the discussion into other topics.

Types of Poorly Constructed Questions

It is difficult to fully appreciate highly effective discussion questions without examining the less effective types as well. Andrews' categories and classroom research provide valuable insight and information on this latter kind, too.

Some of these questions have their place, but they tend not to encourage broad participation and/or higher-order thinking.

Analytic convergent questions may elicit complex, analytical thought, but they have only one correct answer. So they make students edgy and cut the discussion short as soon as someone gives the right answer. It is little wonder that they evoke only 2.0 answers per question. Typically 1.0 of the attempts isn't exactly that right answer. Analytic convergent questions are best used sparingly as knowledge and comprehension warm-ups. At least they get students talking.

Programmed-answer questions are only *implicitly* closed-ended. Although they may have more than one appropriate answer, the instructor conveys (perhaps unconsciously) having only one specific answer in mind. Students regard this type of question as an unwelcomed challenge to read the instructor's mind. Some even consider it manipulative and closed-minded.

Rhetorical questions are those with an obvious answer, usually too obvious for students to take seriously. At best, they inspire a few nods and agreeing facial expressions. While this type of question has its place in a motivating or persuasive speech, it is mainly a momentary time-filler in teaching.

Quiz show questions have a one- or two-word correct answer— e.g., a name, a date, a title—but they only pay off on television. Usually they elicit only factual recall, and they serve poorly as warm-up questions for genuine

discussion. Their average mileage is 1.5 responses per question, suggesting that the first "contestant" guesses wrong about half the time.

Dead-end questions are even less stimulating; they're quiz show questions with a yes-or-no answer. Students simply place their bets. These questions can easily be transformed into useful types in one of two ways. First, you can often change them into true-false items, having students rephrase false statements to make them true. Better yet, restructure them into relational questions by beginning them with a why or a how. With thought now required, students are more likely to participate.

Fuzzy questions are too vague and unfocused for students to know how to approach them. They may be phrased unclearly, such as "Who else knows what else falls into this category?" Or they may be too global, like "What should we do about the breakdown of the family?" Students loathe taking the risk required to attack such grand questions. Other common fuzzy questions represent a well-meaning attempts to help: "Does everyone understand this?" and "Any questions?" You may occasionally get an honest response, but all too often you find out later that not everyone *did* understand and quite a few students *must* have had questions. It is usually better to use classroom assessment techniques (see Chapter 27) to answer such concerns.

Chameleon and ***shotgun*** questions are both a series of weakly related questions "fired off" one after the other in hopes that one will hit with the students. Chameleons change their topical focus through the series until the last one barely resembles the first one, leaving students not knowing which one to try to answer. Shotgun questions, on the other hand, may all go off in the same general direction, but they make the instructor look like a "bad shot"—either desperate for a response or confused about the issues. Students in turn become confused and disoriented in the murk of the inquisition, not knowing which in the series to dodge and which to address. The average series yields only 2.3 responses.

Put-down and **ego-stroking** questions are two sides of the same bad attitude. The former type of question implies that students ought to know the answer and/or shouldn't have any more questions—e.g., "Now that I have explained this topic thoroughly, are there any more questions?" The latter type assumes the superiority of the instructor to the discouragement of the students' individuality. An implicit request to "rephrase the answer the way I would say it" douses students' creativity, self-expression, and often their motivation to answer at all.

Turning the Tables

The person posing the discussion questions need not always be the instructor. If you model good questioning techniques and spend a little time teaching your favorite questioning schema, you can have your students develop discussion and even test questions as homework assignments. You can use the best ones in class and in actual tests and even grade them if you choose. The quality of these questions also tells you how diligently your students are doing their reading (see Chapter 19).

The next chapter offers other teaching formats that put the spotlight and the responsibility for learning on students.

For further reading:

Brookfield, S.D. and S. Preskill. 1999. *Discussion as a Way of Teaching: Tools and Techniques for Democratic Classrooms*. San Francisco: Jossey-Bass.

Browne, M.N. and S.A. Keeley. 2000. *Asking the Right Questions: A Guide to Critical Thinking*, 6th ed. Upper Saddle River, NJ: Prentice Hall.

EXPERIENTIAL LEARNING ACTIVITIES

This chapter covers a potpourri of teaching formats that allow students to "discover" knowledge by direct experience, either simulated or real. These activities rank even higher than discussion on a continuum of student involvement, ranging from moderately student-involving to extremely high. We start with the former and move to the more experiential.

Research documents that more discovery-oriented and student-active teaching methods ensure higher student motivation, more learning at higher cognitive levels, greater appreciation of the material's utility, and longer retention of the knowledge. They also meet a wider range of instructional goals than do more passive methods (see Chapters 3 and 13).

Student Presentation Formats

Oral presentations by students have become rather common course components due to the growing emphasis on communication across the curriculum—not only writing but speaking as well. This relatively new trend reflects the high priority employers place on communication skills (McDaniel and White, 1993; Kimball, 1998), but it may also be a response to their frustration with the communication skills of the college graduates they hire. Formal oral presentations are not in themselves experiential, except to the extent that student learn all the preparation, platform skills, and rehearsal that a truly good presentation requires.

However, oral communication takes many forms, and the activities described in this section give students public speaking opportunities within experiential learning contexts. As such, they add pizzazz to student presentations.

In each case, you assign or have students select the topic, research area, position, role, school of thought, etc. that they will represent. Usually, such formats require advanced research, some even a paper. But you can set up some of these activities spontaneously in a well prepared class. Before you "turn students lose," so to speak, to investigate, represent, and/or question different sides of a controversy, be sure they understand rhetorical structure, the basic rules of evidence, and logical fallacies.

Debate. Every field has topics amenable to a two-sided, fact-based argument. The format need not be any more complex than statements of the affirmative and the negative, plus rebuttals, each with a strict time limit. It is best to assign sides to student pairs or triads.

A variation that involves the

entire class is a *change-your-mind debate*. You designate different sides of the classroom as "for the affirmative" or "for the negative," with the middle as "uncertain/ undecided/neutral." Before the debate, students sit in the area representing their current position, and they can change their seating location during the debate as their opinions sway. After the debate, lead a debriefing discussion focusing on the opinion changers ("What changed your mind?") and the undecided students, who are likely to provide the most objective analysis of both the debate and the issue at hand.

Another variant is called *structured controversy* or *academic controversy*, in which two pairs in a group of four students formally debate each other on an issue, then switch sides, and finally synthesize a joint position (Johnson, Johnson, and Smith, 1996). Done properly, this activity requires that student conduct considerable outside research and write up a final report.

"Expert" individuals or teams.

Designate individual students, pairs, or triads to be the class experts on a certain topic, geographical area, body of theory or research, etc. Following your bibliographic leads, students do outside readings and turn in weekly, annotated reading lists on their area of expertise. Then you regularly query the "experts" in class, asking for informational updates or about the relevance of their area to the day's discussion.

Dunn (1992) applied this format very effectively in his World Affairs course, where he paired off students as "briefing teams" charged with keeping up on the current affairs of nine world regions. On some days he played the role of a political

leader dependent upon his students' briefings, especially to lighten the mood when he felt the need to cajole his class into working harder.

Panel discussion.

Four or five students briefly present different points of view on a topic, either their own or one they are representing. Panel members can even play different noted scholars and historical figures—e.g., Freud, Jung, Adler, Skinner, and Rogers in a psychology course, or Benjamin Franklin, Thomas Jefferson, Aaron Burr, James Madison, and George Washington in an early American history course. Then the class addresses thoughtful questions and challenges, preferably prepared in advance, to various panel members.

Press conference.

You or a student assumes the focal role, posing as a noted scholar, a leader in some realm, or a representative of a particular position or school of thought, while the rest of the class plays investigative reporters, each student or small group with an assigned audience or readership, such as local residents, residents of another area or country, a special interest group, a specific company or other organization, etc. These "reporter" students ask probing, challenging questions of the focal person.

Two planning caveats are in order. First, the focal role should represent a broad-ranging, controversial decision or stance. Defining such a role is easy in political science or history, but in other fields it requires more creative thought. In psychology or sociology, for example, the focal role may be a criminologist or criminal psychologist whose testimony leads to the probation of a violent convict. In economics, the focal role may represent an uncertain intervention strategy. In the sciences and medical fields, it may stand for a controversial environmental or public health position—perhaps on global warming, endangered species preservation, genetically engineered produce, prescription drug restrictions, fetal tissue research, human cloning, or the like.

Secondly, in addition to assigning audiences/readerships to the students playing reporters, you can require them to research and write out their questions and challenges in advance. Having them then write a mock article incorporating the press conference is an optional follow-up assignment.

Symposium. Individual students or student teams present their independently conducted, outside research or papers that express their own ideas. The rest of the class asks questions and gives constructive criticism, which is especially useful if students can revise their work. Additionally, for each class period, you may assign one or two discussants to interrelate and critique the research/ papers. Discussants should have at least a day or two to review the symposium products in advance.

Role Playing

You assign students roles in a true-to-life, problematic social or interpersonal situation that they act out, improvising the script. When one player is not supposed to know the full story about another player's intentions, problem, or goals, you should provide written descriptions for each role. You also must decide what information to give to the rest of the class. Following the enactment is a class discus-

sion of "debriefing" of how the players felt at crucial junctures and what behaviorial patterns the other students observed.

While role playing relies on make-believe scenarios in the classroom, students learn experientially by identifying with the roles they play and observe. You may also play a role, especially when you want to model certain behaviors (e.g., how to conduct a family therapy session, to negotiate a contract, to mediate conflict, or to open a formal meeting).

This technique is used successfully both in therapy and in instruction, especially in the humanities and social sciences. In political science or history, students can take the identity of key leaders or decision-makers in a conflict or the role of collective constituencies that face an important task—for instance, landed elites, Tory loyalists, continental army soldiers and militia, tradesmen, yeoman farmers, ministers, lawyers, etc., all responsible for drafting their positions for a state constitutional convention (Frederick, 1991).

In structuring an original role play, the only rule is to incorporate conflict between the roles and some need for the players to reach a resolution (Halpern, 1994). Here are some applications to inspire your own ideas (Nilson, 1990):
- Professional (doctor, lawyer, pastor, etc.) and client disagree over an approach to the client's problem.
- Executive promises union negotiator (or up-start worker) a major promotion for keeping quiet.
- Worker representatives try to convince executives not to close an unprofitable plant.
- Human resources executive must make a tough hiring

decision among various male, female, minority, and non-minority candidates with different job qualifications and personalities.

- Politician experiences role conflict between partisan and administrative roles or between ideological stance and the need for campaign funds.
- Couple or family argues over money, (un)employment, discipline, authority, autonomy, communication, moving, domestic violence, alcohol or drug use, etc. This scenario may include a social worker's, physician's, or therapist's role.

If you teach a foreign language, feel free to make a role play of any situation your students may encounter while traveling. While they may not learn much through empathy, they will get useful, conversational practice in the target language. If you teach literature, consider casting students in the roles of the characters and letting them play out a hypothetical scene that extends the piece of literature.

Simulations and Games

With computer technology imitating life, two distinct types of simulations are available. The first is the relatively new computerized type. It can take the form of an individual tutorial program (CAI, for "computer-assisted instruction") or a full-blown multimedia simulation (see Chapter 22). One software package on hydraulics, for instance, allows students to solve complex canalization problems by varying the delivery, inflow, outflow, and power of various pumps. In electrical engineering, they can manipulate the performance of an electrical network and study overloading, breaks, and the like. Medical software simulates diagnostic situations, presenting students with a hypothetical patient's symptoms and even a patient's answers to questions the students ask—all through interactive technology (Pregent, 1994). Whose Mummy Is It?®, an adventure game, takes students on a virtual tour of ancient Egypt and other influential societies of antiquity, such as Greece, Rome, China, and Mesopotamia. Other computer simulations include Unnatural Selection® (biology and environmental sciences), SimIlse® and SimWorld® (environmental sciences and politics), and SimCity® (urban planning). There are dozens more to choose from.

The second, traditional type of simulation is a human enactment of a hypothetical social situation that, while not necessarily realistic, does abstract key elements from reality (Mitchell, 1982). Only a thin, gray line distinguishes it from role playing. Similations usually cast the entire class in roles and run longer, sometimes for many hours. In addition, they portray grander, more macro situations, which usually can't be re-enacted in real time or in realistic detail.

Human simulations developed a strong faculty and student following through the 1970s and the early 1980s. So did academic games, variants that rely on boards, cards, dice, etc. They are exclusively competitive, more abstract, and somewhat removed from reality. Still, games and simulations were the most student-involving instructional techniques in broad use at the time. They were not always easy for instructors to develop themselves. Simulations of societies, formal organizations, markets, cultures, world politics, and other grand realms are extremely complex and require an array of supporting materials. So an extensive market of simulations and games sprung up.

To this day, few other classroom formats can bring course material to life as effectively. They allow students to "live out" the hypotheses and implications of theories, giving them intense emotional, cognitive, and behavioral experiences that they will otherwise never have. Indeed, simulations and games still have an important place in instruction.

Some examples. Simulations and games number in the thousands with all their possible variations, and a few have become classics in psychology and the social sciences. Simsoc® and Star Power® simulate societies with an emphasis on class and inequality. Barnga® and Bafa Bafa® sensitize students to cultural differences and clashes. The Prisoner's Dilemma® illustrates a "frame" game/simulation—that is, one that can be played with different scenarios and pay-off rules to highlight different psychological and sociological principles. Hyman (1978, 1981) developed several variations.

Another frame simulation is structured as a mock trial with a suite of genuine cases to choose from (Karraker, 1993). The case options span many disciplines— environmental protection, industrial safety, medical technology, religious practices, securities markets, affirmative action, community development, and individual rights.

The field of business may have the most simulations, and they tend to be marketed under straightforward titles such as Airline, Corporation, Supply Chain, Manager, Marketer, Human Resource Management, Collective Bargaining

Simulated, and Entrepreneur. Bus-Sim® has developed a simulation for just about every business specialty. UNIGAME® and Virtual U® simulate high-level university administration.

Urban planning and politics are two other areas that have spawned numerous simulations built around different controversial decisions, such as locating a freeway and developing a long-term growth plan.

Many academic games are modeled on traditional games, such as Bingo, and television quiz shows, such as Jeopardy, Family Feud, Wheel of Fortune, Password, the Weakest Link, and Who Wants to Be a Millionaire? The questions and answers come from the course material. Students can submit the questions and even run the games. Games are painless, even fun, review formats for factual material.

Simulation and game logistics. Think first whether a simulation or game will truly serve your student learning objectives for a course. A simulation/game and its debriefing take a good deal of class time—at least an hour for the very simplest. Plus, to motivate your students' full attention, you should grade them on their performance, with an emphasis on the quality of their strategy, not their oratory. To get maximum mileage from a simulation or game, piggyback other assignments on it, such as readings, outside research (before or during the simulation), an oral presentation, a response paper, or a position paper.

You can obtain a simulation in one of three ways: 1) you can buy one from a commercial distributor (often a publishing house), which can cost up a few hundred dollars; 2) you can find one free in a journal (see below) or at a teaching conference, though you will probably have to make any needed materials on your own; 3) you can adapt one to your course purposes; or 4) you can design your own.

If you choose the last option, start with the learning objectives you want the simulation to meet. Then delineate the primary goal(s) around which the key roles will conflict and/or compete. Finally, develop the activities, processes, and rules.

In any case, you need to know the conventional wisdom for running simulations. First and foremost, be prepared. Read the instructor's manual or directions at least twice at a leisurely pace well in advance. Mark what directions you will give the students at each stage of the simulation. In general, it's best not to give all the directions at the beginning, as too much information will confuse the students. Rather, parcel out the instructions as needed. List your pre-class set-up tasks. Know the sequence of events and schedule of distributing artifacts and materials. Have a plan for debriefing the simulation and discussing it in relation to the course subject matter. Still, don't hesitate to refer to the manual during the simulation.

Be aware that most facilitators run simulations at too slow a pace. The challenge is to keep the game moving, even if the tempo puts pressure on the students. They need a long enough time to realize the constraints, costs, and benefits of their decision-making options, but not necessarily long enough to answer every question that arises, to come to a full consensus, or to feel completely comfortable with their decision. After all, a simulation must imitate life as much as possible.

To find out more about simulations and games in your subject areas, see your own field's teaching journals and the following journals: *The International Simulation and Gaming Research Yearbook* published by the Society for Academic Gaming and Simulation in Education and Training (SAGSET)

Simages, journal of the North American Simulation and Gaming Association (NASAGA)

Simulation & Gaming: An Interdisciplinary Journal of Theory, Practice and Research, journal of an international consortium of professional associations, including the Association for Business Simulation and Experiential Learning (ABSEL)

Service Learning (SL): The Real Thing

Nothing teaches experientially like direct experience. If you want students to understand the characters in a piece of modern literature, let them talk with the real human counterparts. If you want them to comprehend the dynamics of poverty, let them work with the poor and the homeless. If you want them to appreciate the problems and crises of other countries, let them help the emigres and refugees. If you want them to understand prisoners, children, whomever, let them spend productive time with them.

Service learning is a method by which students acquire knowledge while working in community service. The current generation of college students is distinguished by its volunteerism and service orientation, which may explain service learning's high popularity with students.

According to SL proponents,

instructors, and "graduates," service learning is almost uniformly a positive, life-changing experience for students—the kind they never forget. It imparts new knowledge not just in the abstract but in a concrete, real-world context. The experience also stimulates emotions, which strongly enhance learning and retention (see Chapter 2) and help students progress toward certain affective, social, and ethical learning objectives (see Chapter 3).

Let's examine the accumulated research on the effects of service learning (Eyler, Giles, and Gray, 1999; Gray, Ondaatje, and Zakaras, 1999; Astin et al, 2000). Service learning enhances the following:
• students' personal development (sense of identity and efficacy, spiritual and moral growth)
• students' social and interpersonal development (leadership, communication, ability to work with others)
• students' cultural and racial understanding
• students' sense of civic responsibility, citizenship skills, and societal effectiveness
• students' commitment to service in their career choice and future voluntary activities
• in many but not all studies, students' academic learning and abilities on *some* dimensions: writing skills, ability to apply knowledge to the real world, complexity of understanding, problem analysis, critical thinking, and cognitive development (no clear effect on grades, GPA, or later standardized test scores)
• students' relationships with faculty
• students' satisfaction with college and likelihood of graduation
• relations between the institution and the community.

How positive the SL experience for a given student depends on several factors, however. The single most powerful determinant is the student's degree of interest in the subject matter before the experience. Therefore, service is best reserved for upper-level courses in a major (Astin et al, 2000).

The other known influences are under the instructor's control: how much students can share and discuss their experiences in class; how much training they have for the experience; how well tied the experience is to the course content; and how much written and oral reflection students are asked to do, especially in tying the experience back to the course content (Zlotkowski, 1998; Gray, Ondaatje, and Zakaras, 1999; Astin et al, 2000).

Implementing service learning. Is SL right for your course(s)? First, examine your student learning objectives. Service learning is worth considering if you have objectives that are affective, ethical, or social beyond working effectively in a group, or if your cognitive objectives are served by students' practicing on an outside client. If either of these is true for your course, try to identify community tasks that truly complement your subject matter. For example, if you teach Children's Literature and one of your objectives is for your students to be able to critique works from a child's point of view, then their reading books to children makes sense. If you teach Public Relations, having your students conduct a PR campaign for a local nonprofit organization clearly benefits their learning.

Second, be aware of the ethical questions that *some* SL experiences raise, and check your comfort with your answers. Is it appropriate to have students working for social change (if the SL experience involves it)? Should they be required to give service even if their current politics and ethics don't warrant it? (Requiring SL *is* legal.) Will they be placed in physical danger?

Third, consider your time constraints and commitment. SL requires more planning and coordination than most other methods, especially your first time using it.

If service learning fits well in your course(s) and schedule, begin your upfront tasks at least a couple of months before the term begins. (See Stacey, Rice, and Langer, 1997, a concise and comprehensive instructor's manual.) First, identify one or more appropriate community agencies. You might start with schools, medical and mental health facilities, social service agencies, and the local United Way. Then schedule a face-to-face meeting with the key contact person to find out about the organization's needs and expectations and to explain your own for your course. Ensure that the agency will orient and supervise your students. Alternatively, 1) have students find their own agency and work out the project details, or 2) ask your campus SL or voluntary-service center, if you have one, to identify one or more agencies with needs and expectations that will serve your course purposes.

Then start making course design decisions. Will the SL be required, optional, or extra credit? Will you offer an alternative assignment? How much SL will be required? (Fewer than 20 hours reduces SL's impact.) What previous course component(s) will be eliminated to make time for the SL? How much will the SL count for towards the final grade? What will be the requirements of the SL experience? How will you evaluate and grade the SL experience? How will you link the service to the course content? When will you have students discuss their experiences? What writing tasks will you assign for reflection? (Best to have multiple reflection assignments.) How will you grade these reflection assignments? This information will be needed for your syllabus.

Finally, make the necessary logistical arrangements: getting help with liability issues from your institution's risk management office (e. g., release forms); creating student teams, if appropriate (highly advisable to reduce any physical danger); helping students and the agency coordinate schedules; ensuring students are oriented and supervised at the agency; arranging for student transportation, even if just car pools; and devising a system to monitor students' hours of service.

The books for further reading below offer additional guidance for instructors and a wealth of ideas for solid service learning projects, including exemplars. To stay abreast of the more innovative and successful projects and to tell your colleagues about your own, see the *Michigan Journal of Community Service-Learning* and the *Journal of Public Service and Outreach.*

For further reading:

Stacey, K., D.L. Rice, and G. Langer. 1997. *Academic Service-Learning: Faculty Development Manual.* Ypsilanti, MI: Office of Academic Service-Learning, Eastern Michigan University.

Zlotkowski, E. 1998. *Successful Service-Learning Programs: New Models of Excellence in Higher Education.* Bolton, MA: Anker Publishing.

LEARNING IN GROUPS

Every class conveys two lessons: one in the content and another in the teaching method. Student-active techniques send the message that with expert guidance, learners can actively discover, analyze, and use knowledge on their own. With this participatory "empowerment," students come to understand that they must assume responsibility for their own learning.

One particularly powerful student-active method is cooperative learning, defined as "a structured, systematic instructional strategy in which small groups of students work together towards a common goal" (Cooper et al, 1993). The lesson it conveys is that when people work together, they can accomplish much more than they can as individuals working apart—that is, two heads are better than one, three heads are better than two, and for some tasks, four or five heads are best.

Cooperative vs. Collaborative vs. Team Learning

The teaching format in which students work on a task and learn in small groups has become popular enough to take on many labels. As used in the literature, different terms only reflect nuances in structure. Collaborative learning, the label favored in the sciences, applies to a loosely structured coordination between or among students. Cooperative learning implies a more structured group effort (Millis and Cottell, 1998). Within this latter category, team learning is highly structured version that thrives more on mutual, positive interdependence than on any other characteristic of cooperative learning. Indeed, students take team as well as individual tests and are accountable individually because their course grades largely depend upon their team's grades (Michaelsen, 1997-98).

Two other labels in occasional use is peer instruction or peer tutoring, which usually involves a group or pair of students serving as a more knowledgeable resource to other students.

Cooperative learning is the term of choice here because 1) most of the group-learning research is on "cooperative learning" and 2) structure helps ensure success with the widest variety of students, including the young and the less motivated.

The Case for Cooperative Learning

While cooperative learning is in common use now, it had a slow

128

start in higher education. By 1990, nearly 600 published studies dating back 90 years had compared the effectiveness of cooperative, competitive, and individual approaches to teaching. Many of these studies found overwhelming support for the superiority of cooperative learning, and even those that didn't found no detrimental effects to using it (Johnson, Johnson, and Smith, 1991). But old teaching paradigms and habits die hard. If *we* had no trouble learning with them when we were in college, we can't understand why our students do—which is why the best students can become the worst teachers.

In general, the research on the effects of cooperative learning has focused on three fundamental dimensions: achievement/productivity (i.e., learning), positive interpersonal relationships, and psychological health. Cooperation produces positive results on all of them (Johnson, Johnson, and Smith, 1991; Millis and Cottell, 1998). Astin (1993) studied the effects of 192 environmental factors on various educational outcomes of 27,064 students at 309 institutions. His results indicate that the top two influences on academic success and satisfaction are interaction among students and interaction between faculty and students, each a key component of cooperative learning strategies. In fact, both factors ranked significantly higher than curriculum and content variables. Light (1990, 1992) reported similar results in the Harvard Assessment Seminars.

Johnson and Johnson (1989) surveyed 193 studies comparing the effects of cooperative and traditional techniques on student productivity/learning. More than half the literature reported cooperative learning to have the stronger

impact, while only 10 percent found individualistic methods more powerful. In addition, cooperation enhanced interpersonal attraction in 60 percent of the studies, while competition did so in only three percent. A similar literature survey by Cooper et al (1993) indicated that cooperative learning is more effective than traditional methods in improving critical thinking, self-esteem, racial/ethnic relations, and prosocial behavior.

The superiority of cooperative learning seems to hold at all levels and across student backgrounds and extends as students mature into adulthood (Johnson et al, 1981). Disadvantaged students benefit as well. Frierson (1986) documented that minority nursing students who studied cooperatively for their board exams performed significantly better than those who studied alone. After instituting cooperative, out-of-class enrichment programs for calculus students at-risk at UC Berkeley, Treisman (1986) found that black students in the program received course grades over one letter grade higher than their non-cooperative counterparts.

However, cooperative learning should not necessarily supplant lecture, whole-class discussion, experiential learning, and other methods. The world holds other lessons to learn besides critical thinking, problem solving, social relations, and self-esteem. Moreover, the research cited above indicates that cooperative learning need not be used all the time to have positive effects on student achievement.

It may be helpful, then, to consider cooperative learning a *supplementary* technique (Millis, 1990) and a *format* for various classroom activities. As a *supplement*, it can serve as a student-active break between segments of a lecture (see Chapter 14) or a jump-start for class discussion (see Chapters 15 and 16). As a *format*, it is useful for social and subject-matter icebreakers (see Chapter 7), experiential learning activities (see Chapter 17), case debriefing (see Chapter 23), problem-based learning (see Chapter 24), mathematical problem solving exercises (see Chapter 25), science laboratories (see Chapter 26), classroom assessment exercises (see Chapter 27), and help and review sessions (see Chapter 29).

Changing Methods, Changing Roles

Cooperative learning requires role shifts for both students and instructors (MacGregor, 1990; Johnson, Johnson, and Smith, 1991; Rhem, 1992; Millis and Cottell, 1998). Students must move:

- from passive listeners and note-takers to active problem solvers, discoverers, contributors, and transformers of knowledge;
- from low/moderate to high expectations of preparation for class;
- from a low-risk, private presence to a high-risk public presence;
- from personal responsibility for attendance to community expectation and responsibility;
- from individualistic competition among peers to collaboration among group members whose success depends upon one another;
- from formal, impersonal relationships with peers and instructors to genuine interest in one another's learning and overall well-being;
- from viewing instructors and texts as sole authorities to seeing themselves, their peers, and their community as

important sources of knowledge.

Young freshmen, in particular, can have a hard time making the adjustment, as they may have developed negative associations around cooperation in high school. There, cooperating with authority may have denoted blind or deferential obedience; cooperating with peers may have led to uneven work loads, and group work may have been mismanaged (MacGregor, 1990).

The instructor's role changes, too. No longer is it focused on sorting, classifying, and screening out students. The primary goal is to develop students' competencies and talents. Cooperative learning also recasts the instructor as "a guide on the side" instead of "the sage on the stage." In other words, the role shifts from expert/authority figure to facilitator/coach, one who unobtrusively circulates, observes, monitors, and answers questions (Millis, 1990). Instructors often have what Finkel and Monk (1983) colorfully term an "Atlas complex"; they feel wholly responsible for the success of the course and their students. Cooperative techniques call for placing much of the responsibility for learning squarely on the students' shoulders. Of course, relinquishing control can be difficult at first for an instructor.

Crucial Elements of Cooperative Learning

Cooperative learning techniques share a number of essential features that you must ensure are built into or provided for in the way you assemble groups, design tasks, manage activities, and determine grades (Feichtner and Davis, 1984-85; Kagan, 1988; Millis, 1990; Johnson, Johnson, and Smith,

1991; Cooper et al, 1993; Smith, 1993; Michaelsen, 1997-98; Millis and Cottell, 1998; Felder and Brent, 2001).

Positive interdependence.

For a group to function effectively, each member must feel a sense of personal responsibility for the success of his or her teammates. In addition, each member's success must depend at least in part on the group's success. In brief, members must feel they need one another.

To ensure this element, you can do one or more of the following: assign a group product on which all members sign off and are given a group grade (you can also separately grade individual contributions); give group (as well as individual) quizzes and exams which count toward each member's individual grade; allocate essential resources or pieces of information across group members, requiring them to share (materials interdependence); assign each member a different part of the total task (task interdependence); randomly select students to speak for their group; require that all members edit one another's work using MS Word's "Track Changes" feature (under Tools); and/or assign group members different roles.

Among the possible group roles are recorder, spokesperson, researcher, summarizer, checker/ corrector, skeptic, organizer/ manager, spy (on the progress of other groups), observer, writer, timekeeper, conflict resolver, and runner/liaison to other groups or the instructor.

Individual accountability.

All members must be held responsible for their own learning as well as for the learning of other group members. At the same time, no member should feel that he or she is giving more (or less) than an equal share of effort to the group task. In other words, no freeloaders or hitchhikers allowed.

You can build in this element in several ways, some of which overlap with those above: base final grades predominantly on individual quizzes, tests, papers, and other assignments; count the team grades only for students who are passing individual quizzes, tests, and written assignments; randomly select students to speak for their group; assign group members different roles; assign group members primary responsibility for different parts of the team project, and grade them on their part (e.g., one member conducts the research, another does the write-up, etc.); give teams time early in the semester to discuss and agree on what they will do to sanction non-contributing members; allow teams to "fire" a non-contributing member (after a verbal and a written warning, of course); allow a member to "resign" from a poorly performing team and seek membership in another; and/or base a significant portion of the final grade on peer performance evaluations.

This last strategy deserves elaboration. It can be used only when groups have stable memberships over several weeks or months. At the end of the semester or the group-work unit, have each team member assign each of their teammates a letter grade for group contributions and/or allocate a limited number of points across their teammates. If you use points, you may want to forbid students to allocate points equally across teammates.

It is essential that you give students a list of criteria on which to grade their peers, such as attendance, preparation, promptness, leadership, quality of contributions, quantity of contributions, and social skills. These criteria and your peer evaluation policies and procedures merit explanation on the first day of class. The peer portion of the final grade should reflect the amount and importance of group work in the course—at least ten to 20 percent but no more than 60 percent.

How valid and accurate are peer performance evaluations? Students often give their teammates almost uniformly high evaluations. Does this tendency reflect the fact that cooperative learning motivates students to prepare and perform more effectively than most other formats, as cooperative learning enthusiasts claim? Or are students merely covering up for the poor contributors, as some instructors suspect?

You have to make the call based on your own experience at your particular college or university. If your students are also merciless in penalizing freeloaders, slackers, sandbaggers, control freaks, egotrippers, bullies, whiners, martyrs, and saboteurs, chances are that their positive performance evaluations are valid and accurate. Indeed, earlier studies found this to be the case (Ferris and Hess, 1984-85; Murrell, 1984-85; Jalajas and Sutton, 1984-85).

But if you have reason to suspect that freeloaders and other group-pathological types are getting off easy, try this strategy: Have students write peer performance evaluations two, three, or four times during the semester, and schedule them right after major project sections are due. This way any anger or frustration toward errant group members will come out in the heat of the moment. Another way to counter cover-ups is to say you will toss out any peer performance evaluations that give As to all teams members.

Appropriate group composition, size, and duration. Heterogeneous groups in terms of ability, race, gender, and other characteristics help develop students' social skills and foster understanding among individuals of differing social backgrounds. Research also finds that heterogeneous groups help all students learn the material better (also Heller et al, 1992; Heller and Hollabaugh, 1992). When group composition is diverse, specifically in ability and/or knowledge background, the slower students learn from the quicker ones—often better than they do from traditional methods because students seem to speak one another's language. The quicker ones in turn benefit because, by teaching the material, they learn it all the better. (Of course, very slow students can also hold back the very gifted.)

Depending upon your course, it may be more important that you maximize heterogeneity on some variable other than ability and/or background. For example, if you want your teams to debate ideas and critically examine their own, you might consider finding out students' views the first week of class and assigning teams based on varying opinions and value systems.

Expediency may also have to take priority. If you want teams to meet face-to-face outside of class, you may have to consider students' schedules in assigning groups.

The research indicates that students should not form their own long-term groups. Such a composition only reinforces existing cliques and encourages discussion of extracurricular topics. On the other hand, it also reduces intra-group conflict.

Optimal group size varies with the open-endedness of the task. Several cooperative activities described later in this chapter and in Chapter 14 rely on pairs. But most other activities require groups of three to five to ensure lively, broad participation and to prevent freeloading. A threesome seems to be optimal for mathematical and scientific problem-solving tasks that involve alternative means to one correct answer (Heller and Hollabaugh, 1992). Four or five is best for tasks with multiple respectable answers involving brainstorming, interpretation, and problem solving of a "focal" or "playground" nature (see Chapter 16). Still, teams of up to seven members can function effectively and offer the added benefit of greater diversity (Michaelsen, 1997-98).

It may be wisest to avoid mixing females with a male majority. Heller and Hollabaugh (1992) found that males tend to dominate and overshadow the female(s) when in the majority.

Ideal group duration also depends on the task. Long-term group assignments facilitate major projects and ongoing tasks, since duration fosters group loyalty and refines members' cooperative skills. On the other hand, students can get acquainted with more classmates if groups change with each short-term project or every several weeks. What often happens, however, is that students develop group loyalties quickly and plead to keep the same groups throughout the term.

Ever-changing *ad hoc* groups or pairs based solely on seating proximity may be sufficient for occasional problem-solving and discussion assigments. In large classes where space is tight and chairs are immobile, you may feel limited to these *ad hoc* groups. But you can overcome such limitations by assigning seats.

Face-to-face interaction. Cooperative learning requires that instructors allocate class time to team meetings. However, experience shows that you cannot rely on students to meet and collaborate face-to-face outside of class. Otherwise, group members divide the labor and go their separate ways, defeating the whole cooperative purpose and its benefits. Of course, virtual interaction over email, chat rooms, or discussion boards can and sometimes must substitute for face-to-face meetings. Sometimes you can keep better track of virtual than face-to-face meetings.

Genuine learning and challenge. The cooperative task must make students *learn* something, not just *do* something. It should demand higher-order thinking processes (application, analysis, synthesis, evaluation) and group synergy to complete because it goes beyond what the students have learned in the course thus far. It should require alternative means to an answer and/or multiple answers and pose a genuine challenge that only more than one mind is likely to meet within the given time limit. In brief, it should be a harder task than you'd assign to students working alone.

Explicit attention to collaborative social skills. Working together effectively requires certain behaviors of all the individuals involved: listening actively, taking turns in talking, not interrupting, encouraging others, cooperating, sharing resources, being open-minded, giving constructive feedback, tactfully defending one's views, compromising, and showing respect for others.

Most cooperative learning proponents view these as acquired skills that you must explicitly foster in at least some of the following ways: modeling them yourself; praising them when you see or hear them practiced; having the class brainstorm and discuss them; including them among your objectives for group work; including them among your peer evaluation criteria; and, especially, allowing students time to reflect upon and process the quality of the day's or week's group interactions. Processing may be individual, group, or class and can include questions such as these: How well did I listen? How well did I play my assigned role? Did we include all group members in our discussions? How high quality was our task performance? How could we accomplish our task more effectively? How could we function as a group more smoothly?

Team learning supporters maintain that students intuitively know from their life experience what defines a good (and bad) team member, and they don't need time to group-process beyond writing peer performance evaluations. If they encounter internal conflicts and inequities, they must resolve them on their own without instructor intervention (which may include firing the offending member). After all, the work world will not be interested in their interactional problems and preferences, and one of your jobs is to prepare them to deal with this world.

Management Tips

Beyond the essential elements above are several standard operating procedures that help ensure success and make the management of group activities easier and more predictable for you (Feichtner and Davis, 1984-85; Millis, 1990; Johnson et al., 1991; Cooper et al., 1993; Smith, 1993).

First and foremost, **start small.** Begin by trying out a small-scale, pre-tested technique (like those in the next section) in the class where you feel the most confident. Expect it *not* to work perfectly—any technique can fall short the first time tried—and plan for your time allocation to be off one way or another. A safe launching pad is an optional help or review session.

Second, **use cooperative learning only with a criterion-referenced grading system** (see Chapter 30). Grading on a curve, or "norm-referenced grading," undercuts the spirit of cooperation and the prospect of group success on which cooperative learning relies. An absolute grading scale gives all students an equal chance to achieve.

Third, **introduce the activity to your class by explaining your rationale for using it.** Without getting technical, mention some of the research that documents its superior effectiveness. Perhaps list the crucial elements of cooperative learning and your objectives for the group work. Also reassure your students that they will not jeopardize their grades nor be accused of cheating by helping each other.

Fourth, **give groups a very specific, structured task that requires a written product to show at the end.** The major reasons for group-work failure are the lack of organization and specificity in the assignment and the students' confusion over its purpose and expectations. The written end-product may be no more formal than handwritten notes for the group"s verbal report at the end of the group session. It may be a problem solution, a team exam answer sheet, or notes for a group presentation. Or it may be a major team project for which students meet for weeks to complete.

A word of warning is in order, however. Feichtner and Davis (1984-85) present evidence that large-scale, formal group assignments are more problematic than smaller-scale and less formal ones. Specifically, they caution against assigning more than one major group presentation and more than three written papers or reports per semester. Otherwise, students are more likely to report having a negative group experience. Team exams, however, tend to generate positive experiences.

Fifth, **set and enforce tight time limits and deadlines for task completion,** even for short tasks that pairs or groups can complete in a couple of minutes. It is helpful to bring a timer or stopwatch with you to all cooperative class sessions. For tasks of five to 50 minutes, you might give appropriate ten-minute or two-minute warnings. Larger-scale assignments call for firm deadlines for completing the various subtasks (prospectus, data collection, data analysis, outline, first draft, etc.). It is best to schedule all final product deadlines comfortably in advance of the end of the term. Tight time limits and deadlines help keep teams on task.

Sixth, **ensure the assignment of individual roles within each group.** Many possible roles were listed above in the section on positive interdependence. At the very least, each group of three or more needs a recorder/spokesperson. Role assignments should

rotate at least weekly among the members of stable groups. You can make the first role assignments randomly, or use the following technique for assigning roles in *ad hoc* groups: After breaking students into groups, tell them to point to one fellow member on the count of three. Assign the student receiving the most "points" the task of appointing the recorder/spokesperson and any other necessary roles. The element of surprise makes this technique humorous.

Seventh, **set the rule of "three before me."** That is, you can insist that students take their questions to each other first and not to you until they have asked at least three other students. Or accept only group, not individual, questions.

Eighth, **set rules to control noise levels and maintain order.** Among the most popular ones are "no unnecessary talkin" and "only one group member talking at one time." Another helpful hint is to bring the classroom to silence by informing students that you will signal when time is up by raising your hand. They should then stop talking and raise *their* hands as soon as they see yours up. This technique enables you to silence a huge lecture hall in seconds.

Ninth, to ensure that groups have a genuine learning experience, **conclude each group session with a means of assessing students' progress or mastery of the material.** You might ask for a brief presentation or progress report from each group. Or you can administer a quick quiz or classroom assessment exercise (see Chapter 27). If a quiz, you should set a high standard of mastery that all team members must meet before any of them can leave class. Alternatively, you can select a member from each group at random to take the quiz for the group.

Tried and True Cooperative Learning Strategies

If you are interested in trying out or extending cooperative learning in your courses, consider experimenting with some of the proven formats below. While the levels of success and usefulness vary by discipline and instructor, you can adjust them or create your own versions to serve your needs. The following sampler comes from several sources, including Kagan (1988), Millis (1990), Johnson, Johnson, and Smith(1991), Cooper et al. (1993), Smith (1993), and Millis and Cottell (1998). Many work well between lecture segments as a student-active break (see Chapter 14), and some double as a classroom assessment technique (see Chapter 27). Although a few may sound adolescent, they have all been used effectively at the post-secondary level.

Think-Pair-Share. Give students a question or problem and ask them to think quietly of an answer or solution. Have them discuss their responses with their neighbor, then share them with the class. Set a time limit of one or two minutes for the pair exchange.

Pairs Check. Partners coach each other on worksheet problems and/or check notes for completeness and accuracy. This two-minute activity is similar to *Pair and Compare* in Chapter 14.

STAD (Student Teams-Achievement Divisions). After a lecture, video, demonstration, etc., teams of three or four receive a worksheet to discuss and complete.

When members feel that they have reached acceptable solutions, you give a brief oral or written quiz to the group, a representative, or each individual member to assess their mastery of the material.

Jigsaw. Each member of a "base group" is assigned a minitopic to research. Students then meet in "expert groups" with others assigned the same minitopic to discuss and refine their understanding. The base groups reform, and members teach their minitopics to their teammates.

Structured/Academic Controversy. Pairs in a group of four are assigned opposing sides of an issue. Each pair researches its assigned position, and the group discusses the issue with the goal of exposing as much information as possible about the subject. Pairs can then switch sides and continue the discussion.

Group Investigation. Assign each group or let each group choose a different topic within a given subject area. Groups are free to organize their work and research methods and even to determine the form of the final product (e.g., a video, play, slide show, demonstration, presentation, paper, etc.).

Numbered Heads Together. Each member of a team of four is assigned a number. Pose a thought question or problem, and allow a few minutes for discussion. Call out a number, designating only students with that number to act as group spokesperson. This exercise promotes individual accountability.

Talking Chips. This method ensures equal participation in discussion groups. Each group member receives the same number of poker chips (or index cards, pencils, pens, etc.) Each time a member wishes to speak, he or she tosses a chip into the center of the table. Once individuals have used up their chips, they can no longer speak. The discussion proceeds until all members have exhausted their chips. Then they reclaim their chips and begin another round.

Send a Problem. Each group member writes a question or problem on a flashcard. The group reaches consensus on the correct answer(s) or solution(s) and writes it on the back. Each group then passes its cards to another group, which formulates its own answers or solutions and checks them against those written on the back by the sending group. If groups disagree, the receiving group writes its answer as an alternative. Stacks of cards continue to rotate from group to group until they are returned to the original senders, who then examine and discuss any alternative answers or solutions given by other groups.

Preparing Students for Life

Younger college students are intent on learning about the real world they are about to enter, while older ones want to know how they can function more effectively in it at a higher level. Your objectives as a instructor include preparing students for this rapidly changing world—to make them more knowledgeable citizens, consumers, social participants, appreciators of the arts, and/or science watchers and supporters, as well as more successful professionals and businesspersons. You select your content with this goal in mind. But the methods you choose may reinforce or override your verbal messages.

To prepare students for full participation in our society and the world, it is obvious that student-active techniques are more effective than traditional ones. To prepare students for the business and professional world in particular, cooperative learning is an essential part of their college experience. These days most work is conducted in teams, and for good reasons. The research out of Western Europe, Japan, and North America indicates that teams operating with a cooperative ethos generate more innovative and creative ideas, devise better solutions to problems, and yield greater gains in general than do individuals functioning with a competitive ethos (Demings, 1993).

For further reading:

Michaelsen, L.K., A.B. Knight, and L.D. Fink. 2002. *Team Learning: A Transformative Use of Small Groups.* Westport, CT: Praeger Publishing.

Millis, B.J. and P.G. Cottell. 1998. *Cooperative Learning for Higher Education Faculty.* Phoenix, AZ: American Council and Education and Oryx Press.

Stein, R.F. and S Hurd. 2000. *Using Student Teams in the Classroom.* Bolton, MA: Anker Publishing.

GETTING YOUR STUDENTS TO DO THE READINGS

Active learning depends on your students doing the readings that you assign when you assign them. Their first exposure to the material must be on their own outside of class. If students come to class unfamiliar with the material, they can't do anything with it.

Yet instructors commonly complain that their students don't do the readings on a regular basis, and they don't know what to do about it. In fact, many students don't seem to crack a book until right before an exam, by which time many class periods have been dulled by too many "emergency" lectures and too little student participation.

This chapter examines why students don't do the readings, including how *we* make it easy for them not to do the readings, and how we can change our ways to *induce* them to do the readings. The tools suggested here may not work on every single student, but they will on most. After all, students have a right to fail themselves.

Why Students Don't Do the Readings

Consider all the reasons why students may *habitually* not do the readings—at least not when they are due. So don't worry about the student who occasionally doesn't do the readings due to some short-term life interference, and eliminate those who overburden themselves by trying to combine a full course load with more than half-time employment.

Some students don't enjoy reading. They feel it takes too much time or it's not worth what little they get out of it. Whether or not they even know *how* to read the assigned material, it doesn't matter that much because they'll just pick up the gist of it in class the next day, especially if you normally lecture. Or their friends will tell them about the class. Or they will go to you to get lecture notes. Or they can read your notes on the web. They may also have more attractive options for their non-class time, such as socializing (virtual, phone, or face-to-face), watching television, listening to music, surfing the web, drinking, sleeping, working out, reading a novel or magazine, doing more interesting or important coursework, or engaging in extracurricular activities such as clubs and sports. When you think about it, your course has a lot of competition for their time.

When you examine all the possible reasons why students habitually don't do the readings, they boil down to two: 1) they don't want to and 2) they don't have to—that is, they face no dire consequences if they don't.

Inducing Students to Read

Can you make the students *want* to do the readings? In some cases and to some extent you can. Certainly you can remove barriers to their doing the readings by taking these steps (also see Bean, 1996):

- Choose readings to fit your students' interests and ability levels as best you can.
- Explain to students why you chose the readings that you did from the available alternatives.
- Explicitly teach your students *how* to read and study a textbook, a research article, an essay, a poem, etc. Advise them how each genre of assigned reading is organized, what they should be looking for as they read, how to take notes, and what they should retain for class. Tell them your student-learning objectives for each reading. Alternatively, give them study questions to guide and focus their reading.
- Preview and promote the value of each reading assignment. Place it in the context of the next class and the whole course.

Making the readings more accessible and enhancing their intrinsic value to your students may go far. Once students start doing the readings, they may enjoy the learning and sense of achievement enough to continue reading. But this gentle, persuasive strategy may not go far enough. You may also have to *"make"* students do the readings for extrinsic reasons—that is, to set up incentives and sanctions related to their own self-interest.

We know that most students are motivated by grades, just as people in general are motivated by material and monetary rewards. We also know that people are motivated by pride. They don't want to look bad in front of others, especially superiors and peers. These two cost/benefit values suggest ways to make students accountable for doing the readings. So whether or not they *want* to do them, most students will decide that they *have* to do them to attain their goals and to avoid unfavorable consequences.

Here are four categories of tools that hold students accountable for the readings:

1. homework on the readings;
2. quizzes on the readings;
3. in-class problem-solving or written exercises on the readings; and
4. oral presentations on the readings, either prepared or cold-call (impromptu).

To make these tools work effectively as accountability mechanisms, certain guidelines apply:

- Use these tools or some combination of them on a *regular or near-regular basis* on the class days that readings are due. Your students should *expect* to be held accountable for every reading assignment.
- *Grade* the products in some way, even if on an informal scale, such as 1-to-4 points, √+/√/√-, √/0, or P/F, and count them towards the final grade.
- Make the readings the *only available source* of the knowledge in the readings.

This last factor is critical. It is important that your students can't expect to pick up the knowledge in your lecture. This means that you cannot rehash the readings in class. But you don't have to rehash them if your students are doing them! You can spend class time answering questions on the readings, elaborating and extending them, and leading activities that make students think about and use the knowledge.

It is also important that students can't expect to get the knowl-edge neatly summarized on a web site—at least not in time to be held accountable for it. You can post any summaries later in the term.

Pride becomes an often powerful secondary motivator when the ac-countability tool is an oral presen-tation or in-class group work for a group grade. In this latter situa-tion, most students feel a sense of responsibility towards their team-mates (see Chapter 18).

Specific Tools for Holding Students Accountable

No other printed source assem-bles the many ways that instructors can hold students accountable for the readings. The tools described here—some obvious, others not—come from a variety of sources, some of which suggest the tech-niques for purposes other than in-ducing students to do the readings. Still, all the tools suggested here should serve this purpose well.

Homework. Below are different forms of written homework that re-quire doing the readings to com-plete. With some of them, you may want your students to submit two copies: one for them to refer to and take notes on in class and another to turn into you for a grade. The copy for you may be submitted elec-tronically before class. You may even make the written product a requirement for entering class.
1. Notes on or an abstract of the readings (McKinney, 2001; Bar-rineau, 2001)
2. One or more questions on the readings, on cards or electroni-cally posted (Millis and Cottell, 1998; Martin, 2000; McKinney, 2001). You may ask for specific types of questions (multiple choice, true-false, essay, etc.)

for possible use in future tests.
3. Answers to study, reading-response, or end-of-chapter questions (McKinney, 2001)
4. Solutions to problems
5. Writing-to-learn exercises such as dialectical notes (see Chapter 20) or concept assignments, which are free writes on the readings followed by one sen-tence on each of three impor-tant concepts (Kalman and Kal-man, 1996)
6. Any type of outside material that illustrates an important point in the readings or an ap-plication of them (e.g., a maga-zine or newspaper article, a printed advertisement, a photo-graph, an object, etc.)

Quizzes. Frequent or even daily quizzes are proven account-ability tools (Mazur, 1997; Connor-Greene, 2000; Barrineau, 2001; Thompson, 2002). These days you can administer them either in class or online shortly before class. Ei-ther way, accountability quizzes should focus only on the major points in the readings, not details, and the items should be easy for you to grade quickly, either multi-ple choice or short answer.

With in-class quizzes, you can save paper by dictating the ques-tions or displaying them on a slide or overhead transparency. You can also have students make up the questions as homework. Finally, you can follow the individual quiz with a group quiz and make the double exercise a real learning ex-perience (Michaelsen, 1997-98).

In-class written exercises or problem solving. The options for these exercises are endless. They may be any of a wide assortment of writing-to-learn and classroom as-sessment exercises (see Chapters

20 and 27): e.g., a one-minute paper, a reading response mini-essay, a summary, or an audience-directed paraphrase. They can even be graphical: a summary drawing, a poster, or a concept map. To encourage high-quality work, you can let your students use their exercises as resources during in-class tests. With problems, students can solve them or design new ones for future tests. Most of these exercises are adaptable to teams.

Oral presentations. These need not be only major project-based assignments. They can be daily class exercises, impromptu or prepared, focused on knowledge in the readings—for example:

1. "Randomly" call on students to present their homework on the readings (questions, answers to questions, problem solutions, exercises, outside material, etc.) either in addition to or instead of handing it into you. Over the term you can probably call on *all* your students at least once, maybe many times.
2. Have teams answer questions, do exercises, or solve problems based on the readings, then call on students/teams "randomly" to report on the results.
3. Have students bring in questions on the readings (for future tests, discussion, clarification) and call on other students to answer them.
4. Have students conduct #3 in teams (called "Guided Reciprocal Peer Questioning" in Millis and Cottell, 1998).
5. Use the Socratic method while leading discussions on the readings (see Chapter 13).
6. Have speaking-intensive experiential activities in class, such as debates, panels, press conferences, role plays, and simula-

tions that require the knowledge in the readings (see Chapter 17). Though you may not be able to involve all your students equally, you can induce almost all of them to *prepare* because you might call on *any* of them to play key roles.

Managing Your Workload

Before you conclude that accountability tools would generate too heavy a workload for you, consider how much time the tools actually demand and what other tasks they may eliminate. Yes, you would have to find or devise short assignments, quiz questions, and/or in-class exercises and activities, and you would have to grade them in some fashion. However:

- You can have your students make up questions and problems for you, whether for quizzes, tests, or in-class exercises.
- The grading is very quick and easy (Connor-Greene, 2000; Thompson, 2002). With homework and in-class problems/exercises, you need only check the work for a good faith effort. You can grade orally presented work in class.
- You can give fewer major tests and assignments, saving yourself considerable preparation and grading time.
- You need not prepare lectures.

Finally, consider how much more your students would learn and how deeply you could take them into the material if they did the readings on time. Imagine the class discussions and activities you could lead. In fact, most accountability tools serve multiple purposes and can provide a springboard or an entire framework for a student-active class period. Perhaps they can *save* you time.

WRITING-TO-LEARN ACTIVITIES AND ASSIGNMENTS

Why have your students do in-class or homework-related writing exercises, even those that you don't grade? The reasons are well grounded in research. For starters, writing about the material helps students learn it better and retain it longer—whatever the subject and whether the exercise involves note-taking, outlining, summarizing, recording focused thought, composing short answers, or writing full-fledged essays (Kirkpatrick and Pittendrigh, 1984; Newell, 1984; Young and Fulwiler, 1986; Ambron, 1987; Langer and Applebee, 1987; Hinkle and Hinkle, 1990; Young, 1997; Wright et al, 2001). The power of writing is making students *think actively* about the material.

Secondly, because practice makes perfect, any writing can improve your students' writing skills. They can reap this benefit in any discipline, as long as you explain the appropriate writing format and provide models, practice assignments, and plenty of feedback (Madigan and Brosamer, 1990; also see Chapter 21). Some forms of writing also call for a well defined audience other than the instructor, and these develop students' sensitivity to the interests, values, cognitive levels, and vocabularies of different sectors of society.

A third reason to have your students write is for classroom assessment (see Chapter 27)—that is, to find out *quickly*, while you're still focusing on a particular topic,

exactly what your class is and isn't learning. This way you can diagnose and clarify points of confusion *before* you give the next exam and move on to other topics (Cross and Angelo, 1988; Angelo and Cross, 1993). In fact, the student feedback and questions that writing exercises provide can plan a good part of your classes for you. Reading short, informal writing assignments that do not require grading takes no more time than any other type of class preparation.

Finally, many writing exercises give students the chance to learn about themselves—their feelings, values, cognitive processes, and their learning strengths and weaknesses. Younger students in particular need and appreciate such opportunities for self-exploration (Ambron, 1987).

This chapter covers a number of writing-to-learn activities and assignments that have proven instructional value (from references above, especially Cross and Angelo, 1988, Angelo and Cross, 1993, and Young, 1997).

Free Writes

Students write about a predetermined topic for a brief, specified number of minutes (one to three) as fast as they can think and put words on paper. The objective is to activate prior knowledge or to generate ideas by free association, disregarding grammar, spelling, punctuation, and the like.

Free writes serve as effective warm-up exercises for any class. Usually students walk in "cold," having forgotten the last class, the week's reading, and the lab manual instructions. Frequent free writes also put students notice that they had better keep up with the course. Here are some possible free write topics:

- "Write down all the important points you remember from last Wednesday's discussion."
- "From what you recall from the lab manual, write down what is to be done in lab today, any procedures that confuse you, and what the experiment is expected to create or show."
- You write three key words on the board from the last class or reading and ask students to explain their importance.
- You write a "seed sentence" on the board—that is, a major hypothesis, conclusion, or provocative statement related to class or readings—and ask students to write their reactions.
- You can also use exam review questions for a free write exercise to prepare your students for a tightly timed essay test.

Free writes can also be assigned as homework. In the "concept assignment," students read a section or two of a book, then begin free writing about what they just read and what they don't understand. They read the next section(s) and free write again. At the end of the assigned chapter or unit, they write three sentences, one on each of three key concepts they have identified in the readings. Students usually write three or more pages of notes and reflection (Kalman and Kalman, 1996, as applied to physics). The main benefit of concept assignments is getting the students not only to *do* but to really *think* about the readings.

While it is usually best not to grade free writes, at least not formally, you might collect them and check off those that demonstrate evidence of the student's having listened to the lecture or discussion, done the assigned readings, or studied the lab manual. You can count free writes as part of class participation or as "ungraded but required" assignments.

The One-Minute Paper

With books and notebooks closed, students summarize the "most important" or "most useful" point(s) they learned from the day's lecture, reading assignment, laboratory, or discussion. Time permitting, they also write down questions that remain in their minds. While called a *"one*-minute paper," the exercise usually requires two or three minutes.

Just as free writes can function as a warm-up, a one-minute paper can serve as a "cool-down." It helps students absorb, digest, and internalize new material, moving it from short-term and mid-term memory into long-term. It also makes them think about the material, especially what they didn't understand, which is precisely what you need to know before wrapping up a topic.

As one-minute papers are not graded, they are usually anonymous. You might collect and read each one to find out how well the students grasped the new material. Their summaries and questions will tell you what to review and clarify in your next class.

Journals

Students write down their intellectual and emotional reactions to the lectures, discussions, readings, laboratories, their solutions to homework problems, or other written assignments. They do this regularly at the end of each lecture, discussion, or lab, and/or while they are doing their assignments outside of class. Some instructors require just one weekly journal-writing session, either in class or as handed-in homework, on any or all aspects of a course. Students should have a special notebook solely for their journal.

Journals help students keep up with the course as well as to read and listen *actively*. They also make students think about the material and what they are learning. It is best, however, to provide students with guidelines on what their journals should address. Here are some sample questions:

- What is new to you about this material?
- What did you already know?
- Does any point contradict what you already knew or believed?
- What patterns of reasoning (or data) does the speaker/author offer as evidence?
- How convincing do you find the speaker's/author's reasoning/ data?
- Is there any line of reasoning that you do not follow?
- Is this reasoning familiar to you from other courses?
- What don't you understand?
- What questions remain in your mind?

Journals should be collected and checked off regularly or intermittently, but they usually are not graded. (If they are, they should not count very much toward the final grade.) You might write comments in the students' journals, thus developing a personal, one-on-one dialogue with each student.

One-Sentence Summaries

As an in-class activity or a short homework assignment, students answer these questions on a specific topic in one (long) grammatical sentence: Who Does/Did What to Whom, How, When, Where, and Why? (WDWWHWWW) The topic may be a historical event, the plot of a story or novel, or by substituting another What for Who/Whom, a chemical reaction, a mechanical process, or a biological phenomenon.

This technique makes students distill, simplify, reorganize, synthesize, and "chunk" complex material into smaller, essential units that are easier to manipulate and remember. It is advisable that you do the exercise first before assigning it and allow students twice as much time as it takes you. You can collect and comment on the summaries yourself or have your students exchange them and write comments on each other's.

Learning Logs

After each lecture, reading assignment, and/or problem set, students write two lists: one of the major points they understood and the other of the points they found unclear. Later, at regular intervals, they review their learning logs to diagnose their learning strengths and weaknesses (e.g., reasons for repeated errors) and to brainstorm ways to remedy these weaknesses. This diagnostic process can be conducted in class where students can discuss their learning pitfalls and share study and problem-solving techniques.

Learning logs serve several worthy purposes. Students isolate and review major points presented in the course. They also identify what they aren't grasping. Finally (and most important for some students), they learn about their own learning styles and ways to enhance their learning. This technique is especially valuable in cumulative subjects in which students do similar, graded assignments on a frequent, regular basis.

Do collect and check off learning logs intermittently to ensure students are keeping them up. You might grade them if they comprise a major course assignment.

Dialectical Notes

Students read and take notes on a relatively short, important, self-contained passage that you select from course readings. On the left side of their note paper, they write their reactions to the text as they read it: where they agree, where they disagree, where they are unsure, where they are confused, where they have questions, etc. At some later time, they review the passage and their left-side notes and write their reactions to these notes on the right side of their note paper.

Students can take dialectical notes in class or as a fairly short homework assignment. You can assign the first part (passage reading and reactions) as homework and do the second part (reactions to reactions) in class. Leave some time between them, however— anywhere from a few days to 20 minutes of classroom discussion.

Dialectical notes encourage students to read a text carefully, to analyze it critically, and to reevaluate their initial reactions to it. These notes also demonstrate the nature and value of scholarly dialogue and debate. In addition, they make superb springboards for discussion. After students get used

to the exercise, you might consider collecting and grading their notes.

This technique is especially useful in courses that require close readings of difficult texts, such as philosophy, history, political science, religious studies, law, and social theory. It also adapts easily to mathematics, economics, engineering, and physics problem solving. Students work the problem in mathematical symbols on the left side of the paper and explain in words what operations they are performing and why on the right side. Later in small groups students can read and discuss each other's various approaches and solutions.

Directed Paraphrasing

In their own words, students summarize the content of a reading assignment, a lecture, a discussion, or a lab. Restrict the assignment to a specific length, and define a specific audience and/or purpose for the summary. Students can pretend they are writing to laypersons for the purpose of public education, to public policy makers for the purpose of social change, to practicing scientists for purposes of research needs, etc.

As students must paraphrase material, they must work to understand it in depth and internalize it. Also, since they are writing to a specific audience, they must consider the persuasive and political value of the available knowledge and data—for example, what facts and arguments are important or irrelevant to a given audience.

Directed paraphrasing assignments may be major or minor, in-class or homework, graded or just checked off. Students can also present them orally, and the rest of the class can role play the audience.

Letters Home

Students paraphrase in informal language what they are learning in a course in the form of a letter to their parents, a sibling, or a friend. This technique helps students see the relationship between course material/projects and their everyday lives. It also gives them the opportunity to describe the material in their own words, thus to distill, internalize, and remember the major points. Its value as a pre-exam review exercise is obvious. Letters should at least be collected and checked off.

Other Letters, Memos, Notes, and Electronic Posts

As in directed paraphrasing, you can vary the audience and purpose for letters, memos, and notes. Students can write each other or post messages on an electronic bulletin board about a certain reading, a problem they are working on, a design project, or any other assignment they may share as a team or a class. They can also write real or mock letters on some issue to the editor of a newspaper or magazine, a political leader, a young child, a figure from the past—really anyone that will give them practice in taking the audience into consideration in their message and writing style.

Mock Tests

An excellent assignment for getting students to review and really *think about* the material before a test is to have them make up a test over the material. This exercise can be done in class or as homework, either individually or in groups. However you assign it, students should hear and discuss each other's test questions. The power of this exercise rests in getting students to identify what they believe to be the key concepts and relationships in a body of material. If they miss the mark, they will find out in class *before* the test.

Before giving your students this assignment, you may want to teach them some questioning techniques, such as Bloom's (1956) taxonomy of cognitive operations (see Chapters 3 and 16). You may also find it helpful to specify the test format—so many multiple choice items, true-false, short answer questions, essays, etc. With a little practice, your students may write such good questions that you can actually use in your tests.

Drafts for Peer Feedback

Pre-final drafts of written work (essays, lab reports, proposals, papers, etc.) that will be turned in later for formal grading fall into a gray category that we might call "writing-to-learn-to-write-better" assignments. Just like professionals, students improve their writing in response to well informed feedback on drafts. No doubt you as the instructor can provide the best informed critique, but students can benefit from peer feedback as well, from both getting it and giving it. Peer feedback not only provides students with more varied, immediate, and frequent feedback than any one instructor can give, but also helps students develop communication, critical thinking, collaboration, and life-long learning skills (Topping, 1998; Dochy et al, 1999).

However, the validity, reliability, and accuracy of peer feedback are uneven, some tainted by personal relationships and traits (e.g., race) and typically too lenient, superficial, and unfocused (Orsmond et al, 1995; Mowl and Pain, 1996).

146 This should not be surprising, as students 1) have loyalties to one another and concerns about criticizing a fellow student's work; 2) lack the disciplinary background to know and apply professional standards, at least in lower-level courses; and 3) give only as much feedback as the questions provided absolutely demand. So in answer to "Is the central idea clear throughout the paper?" most students will say only yes or no and will not reference specific passages unless told to do.

Instructors can obtain much more valid, neutral, useful, and detailed student peer feedback by putting a different kind of item on the feedback forms. Rather than requiring an evaluation about the adequacy, effectiveness, clarity, or logic of some aspect of the work, the question can ask students 1) to identify features or parts of the work, as each student sees them, or 2) to give their personal reactions to the work (Nilson, 2002-03, 2003).

For example, instead of forcing a judgment with "Does the opening paragraph lay out a clear thesis statement for the rest of the paper?" rephrase the item as "What do you think is the thesis of the paper? Paraphrase it below" (identification). Rather than asking, "Is the title of the paper interesting, appropriate, and sufficiently focused?" ask instead, "What three adjectives would you use to describe the title of the paper?" (personal reaction). Rephrase the question, "How well written is the paper?" as "Highlight any passages you had to read more than once to understand what the writer was saying" (personal reaction).

The revised items are emotionally neutral and require only basic rhetorical knowledge to answer, yet they demand very close attention to the work and often references to its particulars. They do not allow students to give biased, uninformed, or superficial feedback. Rather, they tell the writer how readers have understood and reacted to the paper, what they got out of it. If most of the readers did not identify the intended thesis, then the writer knows she must strengthen and clarify the thesis statement. If she didn't like the way her readers described her title, then she knows she should change it. If they highlighted several passages as hard to read, she knows she needs to work on her writing. With peer feedback, students find a genuine audience—a role instructors cannot play—and care about how and what they communicate (Nilson, 2002-03, 2003).

Multiple Purposes

Methods that serve multiple teaching purposes, such as accountability tools for getting your students to do the reading (see Chapter 19), are particularly valuable and versatile, and some of these writing-to-learn exercises fall into this category. So they will merit mention again in Chapter 27, as they also provide important assessment feedback about your students' learning.

Writing-to-learn is also called "informal" writing. The next chapter is about teaching your students "formal" modes of writing that conform to the rhetorical and stylistic conventions of your discipline.

For further reading:

Bean, John C. 1996. *Engaging Ideas: A Professor's Guide to Integrating Writing, Critical Thinking, and Active Learning in the Classroom.* San Francisco: Jossey-Bass.

TEACHING YOUR STUDENTS TO
THINK AND WRITE
IN THE DISCIPLINES

A major reason why students can't write well in a given discipline is that they don't know how to *think* in the discipline. While thinking may not always be expressed in writing, writing is *always* an expression of thinking. In fact, writing instruction specialists contend that *writing **is** thinking* (Bean, 1996). Therefore, when you teach your students to write in your discipline—assuming they already know the basic rules of sentence structure, syntax, grammar, and the like—you are teaching them to *think critically* in your discipline.

Crossdisciplinary Commonalities

Not surprisingly, all the academic disciplines share a common ground of thought and expression, and the writing-across-the-curriculum movement defined that territory. Toulmin et al (1984) offer a particularly useful model of crossdisciplinary reasoning and writing. First, all scholarship states a *claim* of some kind: a hypothesis, a thesis, a solution, or a resolution. Secondly, it presents *data* related to that claim—that is, some kind of factual evidence that may take the form of numerical results of an experiment, inferential statistics from a survey, historical documentation, or quotations from a text.

Third, it makes a *warrant*—that is, as persuasive an argument as possible that the data justify the claim and/or make this claim superior to competing claims. Scholars then debate the validity of a given claim in terms of the applicability and the quality of its supporting data and the strength of its warrant.

The claim-data-warrant model is simple enough to teach to undergraduates, and it sensitizes them to the need to include all three elements in every piece of formal writing they do. (Student writing is often missing one or two of them.) It also gives them an easy-to-use framework for evaluating scholarly, rhetorical, and expository writing in general, including that of their peers (Neel, 1993).

However, this crossdisciplinary common ground does not extend very far. The disciplines diverge on the language used, the placement of these elements in relation to each other, the forms of data considered respectable, the standards for an acceptable warrant (Walvoord and McCarthy, 1991).

Teaching Critical Thinking Through the Discipline's Metacognitive Model

Critical thinking has no universal definition or rules. Rather, it is thinking within the usually unspoken conventions that a given discipline has adopted as "legitimate" argumentation and evidence. It is the "disciplinary dialect" that a field speaks, the "disciplinary scaffolding" on which the profession constructs knowledge, the "metacognitive model" on which the discipline operates (Nelson, 1993). Thus, one field's critical thinking may be another field's logical fallacy or unjustified conclusion.

This is not a problem in itself. The problem is that *we fail to articulate our discipline's metacognitive model to our students* (Langer, 1992; Nelson, 1993; Donald, 2002). Maybe it never crosses our minds. Maybe we are so wedded to our model that we forget it isn't common knowledge or common sense. Maybe we assume that students will simply pick it up by osmosis. Some eventually do, of course. Maybe we did. But not everyone does so easily, not without getting C's and D's along the way. And many students *never* get it. They major in another field with a disciplinary dialect that they somehow *do* pick up.

Why not explain your field's metacognitive model to your students up front, especially in introductory courses where their concept is the sketchiest and often the most mistaken? Writing is the natural context for doing so, for three reasons:

1. Writing is the most formal, concrete expression of a student's understanding of the discipline.
2. Most courses give graded writing assignments.
3. These assignments afford students quick feedback on their attempts to communicate in the disciplinary dialect.

Metacognitive Differences among Disciplines

By way of introduction to disciplinary differences, consider the short-answer or essay-question command that often appears on tests and written assignments: "compare and contrast." In the laboratory sciences this typically means "to list" as many similarities and differences as possible. In the social sciences, it implies "to discuss" as many as possible, referring to theoretical texts and/or research findings to buttress one's argument. In literature, however, the command has yet another translation: "to analyze" *one critical similarity* and *one critical difference* at length, staying close to the texts.

It is little wonder then that a literature major in an introductory biology course can write an elegant essay comparing and contrasting plants and animals and never understand why it barely gets a passing grade. Similarly, the biology major in a literature course may be just as puzzled about why his lengthy list of similarities and differences between *The Grapes of Wrath* and *The Sun Also Rises* receives a D. In fact, it is surprising that as many students figure out these disciplinary nuances as they do.

Based on interviews with college instructors, Langer (1992) outlines the major metacognitive differences among three major disciplinary groups, especially as these differences pertain to the written products expected of students. Donald's (2002) work, also based on faculty interviews, fills in some insightful details, especially within the sciences.

Sciences. Students are supposed to apply hard facts and

reliable data to a problem-solving situation, to consider possible outcomes, to hypothesize the most reasonable prediction, to perform a tightly controlled experiment to test the hypothesis, to measure the results meticulously, and to come to probable, carefully qualified conclusions based on the resulting evidence. Student opinion has little or no place in the process, and students should establish the validity of the source when citing someone else's published conclusions.

A lab write-up or report has a specific format, much like a recipe, that students receive instructions to follow. The task involves selecting the relevant information from lab notes and placing it in the proper categories, according to the format. Students are expected to include tables, charts, graphs, drawings, and the like to clarify, simplify, and/or abbreviate the presentation. They should carefully construct and label these visuals. What writing is necessary should be clean, concise, and impersonal with relatively short, non-complex sentences. Under certain circumstances (e.g., lists), incomplete sentences are perfectly acceptable. Sometimes use of the passive voice is recommended.

Within the sciences, physics relies heavily on deductive logic to obtain a reasonable, plausible answer within expected limits. On the other end of the continuum, biology students are expected to think inductively, inferentially, metaphorically and skeptically about their results. Chemistry falls in between. In engineering, students are supposed to use procedural knowledge to solve problems and make design decisions in the absence of complete information (Donald, 2002).

Many subfields in the social sciences and almost all of psychology follow the sciences mode, especially those that rely on the experimental method and the quantitative analysis of large data sets. Students must learn to view their own and others' research results as probabilistic and tentative.

History-based disciplines.
Here the focus is on explaining the relationships between contradictory developments and conflicting documentary evidence. Students are expected to examine concrete historical circumstances and to develop defensible stands on controversial issues, drawing on detailed supporting evidence based on valid documentation. Part of this process entails viewing the conclusions of others with a critical eye, distinguishing true from false positions and main points from subpoints.

In essence, the challenge in writing a paper is to argue clearly and convincingly a historical interpretation using concrete factual, contextual evidence. Content is of greater importance than format. As one history instructor describes the rule of thumb, students should "give at least three different types of reasons relevant to the issues and... details to support those reasons" (Langer, 1992, p. 79).

The fields within this model include art, music, dance, and literary history, some philosophical studies, the historical specialties in the social sciences, and, of course, history. Law is similar in that an argument is won on the basis of factual evidence and a persuasive analysis of what the facts suggest (Donald, 2002).

Literature. As in the history-based disciplines, students are supposed to interpret, but in literary criticism this means something distinctly different. The interpretation is of the meaning of a piece of literature, how it allegorically or metaphorically reflects some aspect of real life. To infer intelligently what an author may intend, students should draw on the major themes and motifs in literature. But personal opinion is an integral aspect of interpretation; in fact, originality of opinion is prized. But an opinion must also have validity, and validity is derived from specific, supporting references to the text. Points in the text are the data or evidence of literary interpretation.

Students are also expected to analyze and evaluate an author's literary style, often comparing and contrasting it with those of other authors. They must incorporate a historical understanding of literary genres and traditions so they know which comparisons and contrasts are interesting. For example, examining stylistic differences between Chaucer and Hemingway might yield an extensive list, but a boring one belaboring the obvious. Of much greater interest are the fewer and more subtle differences between authors who occupy the same or similar literary worlds.

An excellent paper then begins with a novel but thematic slant on a piece of literature and/or a credible analysis of its place within an identifiable tradition, both strongly supported by details and quotations from the actual work. Thus content is critical. But more than in other fields, so is the writing style in the paper itself. After all, literature *is* writing, much like science is the scientific method. Those attracted to literature should be extremely literate and literary themselves.

Along with English, foreign language, and comparative literature, the arts and much of philosophy follow a similar model, perhaps with less exacting standards for students' writing style.

Making Students Better Thinkers and Writers

The purpose of this summary was not to tell you what you already know about your field. Rather it was, first, to heighten your awareness of very different heuristics that students may bring into your course from other courses they have taken outside of your discipline. Secondly, it was to help you determine what facets of the disciplinary dialect and scaffolding that you already share with your students and what else they may benefit from learning. Certainly, the more they know about your discipline's conventions of argumentation and evidence—the more they can "think" like a colleague—the better they will perform in your courses, especially in their formal writing assignments.

While you can explain these conventions to your students, Nelson (1993) suggests a one-hour in-class exercise that allows students to "discover" your discipline's metacognitive model on their own, inductively. Pass out a brief essay-type question along with copies of four different answers ranging in grades from A to D/F, but with comments and grades removed. (Past exams are excellent sources.) Then break students into small groups and have them figure out which answers are better and in what ways. After they develop a list of criteria (which you should verify in class discussion), assign another essay for them to write, either in class or as homework, following these criteria.

According to Nelson, students who have done this exercise report higher-than-expected grades not only in the course in which it is administered but also in their other courses. For many students the experience gives them a whole new gestalt on what disciplines, knowledge, scholarship, and higher education are all about.

Teaching Students to Write for Their Futures

Except for those students who become academics, few of the writing conventions you teach them will carry them into their careers. The workplace has its own metacognitive mode—yet another dialect, another scaffolding that most of your students will have to learn sooner or later. You can help them learn it "sooner" in your course, where the costs of error are comparatively low. They need to know that college graduates spend an average of 20 to 30 per cent of their time in the workplace on writing tasks, and even more as they advance through the ranks (Spears, 1994). No doubt your students will greatly appreciate your instructing them in a skill they will need and use so much.

So if any of your courses can accommodate it, you may want to give your students some experience in business/administrative writing. Such assignments fit in naturally with extended cases, simulations, problem-based learning, and some service learning experiences (see Chapters 17, 23, and 24).

You can build assignments around several different forms: relatively brief memos and letters; lengthy proposals for new policies, procedures, projects, products, and services; and progress reports on projects and transitions. While the briefer forms make excellent individual tasks, proposals and projects reports are often collaborative products in the business/administrative world and thus should be in a course as well.

This type of writing has distinct features not shared with scholarly kinds (most from Spears, 1994). Let us examine them in detail.

Specific audience pitch. As it is always directed to a specific individual or group, either you or your students must clearly define the audience for each assignment. Students then target their message accordingly.

Language and style. Since the audience is usually a non-specialist in a hectic, pragmatic environment, the language must be non-technical, accessible, concise, and direct enough to be skimmed. The preferred words and phrases are clean, short, essential, and powerful— chosen to be quickly informative and/or persuasive.

For instance, wherever possible, adjectives and adverbs replace prepositional phrases; briefer constructions such as "before" and "if" replace "prior to" and "in the event that"; active voice replaces passive.

Purpose. With few exceptions, business/administrative communications ask the audience to take some form of action, whether it be simple approval, change, or funding. Progress reports may ask for more time, more funding, or simply continued faith and support.

Evidence to justify purpose. Standard evidence includes observations, repeated events, interviews, small-scale surveys, and printed materials, usually non-academic. Students can benefit from learning how to collect such data and familiarizing themselves with respected business, administrative, professional, trade, and industry sources.

Format. As in journalistic writing, the purpose and main points appear up front in the introduction. Longer communications such as proposals contain other reader-friendly features that "chunk" the information: a title page; a table of contents; an executive summary or abstract (one-page maximum) focusing on the purpose and the recommendations; short chapters and sections; abundant headings and subheadings; lists rather than text when possible; graphics such as charts, tables, diagrams, and illustrations to minimize and summarize text; a conclusion listing recommendations; appendices with non-essential supporting information; and generous white space throughout.

Accuracy and timeliness. Finally, business/administrative writing must be error-free, which means checked for factual accuracy and carefully proofread, as well as submitted on time. If not, the credibility of the writer suffers or, worse yet, the proposal is not even read. Students must come to understand that the "real world" is much less tolerant and patient than college courses.

The Many Worlds of Writing

No doubt almost all young students enter college with the mistaken belief that they will learn how to think and write well for all purposes, for all the possible nooks and crannies of the world of work where they could land. Just like dualistic thinking, this belief will die hard in their hearts. But this belief may not die at all if instruc-

tors don't explicitly teach and show students the variety of styles and standards of thinking and writing.

They need to know up front that what was good evidence, argument, and writing style in their literature class does not apply wholly in their chemistry course, and that chemistry follows a different set of rules and standards. And so do the worlds of business and government, where they are most likely seek employment. If we don't share with them this basic truth, they may come to think that neither academe nor the world beyond it has any standards and conventions at all.

For further reading:

Bean, John C. 1996. *Engaging Ideas: The Professor's Guide to Integrating Writing, Critical Thinking and Active Learning in the Classroom.* San Francisco: Jossey-Bass.

Donald, Janet. 2002. *Learning to Think: Disciplinary Perspectives.* San Francisco: Jossey-Bass.

TOOLS OF THE TRADE: MAKING THE MOST OF INSTRUCTIONAL AIDS AND TECHNOLOGY

Teaching at its finest demands that instructors consider every educational tool at their command—various techniques, formats, aids, and technologies—to give their students the richest educational experience possible. After focusing on the former two types of tools, we now turn to the latter two.

As Chapter 12 points out, students rely on different learning modalities to different extents. Some students learn best by listening and discussing, some by reading and writing, others through graphic representations, and still others by hands-on experience. Since the traditional college classroom is strongly geared to the digital and auditory learning styles, students who are more visually or kinesthetically oriented are often at a disadvantage. Visual aids and simulated experiences, ranging from low-tech chalkboards and flip charts to the most advanced computer simulations and interactive learning modules, help these students excel while reinforcing everyone's learning.

This chapter is organized starting with the lowest-tech, most readily available visual aids to the (currently) highest-tech instructional technology.

The Ubiquitous Board

You and your students grew up with it. It's in every classroom in the nation—though no classroom seems to have enough of them. You might even have one in your office. It now comes in a few colors and a modern, glossy white version with marker pens. In fact, it's so familiar to all of us in the educational sector that we rarely consider how to use it most effectively. All we notice are the times when it's used *in*effectively, which is often when we can't see it.

Below are a few guidelines for board use, perhaps all of which are intuitive yet all too often forgotten (Bartlett and Thomason, 1983):

- **Write neatly, legibly, and large,** as much as possible on a horizontal (vs. diagonal) line, and only on areas visible to all students. If board writing is not your forte, shift to printing. Be very careful with your spelling, especially if you hold students responsible for theirs.
- **Use thick chalk in a large classroom,** such as "railroad crayon."
- **Use different color chalks and markers** for complex diagrams and drawings to facilitate students' visual understanding of the parts of a process, stages of development, sections of a specimen, etc.
- **Write what you can before class** to save time and energy during class.
- **Outline material on the**

154

board rather than writing sentences, and **use symbols and abbreviations** wherever possible. Not only does this practice save you time and board space, but it also helps students increase their note-taking efficiency. In addition, try to write quickly so you don't lose students' attention.

- **Use the board as an organizational tool.** It is best to work from far left to right, numbering points as you develop them. Divide different topics with lines or spaces, but do connect related ideas with lines as well. Underline new terms when defining them. During pauses, step back to evaluate your board work, and correct and clarify points as required.
- **Be complete in your presentation,** defining critical new terms, giving all steps in a solution, and labeling all parts of your diagrams and technical drawings.
- **Practice writing while looking over your shoulder towards the class.** At least try to avoid spending much time with your back to the class. During the moments that you must, don't bother talking; your students may or may not hear you. It is better to pause, turn around, and explain the material while you are making eye contact with the class.
- **Ask students occasionally whether they can see your board work.** Over an hour, your handwriting may change, or the glare from the windows may settle on different spots.
- **Coordinate your words and your board work to reinforce each other.** It is best to introduce new material verbally, then outline it on the board, then

explain what you've outlined. If you've written out major topics or questions, point to each one as you shift the discussion to it. Also refer to the board regularly to reinforce important points.

- **Use the board to record discussion contributions.** You can reduce redundancy and help your students learn to take notes on discussion.
- **Ask the class before you erase** to ensure that everyone has been able to copy what you've written. (Ever hear the horror story of the math professor who wrote on the board with the right hand and followed closely with an eraser in the left?) If someone needs an extra moment, you might move on to a different part of the board, if available, or use the pause productively to ask or answer questions.
- **Bring students to the board to display their answers** to problems, discussion questions, and the like. They will be less shy about coming up if you begin this routine early in the term and if you assign the problems/questions to small groups. Students don't mind publically presenting a group solution.
- **Avoid wearing very dark clothes on a heavy chalkboard-work day.** Or judiciously try to avoid leaning against the chalkboard. They may call it "dustless" chalk, but it isn't!

The Flip Chart

Heavily utilized at conferences and in boardrooms, the flip chart is rarely seen in a classroom. Yet it has great teaching potential in smaller classes. Some of the same guidelines for board use apply.

Teaching at Its Best

Despite its smaller size, it has three advantages: 1) You can write out much of your material in advance and in any color marker. 2) You can preserve the material, both what you prepare and what evolves during a class, from term to term. 3) Rather than erase, you can tear off pages and tape them wherever you want. It may be worth the minor investment to buy your own flip chart or easel and large pad.

The Overhead Projector

The guidelines for overhead use are similar to those for board use. For instance, if you use marker pens on your transparencies, make sure that the colors you select are easily discernible and that any glare in the room does not obscure the images you are projecting. Also be careful to allow students adequate time to assimilate and take notes on the projected material.

The overhead projector has additional intricacies and guidelines for effective use (Head, 1992; Rogers, 1993). These suggestions are worth keeping in mind the next time you give a conference presentation or an invited lecture.

- **Design your overhead transparencies to project horizontally** on the screen rather than vertically, if possible. The horizontal format fits better on the square screen. In fact, the screen often crops off the lower fourth of a vertical transparency.
- **Use visuals and graphics freely.** The overhead medium is perfect for symbols, graphs, charts, pictures, tables, and diagrams.
- **Focus on one and only one concept in a transparency.** And keep the images as simple as possible. A transparency becomes cluttered and difficult to interpret with more than three or four graphic images.
- **Use key words as heads and subheads,** not complete sentences, to focus students' attention on concepts and relationships.
- **Keep the information on each transparency to a minimum**, not exceed seven lines of seven words each. More than this is difficult to process. Furthermore, the print should be large and clearly legible—at least 3/16" character height. Smaller print may be hard to read from the back of even a small room. For a substantial data set, you may wish to project just a title and to distribute handouts with the actual data— the same for complex graphs, tables, and diagrams.
- **Consider using overlays for sequential diagrams,** such as when you want to illustrate a sequential development, or when you want to reuse some of your transparencies in other contexts. Mathematics, physics, and economics present excellent opportunities for overlaying transparencies: Start with the basic axes, add the curves, then add symbols and explanations. The biological sciences often use overlays to show a succession of specimen sections.
- **Use a pointer,** such as a pencil or a laser, rather than your finger. And it is better to use it **on the overhead projection plate** than to move around in front of the screen. The shadowed image of even a pencil is very sharp, and it commands attention without your making distracting gestures.
- **Eliminate glare by using color transparencies** instead

of the standard clear ones. Several colors are available, including a soft yellow film that is particularly easy on the eye. Brighter colors such as green or red can be interjected for emphasis.

- **Never stand between the projector and the projected images.** Doing so blocks the image and is distracting to the class.
- **Turn off the projector lamp when not in use,** even if you are still talking. This way students stay focused on what you are saying instead of the empty screen.

The Slide Projector

Professionally produced "2 x 2 (inch)" slides are available for many subject areas, and even amateur photographers can make high quality slides. The rules of thumb for using 35 mm slide projectors resemble those for overhead projectors, but with a few unique twists. Daniel (1975) and Head (1992) offer some useful tips:

- **Learn how to load slides correctly.** Many an excellent presentation has been marred by an upside down or backwards slide. To load a slide properly, first examine it to find the way it should be viewed on the screen. Then place a dot or "thumb spot" in the lower left corner of the frame. Your right thumb will cover the thumb spot if you are loading the slide properly.
- **Learn how to use the slide projector** *before* **your presentation.** For instance, know how to focus the image, advance the carousel, and clear any jammed slides, as well as how to replace a blown lamp bulb. A few min-

utes of preparation can save a lot of lost class time spent troubleshooting technical problems.

- **Begin and end your presentation with a black or grey slide.** Bright flashes of light on a white screen can annoy and distract students. If you have a long explanation in the middle of your presentation, insert another neutral slide for the time during which you will be speaking.
- **Visually vary your presentation.** If your slide show consists of photographs or diagrams, break up a long sequence with a slide of text.
- **Keep the show rolling.** For a class, even a minute on one slide can drag the pace of a presentation, unless the image is very complex.

When to Consider High-Tech Alternatives

Low-tech visual aids have proven their teaching effectiveness. But the days of nothing but "chalk and talk" are over. Instructional technology (IT) has taken on a new, broader meaning that encompasses presentation software, course management systems, email, discussion boards, chat rooms, multimedia and interactive presentations on CD-ROMs and web sites, laptops in the classroom and distance learning utilizing the web and one-way and two-way video.

These new alternatives give you greater latitude in designing your courses, but also greater responsibility for choosing and using the various technologies appropriately. You are ultimately your own instructional developer, designer, and and technologist. (Only when you consider unfamiliar techniques and technologies do you typically turn to professionals for advice.) So it is important to view classroom computer technology as only a tool—specifically for communication—and only one of many tools. We can become so fascinated with the bells and whistles that we forget the lower-tech ways to accomplish the same objective. Any computer application should be based on sound pedagogical principles (Knapper, 1982; Albright and Graf, 1992).

What are *appropriate reasons* for using high-tech instructional tools? Lewis and Wall (1988) cite six *good* reasons that faculty give. First, a certain technology may achieve certain course goals and facilitate certain instructional tasks that are impossible to accomplish otherwise. For instance, interactive video technology allows students to experience distant times, places, and events to which they lack direct access. For another example, interactive software allows students to perform lab experiments and procedures that would be too dangerous or too expensive to do in reality (e.g., surgeries and molecular biology experiments).

Second, a certain technology may provide the only realistic means for you to demonstrate a phenomenon. For instance, chemistry and physics instructors can use a computer simulation or display program to show an atomic structure or a chemical or physical force interaction. Such applications are particularly effective when the phenomenon in question is too large, too small, or too dynamic to convey with printed media, static diagrams, or hand gestures.

A third appropriate use of a technology is to allow students to drill and practice at their own pace. No one instructor can regularly give every student individual instruction, although we try to do so when

necessary. Computer tutorials can function in our place, without the time and patience limitations that afflict us mere mortals.

Fourth, using high-tech tools can help students acquire the technological literacy that their future occupations will certainly require. By learning to use word processing software, spreadsheet programs, statistical packages, layout and design software, engineering programs, etc. *now*, students overcome their anxieties as well as their ignorance and broaden their job placement prospects.

Fifth, both you and your students can appropriately use technology to enhance your productivity—in particular, to reduce the time spent on routine record-keeping and communication. Course records for large classes, for example, are most easily managed on a standard spreadsheet. Putting a class journal on a discussion board encourages timely and thoughtful responses, and emailing announcements, assignments, and graded work saves class time. Word processing software streamlines writing and editing tasks. You can even word process your comments on written assignments and essay exams, since students' papers and responses often display similar strengths and weaknesses.

Finally, electronic communication and collaboration can give you and your class some of the conveniences of distance learning with none of the costs. For one example, teams of students can confer and edit projects online at any time. For another, a student who misses a class or an office hour can email the instructor or TA and confer, ask questions, and submit assignments. Or she can pick up the gist of what she missed on the course website.

Let us now take a look at some

of the most pedagogically useful and exciting kinds of high-tech instructional tools.

Presentation Software

While not interactive, presentation software such as PowerPoint can enhance the visual quality and impact of lectures and professional presentations, whether in the classroom or on the web. Such software allows you to create and project text integrated with images, animations, and video clips—all in full color—while playing sound.

Even if you intend to display only text and images, presentation software gives you greater flexibility than overhead transparencies or the traditional slide show. For instance, at any given moment you can highlight the text or zoom in on the section of the image that you are explaining. In addition, you can save the presentation for students to review later.

Cautionary advice. While presentation software is almost essential for conveying knowledge at a distance, it is easy to overuse it in the classroom, especially for text. Such software is merely a complement to lecture, often just an outline of the lecture, and as such it is no more student-active than the lecture. Breaks are just as necessary as during the traditional lecture (see Chapter 14). In addition, a presentation often requires lower classroom lighting than do overhead transparencies, so it can encourage some students to fall asleep in class. This type of software is best reserved for visually-intensive or multimedia material.

When you do make text slides, keep in mind the same rules that apply to text in lower-tech instructional aids: Focus on only one concept per slide; use key words rather than complete sentences; and keep the information on each slide to an absolute minimum. Use the templates to help you arrange your information in a logical and pleasing way.

One more rule applies: Restrain yourself from getting too elaborate with color combinations, backgrounds, clip art, slide transitions and builds, and other design options and special effects. In instruction, usually the fewer the glitzy distractions and the simpler the visuals the better. It is also advisable to keep the same colors and backgrounds throughout a presentation. When in doubt, yellow text on a dark blue background is easiest to read in a dark classroom.

Text slides are easy to produce with the basic presentation software. Inserting images, sound, animation, or video requires additional software and equipment (e.g., a scanner, a microphone), as well as a great deal of computer memory for storing very large files. On your first time through the process, obtain the help of an experienced colleague, knowledgeable student assistant, or instructional technology consultant.

Student presentations. Presentation software is for your students' use as well. It adds the instructional richness and vitality of images and other media to their class presentations. It also makes possible out-of-class and distance-learning student presentations. A slide presentation can be run at any time, preserved and revised indefinitely, and incorporated into a student's electronic portfolio.

Course Management Software

This type of software is actually a *package* of instructionally-useful software. Some of its program components are designed to streamline the instructor's duties—e.g., an online syllabus template, automatic test grading, and a grade book linked to a spreadsheet program. Other features facilitate and expand opportunities for communication and interaction with and among students. This latter function makes this software almost essential in distance learning and very enhancing in "live" courses. It extends the classroom beyond its walls and scheduled meeting times.

Institutions often purchase one course management system for its entire faculty, along with a blanket license, so you may not have a choice of software. However, these are the typical online tools that are bundled in a good product (Sherer and Shea, 2002) or otherwise available to you (e.g., email):
- A course web-page template with an easy-to-insert web-link tool and sub-templates for the syllabus, course calendar, pop-up glossary, and class roster
- Email, with a mailing list option for the instructor
- A class bulletin or discussion board, with "threaded discussion" options
- Team discussion boards
- One or more live chat rooms
- Space for course materials (text, graphics, multimedia), such as assigned readings, lecture notes, instructional programs (if legal to post; see Chapter 6), and student presentations
- Online testing (timed, untimed, and multiple-tries option)
- Automatic grading (of closed-ended items)
- Online grade book
- Automatic test feedback to students
- Online student survey template
- Student web-page templates
- Online help
- Search

Some of these features deserve their own separate discussion.

Electronic Discussion and Collaboration

No longer is conversational exchange confined to face-to-face situations like class time and live office hours. Now instructors have their choice of various electronic forums for class discussion, collaboration, and consultation: email, bulletin/discussion boards, chat rooms, conferencing software, and MOOs. Each has its own special features and strengths.

Whatever the forum, electronic communication augments classroom learning and helps develop students' cognitive skills in important ways. The fact that it is somewhat anonymous and not face-to-face reduces many students' self-consciousness and defensiveness, thereby fostering their involvement and participation. It may also enhance problem-solving skills and creativity (Gallupe and Cooper, 1993).

Electronic communication also seems to stimulate clearer and deeper thinking. As students have to write their questions and responses, the medium encourages them to think more carefully and critically. In addition, as they must frame their messages for clarity and conciseness, they improve their writing skills (Bellman, 1992). But perhaps most obviously, electronic interaction extends your students' learning beyond the classroom, increasing student-active time on task.

Email. Email is a one-to-one or one-to-many (through multiple receivers, cc's, or lists) communication system by which a sender accesses a mainframe system and leaves a message to be read by one or more receivers at remote locations. This communication is called "asynchronous" because a receiver can read the message at any time after it is sent.

One-to-one email with your students can substitute for live office hours and after-class exchanges but without the restrictions of time and place. It also saves class time that would otherwise go to individual student questions, concerns, and Socratic dialogue. Using the attachment tool, students can email you homework assignments, papers, and presentations as well.

With the mailing list option, you can save class time by sending your entire class housekeeping messages, reminders, study questions, and even entire assignments in one mailing. Your students can reply to you individually and confidentially with their questions, to which you can reply individually.

A word of warning: Some students, especially younger ones, keep very late hours and may not realize that you don't. They may email you with questions, especially right before tests, in the middle of the night anticipating a prompt reply. Or they may expect you to be online evenings, weekends, and whenever they are. You should set explicit limits with your classes about your online availability.

If you distribute a class list of email addresses, your students can also communicate with one another, but you will not be able to monitor them unless they "cc" their course-relevant messages to you.

Discussion/bulletin boards. Like email, this form of communication is asynchronous; messages can be sent and retrieved at any time. In addition, they are posted in a "permanent" running record. Once posted, messages cannot be deleted or modified as email messages can be. Thus you can monitor your students' participation. (This is why discussion boards have largely replaced class listservs.)

This communication is strictly one-to-many, but "many" can be a team if your software allows it. Since a class may be discussing a number of topics at any given time during the course, it is best to have "threaded discussions" where contributions are clearly labeled and organized by topic.

If online discussion will be a serious part of your course and/or you will grade students on their contributions, you'll need to develop some explicit standards and procedures like these:

- Explain to your students the importance of online discussion in their meeting the learning objectives of the course (see Chapter 3)..
- Decide how the discussion topics/questions will be generated.
- Establish replies as important contributions (Knowlton et al, 2000).
- Give examples of high-quality and low-quality contributions.
- Define and insist on proper netiquette.
- Give credit to students who answer other students' questions before you do (Weaver, 2002).
- Even if you set a minimum rate or number of contributions and/or grade on quantity, also take quality into account when grading.
- Include peer evaluation of student contributions in the grading.
- Model appropriate participation; do not dominate or direct too

much (Knowlton et al, 2000).
- Ask questions to encourage clarification, elaboration, and correction (Knowlton et al, 2000).
- Over time shift your role from a participant to a facilitator, who may, for instance, synthesize students' contributions around the key points (Knowlton et al, 2000).

Chat rooms, conferencing software, and MOOs. Synchronous, "real-time" communication systems like these are less popular than email and discussions boards for several reasons:
1) they strongly favor those who type fast;
2) they require synchronized schedules of participation;
3) they are infamous for netiquette violations, especially chat rooms;
4) they encourage free-for-all "bull sessions" that wander off the main topic; and
5) they usually allow pairs and triads to splinter off into private side conversations.

Still these tools can play a critical educational role, especially in distance learning. Chat rooms are invaluable for small-group collaboration at a distance, and the instructor can participate. In addition, with conferencing software, you and your students can set up topical folders and transfer any type of computer file within a conference. MOOs (Multiple-user Object-Oriented environments) add graphical interfaces to text-based chat and even allow for video- and audio-streaming of lectures and class activities.

If you intend to use these tools for discussion, consider explicitly setting up standards and procedures similar to those above for discussion boards.

Web-based courses constitute an integral part of distance learning, along with synchronous, "real-time" communication systems, one-way video, two-way video (video conferencing), and local area network (LAN) television. But increasingly classroom instructors are putting parts of their courses on the web, either as a course enhancement or a substitute for some face-to-face class meetings. Course web sites may contain as little as the syllabus or as much as all the lectures, homework, quizzes and tests, multimedia shows, and links to assigned readings and viewings.

Instructional resources. A good reason to have a course web page is to incorporate links to relevant instructional web sites. The web contains a wealth of sites that you may want your students to read/view/hear as an assignment or for course-related research. But this electronic space is so vast that you cannot possibly know when or whether you've located the best resources. Your campus library or instructional technology center may offer web-search workshops that can save you hours, even days, of roaming around on a browser. In addition, your colleagues are invaluable sources in specialized areas. You can post your request for recommended sites on one of your discipline's listservs.

The web offers some rich multimedia resources, as well as a place to develop and publish your own such materials without entailing the CD-ROM production costs. However, it is difficult to find free web-based materials that are truly interactive and have eye-catching images, sound, animation, and video. Still, if they have solid learning value, they also have two added benefits. First, they are accessible to students anytime, anywhere, from any computer terminal with a web browser. Second, they usually contain links to additional sources of relevant information or knowledge located elsewhere in the same document or at another web site. Thus students can select their own pathways to learning and pursue the topics of greatest interest of them.

"Link rot." One reason why you add links to your course web page is to avoid violating copyright laws and guidelines (see Chapter 6). But in relying on links for required readings and activities, you encounter another problem, one particularly serious for distance-learning courses: "link rot." The links may or may not be there the next time you teach the course, or even later in the term when you students get to them. In three graduate-level biochemistry courses at the University of Nebraska at Lincoln, half of the links disappeared in less than five years. The only way around link rot is to make online copies of the web materials and make course links to the copies rather than the originals. But doing this legally requires the written permission of the creators of the materials and *may* entail a fee (Kiernan, 2002).

To post or not to post your own course materials. Of course in distant learning, you may have to post all your course materials. But what if your web site is strictly an enhancement of an classroom-based course? In this case, consider the impact of posting the ma-

terials before you do it.

If you post your syllabus and assignments and make changes during the term, your students may not notice the changes unless you announce them in class and/or over email. What about posting your lecture notes and class exercises and activities? If you do, you might not have students who missed classes coming to you for information and materials. But the more class materials you post, the more your "live" attendance is likely to drop.

"Conservative" posting seems to work best. If you will lecture, by all means post an *outline* of your lecture in advance, allow plenty of space between major topics, and advise your students to print it out and bring it to class for note-taking. This way students will not get lost in your organization. You may also want to post complex visuals for your students to print out for your lecture so they don't have to draw them. In brief, feel free to post materials that are supplementary to, not redundant with, your classes.

But then again, consider the exciting possibilities of making *all* your lectures outside reading/viewing assignments. You then liberate hours and hours of class time for all the discussion, writing-to-learn exercises, cooperative learning activities, and other student-active formats that you may have wanted to integrate into your course but never had the time to include.

Posting homework assignments, study questions, review sheets, the like in advance rarely presents problems, but don't post homework solutions and answers until after you grade and return the work. Of course, putting up answers to your test questions renders those questions and problems unusable in the future.

Instructional Software

This term encompasses a vast market of computer programs and multimedia presentations, some of which are interactive, that are designed to supplement readings and instructor-developed course materials. They can enhance both classroom-based and distance-learning courses. Many of them feature imaginative, high-quality graphics—some even sound, animation and video—to create a multisensory learning experience that accommodates all learning styles (Lamb, 1992; also see Chapter 12). Some arrange the material nonlinearly and interactively, allowing students to select different learning paths based on the decisions they have made earlier in the presentation. With more control over their learning process, they should feel greater ownership of the material.

Many kinds of teaching tools and methods have been packaged in instructional software:

- Realistic demonstrations
- Performances (musical, dramatic)
- Virtual science laboratories for dangerous and/or costly procedures and experiments
- Case studies
- Simulations (Chapter 17 lists examples of such software.)
- Interactive drills and exercises for remediation, practice, or review (e.g., mathematics, reading, foreign languages)
- Interactive quantitative problem solving
- Teacher resources (presentations, exercises, etc.) for K-12 and special education

In addition, we shouldn't forget the career-relevant software that many students have to master before they graduate and seek employment—e.g., spreadsheet, statistical analysis, database management, MIS, drafting, design, and engineering.

Even though your students may have considerable computer savvy, just turning them loose to figure out a new program on their own greatly undermines its instructional effectiveness. Many students resent having to master alien, complex software while struggling through tough new content as well. Only if students can easily navigate through a program can they reap the potential educational advantages. So if you have any choice of software, value simplicity over bells and whistles.

Instructional software is now available for virtually every academic and professional discipline, as well as a number of multidisciplinary combinations (e.g., the Perseus Project, a study aid on ancient Greece that integrates history, archaeology, art history, religion, and linguistics). These products come on CD-ROMs with licenses, a few bundled or optional with textbooks. You can find information on specific products at the Educational Software Cooperative's web site (www.edu-soft.org) and in the journal *IEEE Computer Graphics and Applications*.

As their development costs are high, these engaging instructional aids aren't cheap. They can double the price of a student's textbook, and departments and universities may pay thousands of dollars for a software package and all the needed licenses. But unless you have strong programming skills, developing your own software is not a realistic option. It could take you many months and entail heavy consulting, licensing, and production costs.

Using Laptops in the Classroom

Several universities have mandated laptop computers for part or all of their undergraduate population. They have also set up training programs and incentives to encourage faculty to teach with laptops—with mixed results. It's too early to say if this is the next big high-tech trend in higher education, but it's good to be prepared.

Teaching with laptops. The successful pioneers in laptop pedagogy already have lessons to share. Weaver (2002), such a pioneer who now trains other instructors in using laptops effectively in the classroom, suggests these in-class uses:

• Individual students or teams work online on exercises or problems (either instructor-developed or in an instructional software package) with the instructor present to help.

• Students work online on individual or team projects with the instructor present to help. The projects themselves may be web sites.

• The instructor facilitates a workshop on writing, research methods, web-page development, problem solving, etc. during which the students can actually try out recommended procedures, and get quick instructor feedback.

• Students discuss complex questions (new or for review) posed by the instructor on the class bulletin board. Students have a record of the discussion.

• Students exchange their drafts of assignments to give and receive peer feedback.

• While students are watching a instructor demonstration, a video, or a student presentation, they record and either post or email their observations, questions, and evaluative feedback.

• Students take notes on a presentation, lecture, or discussion, possibly onto a prepared organizational outline.

• The instructor or another student conducts a class survey.

• Team members exchange calendars to set up future meetings.

• Students take timed, online quizzes and tests under the instructor's watchful eye. If these quizzes and tests are objective, students can get nearly instantaneous feedback.

• The instructor can hold class anywhere—at field-research or observation sites, in the library, in galleries or museums, even in a local coffee shop for the atmosphere.

It is possible to add software that can capture a student's screen for projection, and this capability may extend some of these activities.

How essential are laptops to the classroom activities listed above? Certainly laptops enable computer-driven activities without holding class in a computer lab, which usually doesn't allow the instructor and the students to see each other. It is true that some of these activities are quite doable with only low-tech tools. However, laptops enhance the speed and efficiency of these tasks while saving reams of paper and preparing students for an increasingly laptop-oriented work world.

Keeping students on task. Generally students feel comfortable learning with laptops, but many prefer doing other things with their laptops in class: surfing the web, doing their email, talking in chat rooms, or instant-messaging with a friend. No matter what they may believe, they can't concentrate on two activities, neither of which are semi-automatic like driving, at the same time. Weaver (2002) has identified several ways to discourage this discourteous and distracting behavior:

- Tell students to keep their laptops closed unless they are doing an online task that you assigned.
- Set specific objectives for them to accomplish in their in-class laptop assignments, and hold them accountable—e.g., randomly ask students or teams to report their progress to the entire class.
- Set tight time limits for these assignments.
- Walk around the room and stand in the back to monitor their screens during these assignments.
- Have students bring their laptops to class only on certain days, and tell them explicitly *not* to bring them the other days.

The potential of laptops.

Laptop technology is advancing every year. Products are getting lighter, faster, and more reliable, and battery life is increasing. Their use in teaching is in its infancy, and their instructional potential in synchronous distance-learning settings has barely been considered. No doubt, Weaver's (2002) suggested classroom uses are only the beginning. Teaching with laptops invites more creative innovation and experimentation.

Looking Ahead

Faculty and even students have had widely differing reactions to high-tech instructional tools. Most student were raised and schooled with computers, but many were not. Some instructors take to high-tech naturally, comfortably, and quickly, while others do not. Those who don't may find themselves under pressure to adapt to the new technology. They should feel free to ask others for help and to take

training workshops on their own or other campuses. After all, instructional technology is a complex, specialized field in which expertise and proficiency require a B.S. or M.S. degree. Few people can pick it up and stay current on their own.

This chapter just scratches the surface of what there is to know on the topic, which is why the list of additional reading recommendations below is so long. As you can see, entire books are devoted to designing distance-learning courses for various delivery technologies. Even if you teach live courses, material on distance learning may give you ideas for technologically enhancing your courses.

We can reasonably expect the lower-tech instructional tools, such as the board and the overhead projector, to be around in basically their present form for years to come. But ironically, the higher-tech sections of this chapter may be obsolete in just a few years. The "best" software this year may be superseded by another version or product the next.

All we know for certain is that higher education has entered a new world of electronically delivered instruction. You can keep abreast of the latest high-tech improvements, innovations, and products by reading *Syllabus, E-learning, EDUCAUSE Review, IEEE Computer Graphics and Applications,* and the "Information Technology" section of the *Chronicle of Higher Education.*

For further reading:

Brown, David A. (ed.). 2000. *Teaching with Technology: Seventy-five Professors from Eight Universities Tell Their Stories.* Bolton, MA: Anker Publishing.

166

Cyrs, Thomas E. 1997. *Teaching at a Distance with Merging Technologies: An Instructional Systems Approach*. Las Cruces, NM: Center for Educational Development, New Mexico State University.

Cyrs, Thomas E. with Eugenia D. Conway. 1999. *Engaging Students in Distance Learning: Interactive Exercises and Activities for Field Sites*. Las Cruces, NM: Center for Educational Development, New Mexico State University.

Fallon, Diane (ed.) 1999. *Technology and Society: Perspectives*. Madison, WI: Coursewise Publishing.

Moore, Gary S., Kathryn Winograd, and Dan Lange. 2001. *You Can Teach Online: Building a Creative Learning Environment*. New York: McGraw-Hill.

Palloff, Rena M. and Keith Pratt. 1999. *Building Learning Communities in Cyberspace*. San Francisco: Jossey-Bass.

Reiss, Donna, Dickie Selfe and Art Young. 1998. *Electronic Communication Across the Curriculum*. Urbana, IL: National Council of Teachers of English.

Sanders, William B. 2001. *Creating Learning-Centered Courses for the World Wide Web*. Needham Heights, MA: Allyn and Bacon.

Schweizer, Heidi. 1999. *Designing and Teaching an Online Course: Spinning Your Web Classroom*. Needham Heights, MA: Allyn and Bacon.

PART IV.

TEACHING

PROBLEM SOLVING

FOR TODAY'S WORLD

TEACHING PROBLEM SOLVING I: THE
CASE METHOD

In this complex world students must learn how to solve problems. Different disciplines focus on different types of problems, and different types of problems call for different teaching methods. Part IV, which includes this and the next three chapters, gives guidance on implementing four major strategies for teaching problem solving.

Both the case method and problem-based learning (next chapter) help students learn how to solve open-ended, high-uncertainty problems that have multiple respectable solutions—some better than others, however. These two methods are relevant to any discipline with real-world application. Chapter 25 suggests ways to help students reason their way through closed-ended, quantitative problems, as are common in mathematics, physics, engineering, economics, and accounting. Finally, Chapter 26 examines how you can construct laboratories to teach students the real process of scientific problem solving.

The case method exposes students to problematic, real-world situations and challenges them to apply course knowledge to analyze the issues and formulate workable solutions. It is based on real or realistic stories that present problems or dilemmas without a clear resolution. Cases (or "vignettes," if short) are usually printed, but some are available dramatized on video-tape and on interactive CD-ROM.

But you need not depend on "canned" cases; you can write your own to suit your own instructional purposes at no cost but your time. Anyone with a bit of story-telling flair should find case-writing an entertaining activity. This chapter provides guidelines for writing as well as selecting cases.

The Effectiveness of the Case Method

Aside from the fact that students enjoy the case method, good cases are rich educational tools.

- They require students' active engagement in and use of the material.
- They help make up for students' lack of real-world experience.
- They accustom students to solving problems within uncertain, risk-laden environments.
- They foster higher-level critical thinking and cognitive skills such as application, analysis, synthesis, and evaluation.
- They demand both inductive and deductive thinking, compensating for higher education's focus on the latter.
- They serve as excellent home-work assignments, paper topics, and essay questions, as well as springboards for discussion, review, and team activities.

On the student-involvement continuum from didactic methods on the low end (e.g., lecture) to experiential methods on the high end (e.g., service learning), the case method falls somewhere in the middle, depending upon the case. The more it resembles a simulation, the more experiential the learning.

A case more closely approximates a simulation when it is written in the second person (placing the student in the story's key role), in the present tense (happening now), and in extended stages (see "Extended Cases" below. On the other hand, the second person and the present tense may undercut the realism of a hypothetical case, and they obviously don't belong in a "real" case. No matter how they are written, cases are unlike truly experiential formats (see Chapter 17) in that students don't act them out. However, interactive CD-ROM cases almost blur the distinction.

The Appropriate Subject Matter

The case method is made for subjects or courses that have a context for *application* or *use*. This is why professional schools have adopted it as a central instructional method. Business and law did so decades ago; in fact, the Harvard Business School built a whole curriculum and publishing company around it. Medicine, nursing, clinical psychology, educational administration, and pastoral studies followed. Then engineering specialties with incomplete knowledge bases have also discovered cases.

The case method is broadly used in many arts and science fields as well, to a greater or less degree: music history (Chiaramonte, 1994); philosophy (e.g., ethics); economics (e.g., macro, legal aspects); political science (e.g., policy analysis, public administration, constitutional law); sociology (e.g., social problems, criminology, organizations); psychology (e.g., clinical, abnormal, organizational behavior); biology (e.g., resource management, ecology); and scientific methods in general (e.g., design a research study to test a given hypothesis).

Faculty and TA development has also embraced the method. It uses cases portraying problems that instructors may encounter with classes and individual students, for example: challenges to authority, hostile reactions to sensitive material, accusations of discrimination, grading and academic honesty disputes, and difficulties implementing new techniques.

What Makes a Good Case

A good case may be written in the second or third person and in present or past tense. It may be as brief as a paragraph or two or as long as a short monograph; the many hundreds of management and business administration cases advertised in the Harvard Business School Publishing catalog range from a couple to over 40 pages. What is important is that a case have the following qualities.

• *Realism.* Real or hypothetical, a case should depict a currently relevant situation with which students can empathize or identify. Realism is further enhanced by technical detail, character development, historical context, and extension over time or a decision-making process (see next section).

• *Opportunities for students to synthesize course material*. Cases should require students to draw on accumulated kowledge of the subject matter to analyze the problems and formulate solutions. Without some review built into the situations, students may forget to apply the basics in real decision-making situations in their careers.

• *Uncertainty and risk.* While some solutions will be better than others, a case should offer room for multiple solutions and valid debate. Several solutions may be viable, but you may have students select just one course of action and to justify their choice. Or you may ask them to rank-order their solutions. The uncertainty surrounding the solutions may be due to uncertainty in the knowledge base (a trait of all bodies of knowledge), information missing in the case (as is often true in reality), and/or the genuine validity of different approaches to the problem.

Further, the decisions students make must have some importance, even if it is only hypothetical, e.g.: a character's employment, health, or life; an organization's survival or success; a country's welfare; the loss of a legal case; social justice or public security.

Extended Cases

Continuous cases tell an unfolding story in segments over real or condensed time. As real-life situations usually evolve and change over time, this structure adds realism. For instance, some faculty development cases describe an instructor's shifting relationship with a class over a term, with each mini-chapter presenting different issues to consider. Some medical and nursing cases follow the progression of a disease or a pregnancy in a hypothetical patient.

Sequential-interactive cases lead students through a process of narrowing down their solutions/decisions by providing additional information *as the students request it*. Like those on CD-ROM, these cases approach the experiential realism of a simulation and problem-based learning. They cast students in the key decision-making role throughout, requiring that at least their minds act it out.

Here is an outline of how such a case may be structured across subject matter, with the medical or clinical variant in parentheses:

1) Students study a case giving limited information on the nature or root cause of a problem. First, they brainstorm all interpretations/causes (diagnoses) and their solutions (treatment plans). Then they rank-order the interpretations/causes (diagnoses) according to the ease and feasibility for verifying or eliminating them (ease and safety of testing).

2) Students request specific, additional information, beginning with what they have ranked as the easiest/most feasible to obtain (easiest and safest to test), to help them narrow down the possible interpretations/causes (diagnoses).

3) The instructor provides the information they request in turn. (One should have additional information in hand for any likely request.)

4) Students rerank-order the possible interpretations/causes (diagnoses) in light of the new information and repeat step 2.

5) The instructor repeats step 3.

6) Students select the most likely one or two interpretations/causes (diagnoses) and their solutions (treatment plans).

Depending upon the subject matter and the problem, you may also want to include the ease and feasibility of implementing a solution (treatment plan) as a rank-ordering criteria. After all, if students identify widespread poverty as the root cause of a problem, they may not be able to develop a workable, action-oriented solution. Alternatively, you may wish to focus attention on the relative importance or likelihood of a cause. The case method is extremely flexible.

Debriefing Cases

For cases to function well as homework assignments, paper topics, essay exam questions, or discussion springboards, you must guide students through a productive debriefing. That is, you have to challenge them with good questions about the case—questions that engage them in application, analysis, and synthesis of the material, plus critical evaluation of their proposed interpretations and solutions. Brainstorm, focal, and playground questions admirably serve these purposes (see Chapter 16).

The simplest formula for debriefing a case is Problems-Remedies-Prevention, that is: "What are the problems?", "What are the solutions?", and if applicable, "How could these problems have been prevented?" The structure for sequential-interactive cases given above follows this basic formula.

While the problems and solutions are the essential issues, you might ask other questions to direct students back to the course material to find answers. Good cases often contain other matters and important details well worth students' consideration, e.g.: possible reasons behind a character's action or inaction; reasons why such action or inaction fails to solve or even worsens a problem; the impact of the historical context, the organizational culture, or financial constraints; or how the situation might play out if one ingredient were different. Providing your questions in writing will keep the debriefing focused on the key points.

You can launch a case discussion with the entire class (see Chapters 15 and 16) or in a cooperative learning format (see Chapter 18). Using groups offers still more options:

1) All groups can work on the same case with the proviso that each group reach a consensus on its answers (otherwise majority rules). This format works well only with cases that can generate widely different interpretations.
2) All groups can work on the same case, but with each group addressing different questions.
3) After a general class discussion identifying the problems in the case, half the groups address solutions and the other half preventions.
4) Each group works on a different case and presents a descriptive summary and debriefing to the rest of the class.

A Postscript for Pioneers

If the case method is rarely, if ever, used in your field, but you can see a place for it in your course, realize that trying it involves very little risk. It is a tried-and-true method in many fields, and course evaluations show that students find it both highly instructive and enjoyable. The key is in the quality of the case. You might show drafts of your own creations to colleagues before using them in class. Remember, too, that you can continue to improve your cases over time.

For further reading:

Abramson, P.R. 1992. *A Case for Case Studies*. Thousand Oaks, CA: Sage.

Barnes, Louis B., C. Roland Christensen, and Abby J. Hansen. 1994. *Teaching and the Case Method: Text, Cases, and Reading*. 3rd ed. Boston: Harvard Business School.

TEACHING PROBLEM SOLVING II:
PROBLEM-BASED LEARNING

This teaching method is suited to the same kind of "messy" problem that the case method accommodates so well: a real-world, human-situational, open-ended, high-uncertainty problem with multiple respectable solutions, some being better than others. Problem-based learning, sometimes called PBL, shares qualities with experiential learning activities (see Chapter 17). Students can get so involved in the problem-solving that the experience feels real. However, PBL usually doesn't require students to play roles. It's all about solving complex problems, and problems stimulate engagement and learning.

Canadian medical schools developed PBL about 30 years ago for the first two years of their curricula. American medical schools started adopting it during the 1980s (Kaufmann, 1985; Kaufmann et al, 1989; Jonas et al, 1989). But it is applicable in all the same subject areas that the case method is: the social sciences, psychology, history, philosophy, business, law, educational administration, medicine, nursing, clinical fields, the biological and physical sciences, engineering—any discipline or profession that presents "fuzzy" problems.

What PBL Is and
How It Works

To slightly oversimplify, problem-based learning is the case method with the caveat that the course material alone cannot provide viable solutions to the problem. Students must then conduct outside research, which usually makes the problem-solving process a sizable project best conducted by teams of at least four.

Solving PBL problems in steps. The process follows a series of steps. (Bridges, 1992; Pregent, 1994; Duchs et al, 1997-98; Edens, 2000):

1) The team members review the problem, which is typically ill-structured, and clarify the meaning of terms they do not understand.
2) They analyze and define the problem. (You may provide guidance.)
3) They identify and organize the knowledge they already have to solve the problem.
4) They identify the knowledge they need to *acquire* to solve the problem—the "*learning issues.*"
5) They organize and rank-order the learning issues and set objectives for outside research. (You may provide references.)
6) They divide the work among themselves.
7) They conduct the assigned research individually by agreed-upon deadlines.
8) They continue to meet to share research findings and conduct additional research as needed.

9) They merge their newly acquired and previous knowledge into a what they consider to be the "best possible" solution in a finished product. (This step qualifies PBL as a "constructivist" method.)

10) They write up and/or present their solution to the class.

Once the instructor guides students through the basic procedures, the teams should work as independently as possible. Each devises its own internal organization and decision-making rules for evaluating alternative formulations of and solutions to the problem. Members integrate course materials with outside library, internet, interview, and field research. Depending upon the problem, the write-up may take the form of a lengthy memo, a report, a budget, a plan of action, or an oral presentation before a hypothetical decision-making body.

PBL's realism is grounded not only in the problems, activities, and (sometimes) roles, but also in the time factor. Each project proceeds in real time. Solving one problem can entail weeks of lengthy meetings, inside and out of class. In fact, a substantial problem can absorb most of a term. But you can find or design problems that take only a week or two to solve.

Making PBL more experiential. Some elaborate PBL problems allow for adding an optional experiential dimension, which adds this early step: The team members decide on the roles they will play in a kind of open-ended simulation. Students might assume professional roles, such as members of a council with varying political interests to be taken into account. In the lengthy educational administration problem that Bridges (1992) developed, students take the role of personnel-selection committee members, with one acting as project leader, another as facilitator, another as recorder, and the rest as members. He also incorporates specific role plays and mini-simulations, such as conferences, interviews, field observations, in-basket exercises, and progress presentations.

Grading PBL projects. Beyond balancing group and individual grading (see Chapter 18), you must decide in advance the specific dimensions on which you will grade the projects and set bottom-line standards for various grades. You must also convey those dimensions and standards to your students before they begin the project so they will have some structure within which to direct their efforts. Appropriate dimensions may include the clarity of the problem definition, the breadth of outside sources used, the feasibility of the solution, the extent to which the solution resolves all aspects of the problem, and the rationales for the solution selected.

Grading these projects can present real problems because the PBL literature offers no assessment guidance. In addition, it can be difficult to give less than A's to these projects because you don't monitor your students as carefully as you might with other teaching methods; they're supposed to work independently. Another potential complication stems from the high degree of student engagement. Grading down a project can touch emotional nerves unless you can clearly justify your assessments.

PBL's Effectiveness

Pedagogically, PBL has very strong credentials. It is based on the well-tested principle of having students learn by doing (see Chapter 2), and even the simplest projects have them do a variety of things: lead, facilitate, record, compromise, cooperate, schedule, conduct meetings, discuss, prioritize, organize, plan, research, apply, integrate, evaluate, make decisions, persuade, negotiate, and resolve conflict. Beyond these basics, *you* decide and determine what your students will learn to do and what additional knowledge they will acquire by their research in your choice or design of PBL problems.

The research indicates that PBL develops these skills in students (Bridges, 1992; Lieux, 1996; Edens, 2000; Mierson and Parikh, 2000):

- Teamwork
- Project management and leadership
- Oral and often written communication
- Emotional intelligence
- Tolerance for uncertainty
- Critical thinking and analysis
- Application (transfer) of content knowledge
- Research
- Decision making
- Problem solving (of course), often across disciplines

In addition, PBL activates prior knowledge and imparts new knowledge in the context in which they will later be used. In this way, it builds in enough redundancy to ensure the knowledge is well understood and retained (Bridges, 1992). If the problem mirrors situations that students will encounter in their future occupations, PBL also develops career realism as well as skills (Bridges, 1992).

What Students Think

Not all students favor PBL over more traditional methods. While they report developing skills such as problem solving, critical thinking, communication, and taking responsibility, they tend to perceive they are working harder but learning less, even though test results don't confirm this (Lieux, 1996; Edens, 2000). Many students, especially the highest achievers, don't enjoy the open-endedness and ambiguity, the lack of structure and guidance, and the murky expectations for performance (Lieux, 1996; Edens, 2000).

This does not mean that PBL-based courses necessarily get low student evaluations (Kingsland, 1996; Woods, 1996; Mierson, 1998). But instructors new to PBL may not know how to handle certain situations and suffer a temporary drop in their ratings (Lieux, 1996).

Good PBL Problems and Where to Find Them

Good PBL problems and good cases share the same characteristics: realism, opportunities for students to synthesize material, and uncertainty and risk. All the better if they resemble problems that students will experience in their careers. Some generic workplace problems include managerial miscommunications, low organizational morale, negative public relations, moral dilemmas, and difficult policy implementations.

In addition, a good PBL problem for your particular course is one that gives students practice in the abilities that you've targeted in your student learning objectives, and one that directs students to the knowledge you want them to acquire beyond the course material.

You can also judge the quality of problems using Bloom's (1956) taxonomy of cognitive operations (see Chapter 3). A "poor" problem requires only knowledge and/or comprehension, as do typical end-of-textbook-chapter problems. A "fair" problem adds a story element but entails no more than application. A "good" problem demands analysis, synthesis, and/or evaluation to solve. It is highly realistic, full of researchable unknowns, and possibly open to more than one solution (Duch and Allen, 1996). Its description is usually much longer as well.

Here's a simple example. Let's say that the readings, lectures, and class activities have familiarized students in a biology course with the structure and function of DNA, the function of various enzymes involved in DNA synthesis and replication, and radio-labeling techniques. The instructor then gives student teams this PBL problem: *A rare blood disorder has been identified in a particular family in Europe.* [The problem describes the symptoms.] *Devise the least expensive method to determine the disorder's cause and to locate the defective gene, and suggest diagnostic tests for identifying potential victims.*

Presumably solving this problem requires the students to do outside research on topics like blood DNA, DNA research methods, and genetic testing. Once the teams complete their task, they explain their solutions to the class, which then engages in discussion to evaluate the various methods suggested.

Biology PBL problems are quite plentiful and available (Duch and Allen, 1996; Allen and Duch, 1998; Mierson, 1998). Duch and Allen (1996) also describe one for physics. Bridges (1992) proposes ideas for educational administration problems. Edens (2000) gives brief summaries of ten problems in biology, physics, chemistry, business, art history, educational leadership,

medicine, and criminal justice, along with their sources. The two additional readings suggested below also contain a wealth of problems, include a few on Edens' list.

Kudos for Creativity

One of the best things about teaching at the college level is the creativity it affords. Just as you can write your own cases tailored to your course and student needs, so can you create your own PBL problems. In fact, it may be your best if not your only alternative. Generally *you* determine what knowledge and skills your course materials and activities impart, as well what they don't impart, so you control what the potential learning issues may be. One instructor's PBL problem may be your case study because you are teaching what the other instructor's students can only obtain through research. (Recall from Chapter 3 that what your course materials and activities address determines the cognitive level of any given task or question.) So in reviewing published problems, feel free to modify them or to use them just for guidance and inspiration.

For further reading:

Duch, Barbara J., Susan E. Groh, and Deborah E. Allen, eds. 2001. *The Power of Problem-Based Learning: A Practical "How To" for Teaching Undergraduate Courses in Any Discipline.* Sterling, VA: Stylus.

Wilkerson, LuAnn and Wim H. Gijselaers. 1996. *Bringing Problem-Based Learning to Higher Education.* New Directions for Teaching and Learning 68. San Francisco: Jossey-Bass.

Teaching Problem Solving III:

Quantitative Reasoning

One of the most difficult tasks that instructors face in mathematics, statistics, physics, physical chemistry, engineering, computer science, economics, finance, accounting, and all the other quantitatively-based fields is teaching students to be good problem solvers. Quantitative problem solving is quite a different matter from solving "soft," uncertainty-ridden, human-situational problems like the ones the case method and problem-based learning address. Mathematically-based problems may have unknowns that require intelligent estimation, but algorithms are usually available to make the estimations and to solve the problems themselves. (The question is *which* algorithms to use for a given problem.) In addition, this type of problem may have different approaches to arriving at a solution, but usually it has only one correct answer or a definable range of correct answers. Quantitative reasoning, then, has a more precise process and product than does qualitative reasoning.

The Problem with Most Problems

First, let us pose a central question: When is a problem really a problem? According to Zoller (1987), what you may often consider a problem in your courses is really only an *exercise*, since you often give students formulas and specific ways of finding solutions. By this way of thinking, a problem consists of a situation for which the student has no preconceived notion of how to find an answer.

Another important question to consider is whether or not your problem-solving assignments help your students acquire conceptual knowledge. In other words, do the problems you assign elucidate underlying disciplinary principles and the quantitative reasoning process, or are your students merely "going through the motions," repeating the problem-solving pattern you showed them?

Nurrenbern and Pickering (1987) found that, on a chemistry test covering such standard materials as ideal gas problems and stoichiometry as well as conceptual understanding, students performed well on the math sections but demonstrated little comprehension of the physical chemistry behind the questions. Students picked up on a formula and used the "plug and chug" process of selecting the variables necessary to work a solution without understanding *why* they chose the variables they did. In essence, they were using nothing more than an algorithm, a set of mechanical rules, to compute the solution. So problem-solving facility does not necessarily foster concept understanding. For your students to truly develop in your discipline, both these facets must be balanced.

One of the most common methods of teaching students how to solve problems is modeling. You pose a question to the students and show them how to work it on the board. As only one method among many techniques at your disposal, modeling may be a good way to proceed in the early stages. But as an exclusive strategy, it has definite drawbacks.

Bodner (1987) notes that when you work a problem on the board, you are only showing students what experts do when they run through an exercise. You are not actually showing them how to attack a real problem. You are not modeling quantitative reasoning. To accomplish this goal, you must model the cognitive processes involved in genuine problem solving. Only then can students appreciate what problem-solving techniques can do for them.

When students learn only to "plug and chug," several problems usually result (Brookhart, 1990):

1) Students see only one way to arrive at a solution, even though there may be several viable alternatives.
2) They fail to understand the actual reasoning process involved, the rationales behind the facts and rules that justify the steps to a solution.
3) Since instructors rarely make errors, students mistakenly conclude that those "meant for" the discipline easily work through problems with little more than typographical errors.
4) If a problem is at all difficult, it is unlikely that one's first attempt at a solution will be completely correct. But unless students are prepared for some failures, they become discouraged and stop trying.

A Systematic Approach to Teaching Problem Solving

Heller et al. (1992) identify two types of students who are struggling with problem solving in introductory physics. Some students claim to understand the material but not to be able to work the problems. They apparently believe that mathematical problem-solving skills are independent of the physics concepts being taught. Other students say they can follow the problem examples in the text but find the test problems too different and difficult. They seem to view physics as nothing more than a collection of mathematical solutions. Both types should sound familiar to you.

Novice problem solvers of both types often make the same tragic mistakes over and over. In their impatience to find a numerical solution, they dive into algebraic manipulations without fully examining and comprehending the whole problem. They neither qualitatively analyze the situation nor systematically reason through and plan a strategy for solving the problem. When they arrive at any solution, they are satisfied and don't take the time to check it.

To overcome the novice's poor tactics, the Heller team (1992) developed a method for teaching problem solving that is easily adaptable to any of the quantitatively-based disciplines. The heart of the approach is to teach students a five-step problem-solving strategy

that requires them to systematically translate the problem into
different representations, each
more abstract and more mathe-
matically detailed than the last.
Similar multi-step methods have
been developed by Schoenfeld
(1985), Bodner (1987), Samples
(1994), and Bridgwood (1999).

**Step 1: Visualize the prob-
lem.** Sketch or diagram the main
parts of the problem. Identify the
known and unknown quantities and
other constraints. Restate the
question in different terms to make
it more understandable.

**Step 2: Describe in writing
the principles and concepts at
work** in the question. Then translate the diagram into symbolic
terms, and symbolically represent
the target variable.

Step 3: Plan a solution.
Identify the equations necessary to
solve the problem and work backwards from the target variable to
see if enough information is available to arrive at a solution.

Step 4: Execute the plan.
Plug in the appropriate numerical
values for the variables and compute a solution.

**Step 5: Check and evaluate
your solution.** Is the solution
complete? Are the proper units
used? Is the sign correct? Is the
magnitude of the answer reasonable?

Bridgwood (1999) also surveyed
his electrical engineering undergraduates on how helpful they
found his problem-solving strategy,
and they assessed most of the steps
as valuable and the overall strategy
as well worth using in the future.

**An Effective, Innovative
Teaching Strategy:
Cooperative Groups
Solving Real Problems**

Heller and Hollabaugh (1992)
devised the idea of "context-rich"
problems in physics as part of their
approach to promote good problem-
solving skills. These are problems
that are more like those that students encounter in the real world.
Since they are presented as short
stories about real objects and realistic events, they offer a reason for
doing the calculations and finding a
solution. (One such problem involves planning a skateboard stunt,
another deciding whether or not to
fight a traffic ticket.) They may
also have these additional characteristics:

- No specific reference is made to
  the unknown variable.
- Excess information above what
  is needed to solve the problem is
  given.
- Students must supply missing
  information from "common
  knowledge" or educated guessing.
- No specific mention is made of
  reasonable assumptions that
  may be necessary to reach a
  workable solution.

Context-rich problems are designed to be difficult, so students
working alone often fail to derive
satisfactory answers. Thus Heller
and Hollabaugh (1992) recommend
cooperative problem-solving groups
to spread the thinking and reasoning load over several students.
Groups provide a supportive atmosphere for students to discuss the
physical principles behind the problems and possible strategies to
reach a solution. Since students
talk out their different ideas and
evaluate alternative approaches,
group problem solving develops

individual problem-solving skills.

Before obtaining promising results with cooperative learning, the Hellers and their associates experimented with different group compositions, including random, homogeneous, and heterogenous on various variables. They soon found the most successful arrangement.

Initially, they assembled the groups randomly. Then after the first exam, they reconstituted the groups based on abilities, teaming together students of high, medium, and low abilities, as the cooperative learning literature advises (see Chapter 18). Generally, students in these heterogeneous ability groups developed their problem-solving skills as fully as did the homogeneous high-ability groups in previous experiments.

The optimum group size proved to be three, with members rotating among the roles of Manager, Skeptic, and Checker/Recorder. Pairs lacked the critical mass to arrive at more than one or two strategies and were more easily side-tracked on a fruitless path. On the other hand, groups of four or more gave some members the opportunity to free-load on other members' reasoning. Additionally, same sex groups or groups composed of two females and one male worked best, avoiding the dominance posturing of more than one male in a group (Heller and Hollabaugh, 1992).

Heller et al (1992) also found that the students in their experimental program developed higher problem-solving expertise than those taught in the regular lecture and discussion section format with assignments of standard physics problems. As far as student learning is concerned, they concluded that cooperative problem-solving groups working on context-rich problems offer a preferable alterna-

tive to the traditional approach (confirming Treisman, 1986).

With students relying on each other to resolve their concerns and questions immediately as they arise, these groups also free the instructor to circulate and help the students in genuine need. Chapter 18 gives more information on cooperative learning research results and set-up methods.

Identifying and Correcting Problem-Solving Pitfalls

Black and Axelson (1991) identify the often ingrained, poor problem-solving habits that plague many students.

1) Inaccuracy in reading:
- failing to concentrate on the meaning of the problem
- skipping unfamiliar words
- losing/forgetting one or more facts or ideas
- failing to reread a difficult passage
- starting to work the problem before reading it all

2) Inaccuracy in thinking:
- placing speed or ease of execution above accuracy
- performing a specific operation carelessly
- interpreting or performing operations inconsistently
- failing to double check procedures when uncertain
- working too rapidly
- jumping to conclusions

3) Faulty or careless problem analysis:
- failing to break down complex problems into easily manipulated components
- failing to draw on previous experience to clarify a difficult idea
- failing to refer to a dictionary or

text glossary when necessary
- failing to actively construct diagrams where appropriate

4) *Lack of perseverance:*
- losing confidence and admitting defeat too easily
- guessing or basing solutions on superficial understanding
- using algorithms mechanically to arrive at solutions without giving thought to conceptual issues
- failing to carry out a line of reasoning to completion
- taking a one-shot approach and giving up if the singular attempt fails.

Black and Axelson's (1991) elaborate list incorporates the common errors that Bridgwood (1999) identifies:
1) conceptual errors due to ignorance or careless
2) algebraic errors, especially in cancellation and grouping
3) arithmetic errors due to the failure to check one's work.

Helping your students overcome these bad practices is best done during office hours on a one-on-one or small-group basis (see Chapter 10). Black and Axelson (1991) outline a strategy for helping students identify and break these habits in such tutorial sessions.

First, have your students read a problem aloud and specify what is needed to solve it. Then let them try solving it on their own, insisting that they think through the problem out loud. Talking to themselves makes them slow down and improves accuracy and explicitness. As they attack and proceed through the problem, pose questions that make them examine their reasoning, such as:
- What do you know about the problem?
- How can you break the problem into smaller steps?
- What are some possible ways to go about solving it?
- How did you go from step one to step two?
- What is your reasoning for this step?
- What are you thinking at this point in the process?

Given the dangers mentioned earlier, it is best to use modeling sparingly and to demonstrate only a part of the general problem-solving process, not how to get the answer to any specific problem.

Making Traditional Settings Accommodate These Teaching Methods

To teach quantitative reasoning and problem-solving effectively, you need not completely overhaul your classroom nor tutor every student individually. Everything known about how to teach quantitative reasoning boils down to just a few insights: Students do learn problem solving by doing, but they don't learn by doing it wrong, and very few deduce the real *process of problem solving* on their own.

Therefore, most students need to be taught the process as a step-by-step, self-posed question-by-question procedure that incorporates the conceptual principles and reasoning skills being demonstrated. Cooperative group work helps keep the process explicit and generates different problem-solving approaches, weaning students away from the mechanical use of algorithms and making them realize their multiple options. Finally, real-world problems that are meaningful to students furnish more interesting and challenging contexts for them to apply and hone their skills.

Traditional lectures and discus-

182 sion sections can easily accommodate instruction in the problem-solving process. In fact, the interactive lecture provides an excellent forum for intermittent practice applications of the procedures you teach (see Chapter 14). Smaller classes, discussion/quiz/recitation sections, and help and review sessions readily allow for cooperative group problem solving on a regular or sporadic basis. You might even enjoy trying your hand at creating more relevant, updated word problems.

At the very least, it is wise to move away from the standard procedure of simply going over the homework or review problems and effortlessly modeling idealized solutions, while students passively watch. You have to see and hear how *your students* approached and either solved or failed to solve the assigned problems. You can find this out by having them write their solutions on the board or a transparency and explain their reasoning to the rest of the class. They can work individually or in *ad hoc* pairs or triads, as long as *they are doing the work*. To save time, you might select only the more difficult problems for student presentation. Then towards the end of class, give students new problems to solve in small groups.

For further reading:

Donald, Janet. 2002. *Learning to Think: Disciplinary Perspectives.* San Francisco: Jossey-Bass. Chapters 2 and 3.

Gonick, Larry and Woollcott Smith. 1993. *The Cartoon Guide to Statistics.* New York: HarperPerennial.

TEACHING PROBLEM SOLVING IV:

SCIENCE IN THE

LABORATORY

While this chapter is written for everyone who teaches a science at the college level, it addresses two often distinct audiences: the science *faculty* and science *lab instructors*, typically graduate-student teaching assistants. Only in small colleges do faculty members ordinarily design and conduct the laboratories that support the "lecture" part of their course. But dividing the chapter into two sections, one for faculty and the other for TAs, makes little sense. Even if TAs conduct the lab, it is the faculty that has the power to redesign the labs and to define and uphold lab safety standards. While the TAs have little control over the lab and none over the broader course, most of them will soon occupy a position of such control and responsibility for their students' learning.

"Science" and "problem solving" are so closely related that the sciences are the only group of disciplines (along with its more applied progeny, such as engineering and medicine) that uses every problem-solving teaching method we've examined so far: the case method, problem-based learning, and quantitative reasoning (see Chapter 23, 24, and 25). Even so, these don't cover all the types of problems that science address. Science has its own unique brand of problems, along with its own methods to solve

them and to teach the process of solving them.

Most of "real" everyday science is the process of solving problems in a laboratory. (Some sciences locate their lab in the field at least part of the time.) If laboratory work is so central to science, it should also be in science education. The science lab should imitate the reality of *methodological* problem solving—that is, devising hypothesis-testing strategies and procedures using intelligence and trial-and-error—on the way to solving the *content* problem—that is, meeting the experimental objectives with valid and reliable findings.

Where Science Education Falls Short

Thanks to two classic works, Tobias (1990) and Seymour and Hewitt (1997), we know quite a bit about the reasons why so many students come to dislike, lose interest in, and switch out of the sciences (and mathematics and engineering). At the top of the list is poor teaching, manifested as faculty with a weed-out mentality about their courses, poor communication and public-speaking skills, attitudes of indifference and/or condescension towards students, little understanding of how students learn, and lessons that lack application and illustration—all exacerbated by too much material being crammed into too little time (Seymour and Hewitt, 1997). Other important turn-offs is the heavy reliance on lecture, factual memorization, "how" rather than "why" explanations, quantitative operations, and "technique"—all at the expense of theory, creativity, interconnected concepts, and discussion (Tobias, 1990).

Although science engages in the discovery and identification of facts, it is certainly not just a mountain of factoids. Yet undergraduate science education often gives that impression. The reason probably lies with science's predominant teaching method: the lecture. It is usually the instructor's technique of choice because it maximizes the amount of factual information that can be conveyed. It also feels comfortable and easy to manage, especially with large classes. The instructor exercises total control while the students merely—or hopefully—listen.

The lecture has its appropriate uses, but it is not very digestible as a steady diet. As Chapter 14 explains in detail, lecturing beyond 15 minutes or so pushes the students' ability to process and retain the material and becomes counterproductive.

In addition, the lecture does a relatively poor job of teaching students how to *do* something, such as writing, speaking, thinking critically, formulating a hypothesis, solving problems, or designing and conducting an experiment. Since science is both a mental and a physical activity, the lecture is not well suited to it. It is especially ill-suited to strongly kinesthetic learners, who are particularly attracted to science and its professional offshoots (e.g., medicine and engineering). These learners benefit most from physically acting out or performing the lessons, then inducing the conceptual point on their own (see Chapter 12). In short, they learn best working in the lab or the field.

Finally, while an excellent lecture can be very motivating, a standard one rarely allows students to understand and appreciate the sense of discovery that makes science exciting.

Real science happens in the lab. Only in that setting can students learn how to *think about* and *do* the discipline. The lab extends science education to exploring questions and solving genuine problems rather than constraining students' imaginations with the recitation of preconceived answers.

But all too often labs are treated like second-class, tacked-on learning experiences at best—poorly coordinated with the readings and lectures, hampered by a shortage of functioning equipment, and dulled by cookbook procedures leading to predictable answers that haven't been of scientific interest for decades. Under these circumstances, students come to regard labs as tedious, irrelevant tasks to hurry through, get done, and forget.

Making the Lab a Meaningful Learning Experience

Starting off the lab. Recall that science defectors cite a lack of theory and conceptual links as reasons for leaving. When the lab is disembodied from concepts, it lacks meaning and relevance. So it is critical to place the lab in the bigger scientific picture before proceeding into the actual activities.

Given the time constraints of many lab exercises, you may be tempted to forego discussing the principles to be illustrated and just launch into the day's work with a brief synopsis of the procedures. While this short-cutting gets students out of the lab quicker—which they usually appreciate—it robs the lab of its educational value. And it isn't necessary because you can introduce the principles efficiently while simultaneously preparing students to perform the day's tasks.

Begin a lab by asking students to review the previous week's material. You might have them do a two-minute free write to activate their memory (see Chapter 20). After you ask a couple of students to read their responses aloud, tie this particular lab to the course's progression of topics and labs, sketching as cohesive a "big picture" as possible. Then introduce the day's principle, eliciting lab manual information (e.g., the experimental hypotheses and predictions) from the students.

The design of the lab itself.
The shortfalls of science education have inspired quite a number of successful and innovative reforms in the past two decades (e.g., Penick and Crow, 1989; Hufford, 1991; Felder and Brent, 2001; Kimmel, 2002; Odom, 2002). Almost all of them have involved radically redesigning the laboratories. The new labs all share these characteristics:

- They are "discovery-based," "inquiry-based." This means they challenge students to conduct real scientific investigations, identifing and solving problems the way scientists actually do. Students must independently develop a *strategy* to test a hypothesis and/or find answers to questions, along with the *procedures* to carry out the strategy. The lab manual provides neither, and the lab results are not predictable.

- They focus on developing students' critical thinking, decision-making, and complex reasoning skills by giving students opportunities to *practice* these skills. In addition to developing an experimental strategy and procedures, they must explain unexpected results in their lab reports.

- They foster genuine teamwork and collaboration. Since the labs are novel and challenging, students mutually need each other, as they would in a professional setting. In many innovative courses, each lab group turns in one report and shares a group grade. (In Kimmel's labs, students also keep their own individual lab notebook, which is graded.) In addition to sharing their discoveries, results, and conclusions, students may even exchange their lab reports for peer review (Odom, 2002).

- They feature modern technology, such as industry equipment in current use and/or updated software for analyzing the data and displaying the results (spreadsheet, statistical analysis, etc.).

An example of an actual discovery-based lab may clarify the specifics. Let us look at Odom's pendulum lab in a sophomore-level calculus-based physics course. Students enter the lab with a background in the basic mechanics of a pendulum, including the equation to describe its period and the simplified version for small angle approximations (first-order expression). They first receive the two lab objectives:

1. Determine the maximum angle for which the period of a simple pendulum is valid. In other words, ascertain the cutoff angle for when the small angle approximation fails.

2. Use a simple pendulum to determine the value of g, the acceleration due to the earth's gravity.

Student lab groups get this equipment: a pendulum stand, clamp, string, and bob (an aluminum rod with its center of gravity marked); a protractor; a computer timing device (on the lab web page); and meter sticks (located around the classroom). They also receive 10 nudge questions for the groups to answer and a lab report template (on the web page) with five problems for individuals to solve—all of which lead the students through the process of meeting the lab objectives. They receive no other directions (Odom, 2002).

This lab requires about six hours over two weeks. Odom (2002) also got rid of the one-weekly-three-hour-lab restriction that constrains most science curricula.

The results of this and the other experimental programs have been so positive that the hosting departments have adopted them into their regular curriculum. Students actually discuss and even argue about the best plan of attack, and they divide the labor on their own. Compared to student performance in the courses with the old labs, they hand in higher-quality lab reports, do significantly better on the tests, have higher final grades, and give the course higher evaluations (Penick and Crow, 1989; Hufford, 1991; Felder and Brent, 2001; Kimmel, 2002; Odom, 2002). In Kimmel's labs the C students have shown the greatest gains in achievement. Kimmel also compares student attitudes in the old and new labs, finding far better attitudes in the new ones—specifically, higher motivation, greater engagement, greater perceived learning, higher valuation of the labs as learning experi-

ences, and higher assessments of team functioning. The traditional lab designs and manuals are clearly outmoded and ineffective.

The Essentials of Lab Safety and Management

Unless all your labs are on instructional software, safety must be of paramount importance to you and your students. With so little lab experience, student tends to be careless. So it is your responsibility to make them aware of lab hazards and safety measures.

Student need explicit instructions on proper procedures, especially when working under potentially hazardous conditions. For example, if certain chemicals require special disposal protocols, students must thoroughly understand the reasons for them. For the visual and kinesthetic learners, an instructor should demonstrate as well as describe the proper construction and handling of apparatus.

As the most experienced scientist in the room, you must also be able to act promptly and effectively should an emergency arise. Know the standard procedures practiced by your department. If you are unsure of how to proceed in any given situation, ask a(nother) faculty member, a lab staff member, or the departmental safety officer.

Responding to medical emergencies. In the event of a lab accident, rule number one is to remain calm. Make sure you know the location of the first-aid kit, fire extinguishers, fire blankets, emergency showers and eye washes, bleach solutions, and hazardous waste clean-up kits. Familiarize yourself with the uses of each so that your emergency response will be swift and decisive.

First-aid training may not be required of lab instructors at your institution, but your knowing first-aid principles is essential. At least study a first-aid manual such as the one published by the American Red Cross. Better yet, take first-aid and CPR certification training courses.

If a student is injured in your lab, *stop to assess* the situation, then take proper action. Small cuts and scrapes may be inconsequential, requiring nothing more than a bandage. But today due to AIDS, it is best to treat all injuries involving loss of blood as hazardous situations. So do not touch a student who is bleeding unless you are wearing gloves. Isolate the blood spill area and immediately swab the surface twice with at least a 10% bleach solution. Label biohazardous materials accordingly and dispose of properly, as per your institution's standards. Contact the student or employee health center for more information on AIDS and how to protect yourself.

Below a brief quiz presenting several typical lab emergencies. It will help you assess your own and/or your lab TAs' emergency preparedness.

Preventing lab emergencies. The generic guidelines below apply across the scientific disciplines. Your particular field may call for additional rules:

1) Be prepared. Rehearse new or unfamiliar procedures before the lab. Be able to identify pitfalls and problems. If students sense you don't know what you are doing, they will say so on your teaching evaluations.

2) Direct students to keep the lab as clean as possible. Not only is this good practice for them, but it also reduces the prep staff's work load.

3) Give students dress codes, and show them how to use safety equipment such as goggles and face shields. Then explain the reasons for the rules, and

---

Quiz Yourself on Lab Safety

If you now or ever will supervise a lab, the chances are are good that you will face a lab emergency during your career. With some procedural knowledge and preparation, you should be able to handle most situations. Quiz yourself on how you would respond to emergencies like these:

- A student tries to force a glass rod into a rubber stopper. The rod breaks, driving the sharp end into the palm of his hand.
- A student wearing a loose sweater is working with a Bunsen burner. As she turns away from the burner, her sleeve catches fire.
- A student spills 12 M HCl on his hand.
- A student tips over a boiling water bath, scalding his feet.
- During an experiment, a student goes into respiratory arrest.
- A student is shocked while plugging the cord of a piece of equipment into a wall socket.
- A student splashes a large quantity of a corrosive chemical into her eye.
- A student's error releases a massive quantity of bromine gas in the lab.

enforce them. Typical clothing codes include long pants, tied-back hair, shoes with tops, no excessively loose clothing, and no encumbering jewelry.

4) If your lab has a traditional manual with directions and procedures, you must make your students read the manual carefully before coming to lab. The better informed students are, the smoother and safer the conduct of the lab. Chapter 19 offers dozens of ways to induce students to do the readings when they are due. (You need to have input into their lab grade.) You may have to schedule some time at the beginning of lab for a brief accountability activity (e.g., quiz, writing exercise, oral presentation, etc.), but this will take you less time than going over the directions in the manual.

5) Discuss procedures thoroughly. You can be redundant where safety is concerned.

6) Be especially aware—and continually remind students—of any particularly dangerous procedures.

7) Demonstrate proper techniques and correct students when necessary.

8) Encourage student questions.

9) Move around the lab. While you can't be everywhere at once, be readily available for consultation.

The Importance of Science Education

In a truly enlightened, democratic society, people must be "scientifically literate"—not only conversant in but also comfortable with science. Everyone who teaches in the sciences and its applied offshoots plays a crucial role in fostering a society that is well informed enough to govern itself intelligently. Self-government requires not only a well informed populace but also one that can solve its own problems. Problem solving of every type—open-ended and closed-ended, qualitative and quantitative, high-uncertainty and formulaic—is science's stock-in-trade. This fact alone makes science an essential component of higher education. But we have to ensure that students learn how science *really* proceeds—not like a well-ordered textbook, but in a zigzag, trial-and-error, collaborative manner that demands complex reasoning, strategic thinking, and inventiveness.

For further reading:

Astin, Alexander W. and Helen S. Astin. 1993. *Undergraduate Science Education: The Impact of Different College Environments on the Educational Pipeline in the Sciences.* Los Angeles: Higher Education Research Institute, UCLA.

Independent Colleges Office. 1991 and 1992. *Volume I: What Works: Building Natural Science Communities* and *Volume II: What Works: Resources for Reform.* Washington, DC: Project Kaleidoscope.

Seymour, Elaine and Nancy M. Hewitt. 1997. *Talking About Leaving: Why Undergraduates Leave the Sciences.* Boulder, CO: Westview Press.

Tobias, Sheila. 1992. *Revitalizing Undergraduate Science: Why Some Things Work and Most Don't.* Tucson, AZ: Research Corporation.

PART V.

ASSESSMENT/

MEASURING OUTCOMES

ASSESSING STUDENTS' LEARNING IN PROGRESS

No doubt you can recall class periods when you would have liked to have known what your students were learning from your lesson and whether or not you should proceed with the next one. Perhaps you found out what they missed from a test you gave three weeks later. Obviously, it is much more cost-effective to assess your students' learning while in progress, before their shortfalls in understanding adversely affect their grades and motivation. Such information can also help you determine, and ultimately enhance, your teaching effectiveness. It can even direct your students to the areas on which they need to focus their studying.

Classroom assessment techniques (CATs) were developed precisely to serve these purposes (Cross and Angelo, 1988; Angelo, 1991a). You can use them regularly or intermittently without violating the structure and content of your course and quickly identify trouble spots of an entire class or given individuals. Knowing what your students didn't absorb the first time through the material, you can turn around a bad situation.

Perhaps classroom assessment isn't all that much different from the informal, sometimes unconscious gauges you already use: reading students' expressions and body language, asking and answering questions, and the like. But these are unreliable and rarely encompass the whole class. CATs formalize and systematize the process, ensuring all students are included in your assessments.

Four-Dimensional Assessment

To assess students' learning, it is helpful to view it as four-dimensional (Angelo, 1991b). First, *declarative learning* is "learning what"—that is, learning the facts and principles of a given field. In terms of Bloom's (1956) taxonomy of cognitive operations (see Chapters 3 and 16), declarative learning focuses on knowledge and comprehension at the lower end of the scale. *Procedural learning* is "learning how" to do something, from the specific tasks of a given discipline to universal skills such as writing, critical thinking, and reasoning. Its emphasis is application. The third dimension, *conditional learning*, is "learning when

192 and where" to apply the acquired declarative knowledge and procedural skills. Too often taught only implicitly through example and modeling, it can be better taught *explicitly* using the case method, problem-based learning, role playing, and simulations (see Chapters 17, 23, and 24). While conditional learning clearly entails application, it also involves analysis and synthesis. Finally, *reflective learning* is "learning why," which engages students in analysis, synthesis, and evaluation. It directs their attention to their beliefs, values, and motives for learning about a particular topic. Without this dimension, higher education is little more than job training.

Different CATs are designed to measure students' progress on different learning dimensions. So before selecting a CAT, consider which dimension you wish to assess.

Characteristics of Classroom Assessment Techniques

All CATs share these features (Angelo and Cross, 1993).

Learner-centered. While no substitute for appropriate teaching methods or graded examinations, classroom assessment aims to help students to learn better, whether by improving their study habits or by changing their metacognitive model of the discipline. In this respect students take responsibility for their learning.

Teacher-directed. You have total freedom to decide what will be assessed, how it will be assessed, how the results will be analyzed, and how they will affect further actions. Be sure, then, that your

CATs address factors that you are willing and able to change or improve.

Mutually beneficial. As students actively participate in the process of classroom assessment, CATs reinforce their learning of material. Like the student-active lecture breaks described in Chapter 14 and the writing-to-learn exercises covered in Chapter 20, good CATs make your students review, retrieve, apply, analyze, and/or synthesize the material from your lectures, classroom activities, and reading assignments as well as their prior learning experiences. Further, as classroom assessment underscores your interest in your students' progress, it also enhances their motivation. In turn, you benefit from the feedback on the effectiveness of your formats and methods. By working closely with your students, you enhance your teaching skills.

Formative. Unlike summative evaluations such as graded quizzes and exams, CATs are usually anonymous, ungraded, and geared strictly toward student learning.

Context-specific. CATs work differently in different classes. Since you know your classes best, you can tailor CATs to their specific "personality" and needs, as well as to your discipline, material, time constraints, and informational priorities.

Ongoing. Ideally, CATs provide a continual educational "feedback loop," informing you about your students' learning, to which you in turn adjust your teaching, back and forth until the end of the term.

Rooted in good teaching practice. Classroom assessment builds on current teaching practices, making them more systematic, effective, and flexible. For example, by using a simple diagnostic pre-test, you can find out how closely your students already meet your objectives. You can then pitch your presentations to their actual level, possibly covering more material than you might have otherwise.

Getting Started with Classroom Assessment

Angelo and Cross (1993) suggest a three-step plan for successfully launching classroom assessment.

First, *start small.* Select one "friendly" class in which you are confident things are going well and a simple, short, low-effort CAT (e.g., the One-Minute Paper, the One-Sentence Summary, Directed Paraphrasing, and the Muddiest Point).

Second, *give detailed directions and a rationale.* It is best to tell students what you are doing and why. They will need explicit instructions on the board, a slide, or an overhead transparency and the assurance that their responses will be anonymous and used solely for mutual improvement. Allocate a few extra minutes the first time through any CAT.

Finally, *respond to the information you gathered.* After you have reflected on your students' responses, it is advisable to take some time to share them with your class. If you decide to change your teaching formats or methods as a result, tell your students what you will initiate or do differently, and why. Equally important, give *them* pointers on how *they* can improve their learning.

Some Tried and True CATs

Chapter 20 introduced several popular CATs that also serve as writing-to-learn exercises: the *One-Minute Paper,* the *One-Sentence Summary*, *Directed Paraphrasing, Dialectical Notes,* and *Learning Logs*. Angelo and Cross (1993; also Cross and Angelo, 1988) describe dozens of other techniques, among which are the following:

Background Knowledge Probe. (Moderate instructor effort; low student effort.) This is essentially a diagnostic pre-test to administer on the first day of class and/or when you begin a new unit of instruction. It can consist of two or three short answer or essay questions or 15 to 20 multiple choice items about students' attitudes and understanding.

This CAT provides information not only on your students' prior knowledge but also on their motivation, beliefs, values, and, if you use open-ended questions, their writing skills. The results also tell you what material to cover and what existing knowledge you can use to map on new knowledge. Finally, probes activate students' prior knowledge, readying them for additional learning.

Focused Listing. (Low instructor and student effort.) You can use this technique to activate students' prior knowledge before you teach a topic and to help them review afterwards. Direct students' attention to a single important name, concept, or relationship and ask them to list as many related concepts and ideas as they can. You might limit the exercise to two to three minutes or five to ten items. With these constraints, the results give you a pretty accurate picture of the

194 features students identify and recall as salient and not just those they think you want to hear.

Memory Matrix. (Moderate instructor effort; low student effort.) Memory matrices stress recall of course material, but they also require students to organize it in a framework you provide. Start by drawing a matrix with content-appropriate row and category headings. Leave sufficient space for several one-word or phrase responses in each cell. Distribute copies for your students to fill in, with a limit on the number of items they can write in each cell. This limit keeps students from stalling in search of the one best answer. Collect and examine the matrices for completeness and correctness.

Memory matrices show you how your students organize knowledge and whether or not they properly associate principles and concepts. Additionally, matrices help visual learners excel, facilitate students' retrieval of large amounts of information, and are easy to evaluate.

Muddiest Point. (Low instructor and student effort.) Very simply, ask your students to write down what they perceived as the muddiest point in a lecture, a homework assignment, a film, a demonstration, a discussion, etc. Reserve some time at the end of class to ask and answer questions, then collect the student responses. You can then clarify the muddy points during the next class.

Perhaps the easiest CAT to implement, it can be used on the spur of the moment. Struggling students who are not comfortable asking questions publicly find it to be a lifeline. Additionally, it enables you to see the material through your students' eyes, reminding you of the many ways they process and store information. Finally, knowing they will have to identify a muddy point induces students to pay closer attention in class.

Concept Maps. (Medium to high instructor and student effort.) Concept maps are diagrams that show the mental connections students make among various concepts. For instance, you might ask your students to diagram the important features around racism, democracy, or natural selection and have them show how the features interrelate by drawing lines and arrows between them.

As few students are accustomed to drawing causal or associative models, it is best to work through your first concept map with your class. Start by writing a focal concept on the board or an overhead transparency, then spend a few minutes brainstorming related concepts and terms with the class. Begin with primary associations, then secondary and tertiary. Feel free to try different types of diagrams (e.g., concentric circles, a wheel with spokes, branching models, causal models, etc.)

Concept maps help visual learners get their minds around abstract relationships. Using low-tech materials, they also give you a graphic view of your students' conceptual association skills.

Paper or Project Prospectus. (Moderate to high instructor and student effort.) A prospectus is a detailed plan for a project or paper—perhaps even a rough draft—that focuses students on the topic, the purpose, the issues to address, the audience, the organization, the time, skills, and other resources needed—in fact, whatever guidelines you provide for the final product. First, students need to understand these guidelines, that is, the important facets and likely pitfalls of the assignment. For the prospectus itself, you might compose a list of three to seven questions that students must answer. Of course, advise students not to begin substantive work on their actual assignment until they receive feedback on their prospectus from you and possibly other students. As this CAT is a major assignment in itself, you may want to make it required and give some credit for good work.

The prospectus accommodates many different types of sssignments and teaches crucial, transferable planning and organizational skills. In addition, it gives students early enough feedback to help them produce a better graded product.

Everyday Ethical Dilemmas.
(Moderate to high instructor and student effort.) For this CAT, you begin by locating or creating a brief case study that poses an ethical problem related to the material (see Chapter 23). Then write two or three questions that force students to take and defend a position. Let your students turn in their written responses anonymously, thus giving you an honest overview of the prevailing class opinions and values. Students will need some time to think reflexively and to develop their arguments, so you might assign this CAT as homework.

Ethical dilemmas encourage students to "try on" different values and beliefs, thus helping them develop moral reasoning skills. This CAT also affords you probing, personal glimpses into your students' ethical and cognitive maturity. With these insights, you can foster their continuing growth

by introducing values and opinions that they have not yet considered.

Self Confidence Surveys.
(Low to medium instructor and student effort.) As the name implies, this CAT consists of a few simple questions about your students' confidence in their ability to perform course-related tasks. Design a brief, anonymous survey focusing on specific skills and tasks. Find the low-confidence areas in the results, and give additional instruction and practice accordingly. Self confidence surveys help you identify your students' areas of anxiety and establish the minimal levels of self confidence necessary for success in the course.

Punctuated Lectures. *(Low instructor and student effort.)* After your students listen to your lecture or demonstration, stop for a moment and ask them to reflect on what they were doing during your presentation and how it helped or hindered their understanding. Have them anonymously write out and turn in their reflections. After reading their responses, offer suggestions on how they can improve their listening and self-monitoring skills. Through your feedback, this CAT helps students hone these skills, both of which are highly transferable. It also better acquaints you with your students' processing styles and pitfalls.

RSQC2 (Recall, Summarize, Question, Connect, and Comment). *(Low to medium instructor and student effort.)* This technique assesses your students' recall, comprehension, analysis, synthesis, and evaluation of recent material. Begin by having students list the most important points they can remember from the last class (or

the assigned reading). Second, ask them to define as many terms as they can in one-sentence summaries. Third, have them write one or two questions about each point that still confuses them. Fourth, ask them to connect each important point they identified either with other important points or with your course goals. Finally, have them write an evaluative comment about the course, the class period, or the material (e.g., "What I enjoyed most/least...."; "What I found most/ least useful....").

Each of the five activities requires at least two minutes. If you can spare the time, let students compare their responses among themselves. Of course, feel free to pick and choose the activities you find most useful.

RSQC2 gives you timely feedback on what your students consider important material and what they value about your course. By having them recall the previous class and make connections, this CAT also builds bridges between old and new material.

Student Portfolios

While very different from anonymous, one-time CATs, student portfolios allow you to assess and document your students' progress across written products without attaching grades. A portfolio is a collection of samples of a student's work during the term, one that you and she may assemble together, along with the student's written reflections on the products and/or her intellectual progress through writing them. The samples may be the student's best work, the widest variety of his/her good work, and/or the "history" of one or more major pieces of work (e.g., notes, outlines, peer and instructor reviews, and

multiple revisions in response to those reviews). You grade only the total portfolio and the student's reflections, typically at the end of the term (Bernhardt, 1992).

Student portfolios became very popular among English instructors from primary through post-secondary levels in the 1980s. Those who use them testify that portfolios encourage constructive dialogue between students and the instructor and motivate students to attempt more varied and adventuresome writing, to take instructor and peer feedback seriously, and to revise their work, often several times. Instructors in many disciplines, even mathematics, have developed their own versions of the portfolio, most of which either permit or require much more creative demonstrations of learning than do traditional assignments and tests (Belanoff and Dickson, 1991; Crowley, 1993).

Consider, for example, the imaginative range of assessments artifacts that a mathematics portfolio can contain: samples of journal entries; written explanations for each mathematical step of a complex problem solution; a mathematics autobiography focusing on changing attitudes and new insights; multiple solutions to a challenging problem, each reflecting a different approach; an elegant proof, either intuitive or formal depending upon the student's abilities; student-developed lesson plans for teaching a particular mathematical concept; student-developed word problems; student-drawn visual representations of problems; student-made concrete representations; and reviews of mathematical books and journal articles—all in addition to examples of traditional student output, such as tests, quizzes, and homework

(Stenmark, 1989, 1991; Crowley, 1993).

Portfolios are not without their problems, however. For example, postponing grades until the end of the term will not necessarily save you grading time. Quite the contrary. While you may not have to affix letters to students' work till the end, you will probably assign more and more varied writing projects and put more time and effort into writing formative feedback and holding student conferences on each project during the term. Without this detailed, personalized feedback, none of the potential benefits of portfolios will acrue. In addition, you will otherwise suffocate at the end of the term under an avalanche of notebooks and folders filled with only vaguely familiar writing samples. In the terms used above to describe CATs, portfolios entail very high effort on both your own and your students' part (Bernhardt, 1992).

Another serious problem for many students is the lack of letter grading during the term. Often they are anxious not knowing where they stand and how they are doing, and some need to know early in the term to decide whether to stay in the course. Academic regulations may not even allow such postponement of grades. Some university require faculty to disclose midterm grades or to submit deficiency reports on students earning a "C-" or lower, and curriculum committees will not approve new courses unless a substantial part of the final grade is determined by the middle of the term.

A final problem with portfolios pertain to grading standards. If a portfolio contains only the students' best work, how can anyone in the class not receive a good grade? But the converse problem also arises:

Some instructors resist assigning deservedly low grades to students who have worked so hard during the term. Even with herculean effort, some students barely pass a course, and it can be very difficult for an instructor to break the bad news to them after all the time she has talking with and working with these students.

Therefore, before adopting student portfolios, consider the following issues about delayed grading: how your students might respond to it; if your institution's academic regulations accommodate it; and whether you can uphold your quality standards in spite of it. Then ask yourself if you can make the time to give your students' writing the detailed, ongoing feedback that is required.

Extending Classroom Assessment to Classroom Research and the Scholarship of Teaching

If you are collecting and examining systematic data on the teaching effectiveness or student appeal of one method over another, why not write up and publish your more interesting results? This type of research is the backbone of the college teaching field as well as the foundation of this book. It has been called "classroom research" and "action research," but it has recently taken on the more general label of "the scholarship of teaching."

You probably already know how to conduct this kind of research, especially if you are in psychology, education, or the social sciences. Research on teaching typically relies on a quasi-experimental or a survey design, or it describes and assesses an innovative method or curriculum (Nilson, 1992). The

198

proper design may require your collaborating with colleagues who are teaching the same or similar courses (Cross, 1992) or your conducting a longitudinal study of classes before and with the "treatment."

If you will be surveying students or using student products for your research, you must contact your university's Institutional Review Board (IRB) before you begin. Typically IRBs give classroom research an exemption, but you need evidence of their review. A violation can cost your institution federal funding.

In addition, you may have some background reading to do. Much of the scholarship of teaching is anchored in learning theory (Cross, 1992), and your particular research topic may have already inspired a body of literature.

You can search for relevant literature and find publication outlets in the many journals on college teaching (well over a hundred) and the dozens of national newsletters. Some specialize in a given discipline, a few in a specific teaching method (e.g., cooperative learning, instructional technology), but most are general. Though each journal favors one or two types of articles, they collectively publish standard research studies, literature reviews with insightful conclusions, evaluative descriptions of teaching innovations ("how to" articles), philosophical statements, and analyses of current educational policies, problems, and trends (Nilson, 1992). You might skim several of these journals to find some that publish articles similar to yours. Look for such periodicals in your institution's main library, education library, and teaching center library.

Research on teaching is not new. Decades before Cross and Angelo started promoting the idea (1993), economics ushered in scholarly, scientific inquiry into student learning/achievement, the most important outcome we can assess. This field has been on the forefront ever since, largely because economists have been able to agree on the learning objectives for certain courses and to develop standardized tests to measure their attainment. Until other disciplines can reach a similar consensus, their research predicting to student learning/achievement will be limited to small classroom samples.

For further reading:

Angelo, T.A. and K.P. Cross. 1993. *Classroom Assessment Techniques: A Handbook for College Teachers.* 2nd ed. San Francisco: Jossey-Bass.

Teaching at Its Best

TEST CONSTRUCTION

How does test construction fit into the overall scheme of teaching? As Chapter 3 explained, the process of teaching begins with developing student learning objectives. These objectives direct your selection of teaching methods to foster the learning desired. They should also direct your construction of assessment instruments so that you measure your students' success in meeting these objectives. In the end, all three phases of instruction—objective setting, teaching, and testing—should be woven into a multifaceted arrangement of interdependent parts, each strengthened by the others.

While instructors can evaluate student learning in many ways, graded quizzes and examinations are the most common way. This chapter examines the advantages and disadvantages of many of the popular types of test questions and suggests techniques for constructing meaningful tests.

Thinking about Testing

Before you begin writing a quiz or an exam, think seriously about what you are trying to accomplish with it. A test can assess merely students' short-term memory skills or their abilities to comprehend, apply, analyze, synthesize, and evaluate the material as well. Chapters 3 and 16 give details on Bloom's six levels of cognitive operations and questions.

Review your learning objectives and identify each one's cognitive level. If they focus primarily on knowledge, comprehension, and application, then so should your test questions. Unless you have taught your students to work at the higher levels, questions pitched at these levels will not measure their goal attainment. Your students will also be doomed to perform poorly (Jacobs and Chase, 1992; Walvoord and Anderson, 1998).

General Testing Guidelines

The following suggestions were adapted mostly from Lacey-Casem (1990) and Ory and Ryan (1993).

Test early and often. Early testing gives students feedback that tells them how to optimize their course performance. Frequent testing gives more opportunities for success, reducing the penalties for any single poor performance.

Compose test questions immediately after you cover the material in the class. The material and the cognitive level(s) at which you taught it are fresh in your mind. Practiced regularly, this strategy ensures you a stock of questions to use when quiz and exam times arrive.

200

Give detailed, written instructions for all exams and quizzes. Remind students about your and your institution's policies on academic dishonesty (see Chapter 9), and specify the test time limit, the number of each type of question to answer, the point values of different items, where to record answers, whether to show work, whether books, notes, or calculators can be used, etc.

Start the test with some warm-up questions. Asking a few easier questions at the beginning of a quiz or exam induces students to start thinking about the material and builds their confidence.

Proofread the test form for errors. Check for spelling, grammar, split items (i.e., items that begin on one page and continue on the next), format consistency, format errors, instructions for each type of question, and adequate space for constructed responses. It is best to have another set of eyes proofread it, too (e.g., a colleague, your TA, or your supervising professor).

Have another instructor evaluate the test for clarity and content, especially if you are somewhat inexperienced, but even if you are seasoned. You may have written a quiz or exam that seems crystal clear to you, only to find out later that certain items were double-barrelled, ambiguously phrased, or awkwardly constructed. Writing good test items is a hard-to-learn craft, and you needn't learn it all by bad experience.

Types of Test Questions

In general, test questions come in two types (Ory and Ryan, 1993).

Each type has its place, and different students do well with different types of questions. Using a variety of questions on an exam allows students to feel more secure with the test format.

Objective questions. Multiple choice, true/false, and matching items measure knowledge and comprehension very effectively. Inexperienced instructors sometimes think that objective questions are easy to construct. In truth, a good, unambiguous multiple choice question takes time and thought. Professional test writers often produce only eight or ten good questions a day. In addition, well written objective questions can measure higher-order thinking.

Constructed response questions. Completion, short answer, essay, and problem solving allow students to do more than just choose among given, possible answers. Here students write and often justify their own answers.

This type of question is commonly misnamed "subjective," a term that should not be used because it gives students the impression that instructors have no clear standards for judging students' answers. We do have standards (see Chapter 30), but they may not boil down to a dualist scale of a right or wrong answer.

While easier to compose than the objective type, constructed response questions are much more difficult to grade. You must interpret students' sometimes rambling thoughts and judge among variable answers. Consider giving students a choice among several such questions. Having options lowers their anxiety and allows them to show you what they've learned best.

This section lays out the strengths and weaknesses of different types of tests questions and gives construction guidelines (Lacey-Casem, 1990; Jacobs and Chase, 1992; Ory and Ryan, 1993; Brookhart, 1999). Bear in mind that you can teach your students to write questions for you before the test (see Chapters 19 and 20).

Multiple Choice

Advantages:

+ Easy/quick to grade by hand or optical scanner.
+ Reduces some of the burden of large classes.
+ Can assess knowledge, comprehension, application, analysis, and evaluation.
+ Useful as a diagnostic tool since student choices can indicate weaknesses.

Disadvantages:

- Difficult/time-consuming to construct.
- Encourages instructors to test trivial and factual knowledge.
- May be ambiguous; students often misinterpret.
- Particularly subject to "cluing," i.e., students can deduce the correct answer by elimination.

Construction:

• Estimate one to five minutes for students to answer each question.
• Address one problem or concept per question. Avoid questions with multiple correct answers, as these confuse students.
• Phrase items with clarity and internal consistency. The item stem should be a direct positive statement expressing a complete thought. The response alternatives or options should be brief and similarly structured. Avoid wordiness.
• Include any words in the stem that can be repeated in the response alternatives.
• Avoid items that merely ask a series of true/false questions.
• If you use negatively stated stems, italicize or capitalize the negative word(s) to avoid confusion.
• Use familiar language, i.e., similar to the language that you or the readings used to explain the concept, process, relationship, etc.
• Make sure there is one correct or best response.
• Minimize the use of *all of the above* and *none of the above*.
• Use three to five alternatives per item.
• Make alternatives equally plausible and attractive. Absurd options only make guessing easier.
• Present alternatives in some logical order or alphabetize them to reduce your likelihood of falling into a pattern.
• Avoid grammatical cues to correct answers.
• Incorporate sketches and diagrams where appropriate.

True/False

Advantages:
+ Easy to prepare and to grade.
+ Can test a lot of material in a short time.
+ Can assess both lower and higher levels of cognition.
+ Can tap higher levels by having students correct the false statements.
+ Useful as a diagnostic tool if students correct false statements.

Disadvantages:
- High guessing factor for simple true/false questions.
- Encourages instructors to test trivial and factual knowledge.
- May be ambiguous.
- May include irrelevant clues.

Construction:
• Allow 30 seconds to one minute per item.
• Use only statements that are entirely true or entirely false.
• Focus each statement on a single idea or problem.
• Write positive statements. Negative and double negative statements are confusing.
• Avoid verbal cues to the correct answers. For example, questions with *usually, seldom,* and *often* are frequently true while those with *never, always,* and *every* are commonly false.
• Use familiar terminology.
• Balance the number of true and false answers.
• Avoid always making true statements long and false statements short, or vice versa. Students quickly pick up on these patterns.
• Avoid direct quotes from lectures or readings requiring only rote memorization.
• Add cognitive challenge and assessment validity by having students rewrite false statements to make them true.

Advantages:
+ Easy to grade.
+ Assesses knowledge/recall well.
+ Relatively unambiguous.
+ Can test a lot of material in a short time.

Disadvantages:
- Difficult to construct a commo set of stimuli and responses.
- High guessing factor.
- Cannot assess higher levels of cognition.
- Not useful as a diagnostic tool.

Construction:
* Allow 30 seconds to one minute per item.
* Keep stimuli and responses short and simple.
* List possible responses in some logical order (e.g., alphabetical or chronological) to reduce student search time.
* Add challenge with one or two unmatchable responses.
* Say whether response items can be used more than once or not at all.
* Limit stimuli and responses to 15 or less.
* Keep all stimuli and responses on one page.
* Have students identify their response choices using only capital letters to avoid ambiguity.

Completion (Fill-in-the-Blank)

Advantages:
+ Easy to prepare and grade.
+ Assesses knowledge/recall and vocabulary well.
+ Eliminates guessing.
+ Can test a lot of material in a short time.

Disadvantages:
- Cannot assess higher levels of cognition.
- Highly structured; requires an all-or-nothing response.
- Not useful as a diagnostic tool.
- May include irrelevant clues.
- Difficult to construct so that the desired response is clear.
- May be difficult to grade if more than one answer may be correct.

Construction:
• Allow 30 seconds to one minute per item.
• Use clear wording to elicit a unique response.
• Avoid grammatical cues. For instance, use *a/an* and *is/are* to reduce cluing.
• Omit only significant words from the statement.
• Omit words from the middle or end of a statement, not the beginning.
• Make all fill-in lines the same length.
• Place the response lines in a column to the left or right to facilitate grading.
• Use familiar language.

Short Answer

Advantages
+ Easy to construct.
+ Can assess levels of cognition from recall to analysis.
+ Requires a command of vocabulary and/or problem solving skills.
+ More useful as a diagnostic tool than any objective types.
+ Encourages instructors to give students individual feedback.

Disadvantages:
- Time-consuming to grade.
- Difficult to standardize grading due to variability across answers.

Construction:
• Estimate two to five minutes per item.
• Be very specific and concise in identifying the task students are to perform. See advice below for constructing essay questions.
• Indicate whether diagrams or illustrations are required or are acceptable in place of a written answer.
• Extend the cognitive process involved by asking for a case analysis, diagnosis, or hypothesis.
• Require students to show work for full credit on problems.
• Leave an appropriate amount of space for the answers. Too much space invites students to write too much.

Advantages:

+ Quick and relatively easy to construct.
+ Can assess all the higher levels of cognition.
+ Assesses students' abilities to logically compose and present an argument.
+ Encourages creativity and originality.
+ Requires students to really know the material.
+ Develops writing skills.
+ Encourages students to study in a more integrated/synthetic manner.
+ Discourages last-minute cramming.
+ Encourages instructors to give students individual feedback.

Disadvantages:

- Time-consuming to grade.
- Difficult to standardize grading because of variability across answers as well as length of answers.
- Cannot test a lot of material on any one exam.
- Penalizes students who read or work slowly, have poor writing skills, or are non-native English speakers.
- May be ambiguous if students don't understand test verbs or don't read the entire question very carefully.
- Encourages grading protests because the scoring may seem subjective and inconsistent.
- Easy to make questions too broad for students to zero in on the answer.
- Allows students to pick up points for bluffing.

Construction:

- Estimate ten minutes to one hour per item.
- Estimate how long an answer should take to help students budget their time accordingly.
- Give the point value for each question.
- Give several shorter essay questions rather than one or two long ones. This strategy covers more material and spreads the risk for students.
- Use original problems, cases, diagrams, graphs, data sets, etc.
- Identify the key points that must be addressed in the answer.
- Be very specific and concise in identifying the task you want students to perform. Rather than beginning a question with an interrogative pronoun such as why, how, or what, start with a descriptive verb (see Chapter 29 for a list of common test verbs and their definitions) and specify exactly how elaborate the answer should be (e.g., "*Describe three ways* that social integration could break down in the modern world, according to Durkheim. Then *assess* how closely *each one* applies to the United States today.").
- If a question is controversial or value-based, assure students that grading will be based on the validity of their arguments, the strength of their evidence, and/or the quality of their presentation—not the opinion expressed.
- If you let students choose among several questions, limit the choices (e.g., to five out of seven rather than two out of five).

Tests: The Ultimate Teaching Evaluation

The time and effort invested in writing a good test are not without their rewards. It is heartening to see your students perform well on your challenging exam or to receive a compliment on it from a student. Both indicate that your test was probably a learning as well as a "fair" evaluation experience.

But even more important, the tests you design are the most important instruments you have for assessing *your* teaching effectiveness. So for *your* sake as well as your students', they should measure what you set out to teach. Student, peer, and self evaluations are other instruments, and student opinions of your success generally carry the most weight. But they merely take the place of the *only real teaching evaluation, which is how much students have learned.*

In the best of all possible educational worlds, each course exam would be tested to ensure high reliability and validity. Then student performance would be used to evaluate the instructor's teaching success relative to other instructors teaching the same course. Of course, such an ideal could only come to pass if faculty could agree on a standardized content and testing instrument for each course—an idea that goes against academic freedom and autonomy.

Still, how your students perform on well designed tests is your best data for your personal self-assessment of your teaching.

For further reading:

Brookhart, S.M. 1999. *The Art and Science of Classroom Assessment: The Missing Part of Pedagogy.* ASHE-ERIC Higher Education Report Vol. 27, No. 1. Washington, D.C.: The George Washington University, Graduate School of Education and Human Development.

Jacobs, L.C. and C.I. Chase. 1992. *Developing and Using Tests Effectively: A Guide for Faculty.* San Francisco: Jossey-Bass.

Ory, J.C. and K.E. Ryan. 1993. *Tips for Improving Testing and Grading.* Vol. 4. Thousand Oaks, CA: Sage Publications.

Walvoord, B.E. and V.J. Anderson. 1998. *Effective Grading: A Tool for Learning and Assessment.* San Francisco: Jossey-Bass.

PREPARING STUDENTS FOR TESTS

Think back to your undergraduate days. Did you ever experience anxiety or a sense of dread when your professors announced an exam? Did you ever walk into a test feeling well-prepared, only to "freeze" when you saw the first question? Did you ever leave an exam feeling that you "aced" it, only to be sorely disappointed in your grade? If even one of these situation rang true, you can probably empathize with some of the emotions your students are experiencing now.

The first question you usually hear when you announce an upcoming exam is "What will be on the test?" While this is not a valid question, another common query, "What will the test format be?", is perfectly valid. We'd like to believe that students will perform well on any type of test with adequate study. But different types of exams call for different types of study strategies, and most students learn based on how they are tested (Wergin, 1988). Factual memorization for a recall-oriented objective test takes a different kind of study effort than that for analyses of problems or situations. It is that latter type of studying that helps students develop critical thinking skills, and students need experience in the higher cognitive processes of analysis, synthesis, and evaluation.

Preparation Techniques

If we accept that tests can be instruments of instruction as well as evaluation, then preparing students to perform well on tests is also an excellent teaching strategy. Here are some easily implemented ways to help students prepare for exams (some adapted from Lacey-Casem, 1990):

Study groups. Many of the chapters in this book (e.g., 17, 18, 25, and 26) point out the teaching effectiveness of cooperative learning groups. Cooperative *study* groups that meet regularly outside of class are also very helpful (Treisman, 1986; Hufford, 1991). Since student commitment can make or break them, you may want to formalize them by having students sign up for study groups very early in the semester. Then distribute a list of all the groups with their members' names and phone numbers.

Review sheets. This study aid helps many students, especially freshmen in introductory courses. You can make a review sheet as simple as an outline of important topics that you have emphasized or as elaborate as a sample exam. The sample test method involves much more time and effort, since you will not want to duplicate sample items on the real test. But it is highly effective, and you can use a previous test if it accurately reflects your current course.

Between the simple and the elaborate is the list of review questions. The questions should illustrate the variety of question formats that will appear on the test. If you plan to test with some objective multiple choice questions, ask some objective review questions. If you intend rather to test analysis and synthesis, develop review questions that require the same cognitive operations.

Review sessions. As do many instructors, you may wish to set up a special review session shortly before an exam. But it is likely to work well only if students have already made significant progress in their independent or small group studies. Therefore, you should make it clear that you will not be summarizing the last few weeks of lectures and readings nor dispensing the answers to the review questions.

The most productive way to conduct a review session is to *insist* that students come prepared to 1) ask specific questions on the material and 2) answer the review questions on their own. With respect to their questions, always ask the class for answers before answering the questions yourself. With respect to the review questions, have the entire class participate in brainstorming and refining the answers, and assign different questions to small groups and have them develop and orally present their answers. Invite other students to evaluate the groups' answers, then offer your own assessment.

Chapter 14 describes another version of this format called *pair/*

group and review, in which student pairs or small groups develop and present their answers to the class, while you mock-grade them and explain your assessment criteria. You can also have the rest of the class mock-grade the answers to help students learn how to assess their own work.

Help sessions or course clinics. This method takes the review session one step further by establishing weekly meetings of two or more hours during which the professor or the TA answers questions. A regularly scheduled meeting encourages students to keep up with the course and not wait until the last minute to cram for a test. It also reduces stress by having students study without the impending threat of an exam.

Definitions of key test terms. Students, especially freshmen, often do poorly on a test because they are not exactly sure what a particular question, especially an essay question, is asking. So it may be safest to provide them with written definitions of common test verbs, along with review questions that give students practice in the operations. Consider sharing the definitions below with your classes (Ellis, 2000, p. 172; Lacey-Casem, 1990, pp. 41-42).

Analyze: Break something down into parts, such as a theory into its components, a process into its stages, or an event into its causes. Analysis involves characterizing the whole, identifying its parts, and showing how the parts interrelate.

Assess/Criticize/Evaluate: Determine or judge the degree to which something meets or fails to meet certain criteria. If not provided in the question, develop criteria for making judgments.

Classify: Sort into major, general groups or categories that you name or identify.

Compare/Contrast: Identify the important similarities and/or differences between two or more elements in order to reveal something significant about them. Emphasize similarities if the command is to compare and differences if it is to contrast.

Define/Identify: Give the key characteristics by which a concept, thing, or event can be understood. Place it in a general class, then distinguish it from other members of that class.

Describe: Give the characteristics by which an object, action, process, person, or concept can be recognized or visualized.

Discuss/Examine: Debate, argue, and evaluate the various sides of an issue.

Explain/Justify: Give the basic principles of or reasons for something; make it intelligible. Explanation may involve relating the unfamiliar to the more familiar.

List/Enumerate: Give essential points one by one in a logical order. It may be helpful to number the points.

Interpret/Explain: Say what the author of a quotation or statement means.

Illustrate: Use a concrete example to explain or clarify the essential attributes of a problem or concept.

Outline/Trace/Review/State: Organize a description under main points and subordinate points, omitting minor details and classifying the elements or main points.

Prove/Validate: Establish that something is true by citing factual evidence or giving clear, logical reasons.

Combating Test Anxiety

Some anxiety is normal before an exam and indeed has a motivating effect on students. Mealey and Host (1993) reviewed test anxiety literature and identified three categories of anxious students. Students of the first type lack adequate study skills and are aware of the problem. They are not well prepared for exams and worry about poor performance. The second category includes students who have adequate study strategies but become distracted during testing. Other research confirms these two types (Naveh-Benjamin et al, 1987). The final group is composed of students who mistakenly believe that they have adequate study skills but do poorly on exams, then wonder what the problem could be.

Mealey and Host (1993) asked students how instructors reduce or heighten student anxiety before, during, and after an exam. They received four kinds of responses:

1) Students resent interruptions during a test, even if they are to correct or to clarify exam items.

2) Seventy-five percent of the students want the instructor to conduct some kind of review before the test. They feel more confident if they are sure they have correct information in their notes.

3) Students do not like an instructor to walk around the room and look over their shoulders. While it may keep cheating in check, it also raises the anxiety level of stress-sensitive students.

4) Students do not respond well to hearing how hard a test will be. They do not mind a challenging exam, but they would prefer to

hear how they should study, followed by some words of reassurance.

Lacey-Casem (1990) suggests some other practical methods to help alleviate test anxiety:

5) Establish (in writing) your test schedule along with policies on missed exams.
6) Explain and follow a clear grading system.
7) Test frequently. The more grades you have, the less that a poor performance on any one exam will cost your students.
8) Allow students to drop one low test or quiz. Everyone can have a bad day.
9) Make sure your exams can be completed in the allotted time. It is discouraging to near the end of the hour and have many items unanswered.
10) Teach students to relax. Deep breathing exercises, counting to ten, and visualizing a successful test session (Hebert, 1984; Ellis, 2000) are all useful ways to combat nervousness.

Occasionally, you may have a student for whom test anxiety is a debilitating problem. As with other emotional and psychological problems, refer such a student to your institution's counseling center and/or its learning skills/academic assistance center.

What the Effort is Worth

Preparing students for tests is one way to ensure your students review, synthesize, and retain the material. It can also help you organize and plan your exam. Whatever you can do to reduce your students' test anxiety allows them to demonstrate more accurately their actual learning. It is only by seeing their honest achievement that you can assess how succesful

your teaching has been. In your performance review, you may also want to use some of your students' tests to document the effectiveness of your teaching, a topic addressed in Chapter 31.

For further reading:

Ellis, D. 2000. *Becoming a Master Student.* Boston: Houghton Mifflin.

GRADING:

TESTS, ASSIGNMENTS, AND COURSE PERFORMANCE

Grading is a task you may view with dread and disdain, but it provides essential feedback to your students on their performance and to you on your teaching effectiveness.

Historically, grading is a relatively new phenomenon in the academy (Hammons and Barnsley, 1992). Yale University was the first American institution to assign grades, starting in 1783. Professors used Latin descriptors ranging from the exceptional *optime* to the dismal *pejores* to classify student performance. In 1800, Yale adopted a numerical scale of 0 to 4, thus beginning the grade point average. Later the College of William and Mary adopted a similar scheme.

In 1850, the University of Michigan introduced a pass/fail system that set the passing grade minimum at 50 percent. Harvard began using letter grades in 1883. This system soon swept the country, but with tremendous disagreement on the grade cut-off points. For instance, Mount Holyoke set the failing grade at 75 percent, while Michigan maintained a 50 percent standard. Harvard's failing mark was a low 26 percent. Even with such broad discrepancies in the scale, higher education has made few major changes in this system, except to add +/- modifiers.

The Meaning of Grades

Pollio and Humphreys (1988) note that instructors, students, parents, and business people do not agree on the meaning of grades. For instance, when asked how long the impact of receiving a "C" vs. an "A" would last, a full 53 percent of the faculty respondents expected it would last at least two to five years. So did a third of the parents and business people. But only 14 percent of the students surveyed agreed, and 45 percent anticipated no impact at all.

While many students may not want to believe that grades are important to their futures, one of your major responsibilities is to evaluate their achievement and assign grades accordingly. In addition, you are responsible for upholding the value of the grading currency—i.e., combatting grade inflation. So it is worth reviewing the level of performance each grade represents.

An "A" signifies an exceptional level of achievement. The student displays a superb command of the subject matter and can creatively apply it at many different levels. "A" students tend to be very committed and motivated.

A "B" indicates an above average but not outstanding level of

212 achievement. "B" students demonstrate a good grasp of the material and the ability to apply at several but not all levels.

A "C" represents an average level of achievement. The student shows some mastery of the material and a narrow application range. This grade may indicate poor study skills or a lack of motivation or interest. Some "C" students get by on their decent test-taking skills.

A "D" means that the student has little or no true understanding of the subject area and may not be interested in learning any more.

An "F" denotes a performance below the level of random chance. The student may totally lack interest, motivation, and/or ability.

Summative Assessments and Grading Systems

Pregent (1994) describes two types of evaluation: *summative* and *formative*. A **summative evaluation** is an assessment of the knowledge that has been accrued after the learning has ended, at the end of a part or all of the course. It typically follows one of two basic grading systems (Wergin, 1988; Hammons and Barnsley, 1992; Ory and Ryan, 1993; Pregent, 1994):

Norm-referenced grading (NRG). The first type of summative grading system assesses each student's performance relative to all other students' performances. Usually called "grading on a curve," it places students in competition with each other for class ranking; the best and worst performances set the parameters within which other performances are judged. While this system assures any class GPA an instructor may want, it has some serious flaws. First, it statistically assumes a bell-shaped

("normal") distribution of student scores—a phenomenon that doesn't always occur. Second, the grades it yields are unrelated to any absolute performance standard. So if all students in a class perform poorly, some inadequate performances will receive an "A" anyway. Conversely, in a high achieving class, many good performances will unjustly get a "C."

Criterion-referenced grading (CRG). This second grading system eliminates such inequities (Wergin, 1988). It requires instructors to set absolute standards of performance (grading criteria) in advance, giving all students sole responsibility for their own grades.

Comparing these two grading schemes, you can see that the primary purpose of NRG is discrimination or selection, while CRG focuses on diagnosis and mastery. NRG tests general course objectives, while CRG assesses student learning objectives. To be statistically viable as well as fair to students, NRG requires a wide variability of scores—an irrelevant issue in CRG. Finally, NRG yields only the students' relative class standing; CRG measures their actual learning and abilities.

To be sure, criterion-referenced grading has its drawbacks. In particular, it is difficult to develop meaningful, valid standards for assigning grades based on absolute knowledge acquisition (Ory and Ryan, 1993). Instructors who are unfamiliar with their student population may have no idea how scores may distribute on any given test or assignment. (As the nightmare goes, the scores may all cluster around 95 percent or all lag below 70.) But once you have a term's experience, criterion-referenced grading is the superior

Teaching at Its Best

summative scheme, especially if you stress achievement, competence, and excellence in your students.

Formative Assessments and Feedback Guidelines

A *formative evaluation* is an assessment of student performance at any point *during* the learning process, with the goal of helping the student learn the material better (Pregent, 1994). While formative assessment may involve grading, the scores are not calculated in the final grade; rather, they are intended as qualitative feedback to help the student improve. When you comment on rough drafts of papers—or you have your students assess each other's drafts—you are providing your students with formative assessment.

This type of feedback benefits both you and your students in several ways. For them, it encourages steady writing and work habits; it gives them criteria on which to revise and improve their work and their writing in general; and it teaches them the real, professional writing process, which always involves extensive rewriting. For you, it yields much better student products, practically eliminates plagiarism, and changes your role from judge to facilitator.

These few suggestions will make formative assessments of papers more productive:

- Strictly enforce deadlines for students to find topics, gather resources, develop an outline, and submit a first draft. Formative evaluation takes time.
- Comment more on major writing issues, such as content, reasoning, and organization, and less on style and grammar.
- Make your comments constructive, personalized, and informal. Give praise where deserved, as students often do not know what they are doing right.
- Teach your students to give each other useful, specific feedback drafts and informal assignments (see Chapter 20). Give your own detailed comments on the first drafts of the first paper, review your feedback methods with your students, then oversee their comments on the drafts of the second paper. After that, students should be able to provide good feedback on their own.
- Make sure students understand that formative evaluations focus on *major* problems in their papers and that making the suggested changes does not guarantee them an "A."

Accuracy, Consistency, and Learning Value

A sound grading scheme is *accurate, consistent,* and *valuable to learning.* Larger classes require special efforts to ensure these qualities, especially consistency. The following guidelines should help (Lacey-Casem, 1990; Jacobs and Chase, 1993; Ory and Ryan, 1993; Walvoord and Anderson, 1998):

Accuracy:
- A final grade based on many and varied assignments and tests.
- Well constructed quizzes and exams reflecting your student learning objectives (see Chapter 28).
- Point values that reflect the relative importance of the concepts and relationships tested.
- Grading keys and rubrics that allow for the possibility of more than one correct answer.

- Valid items. Be willing to discard a test item that practically all the students have missed; there is probably something wrong with it.
- A grading standard appropriate for the level of your students.

Consistency:
- Written guidelines for correct responses, particularly if multiple graders are involved.
- Consensus among multiple graders, which will require discussion of problematic answers.
- Maintenance of student anonymity to avoid grading biases.

Learning:
- Commenting generously, including on what the student did right. Too many negatives are overwhelming and counterproductive.
- Identifying a few key areas for improvement and specific remediation methods. Once again, if you try to fix everything at once, students become overwhelmed and tune out.
- Directing comments to the performance, not the student.
- Making specific comments, not a cryptic "what?" or "?".
- Allowing revisions after formative assessments on first drafts.
- Providing samples of exemplary work and helping students understand what makes them excellent.
- Providing a detailed key or scoring guide.
- Reviewing exams when you return them so that students understand what you wanted and how they can improve their performance. Focus on frequently made errors.
- Sharing studying, writing, problem-solving, and test-taking techniques, and referring some students to your institution's learning skills/academic assistance center for special help.

Grading Constructed Responses and Papers

Grading answers to constructed response questions requires considerable thought and strategy to ensure accuracy and consistency within reasonable time frames. You can choose from two popular grading methods (Neel, 1993; Ory and Ryan, 1993; Rodgers, 1995).

Analytical (or atomistic) grading. Begin by developing a "key"—that is, listing the components of an ideal response or paper. Then allocate point values among the components. As you read a student's work, check off the components on your list or write the number of points earned next to the component on the student's work. You may give partial point values to an incomplete or partially correct answer. Then total the point values for the grade. This approach helps inexperienced instructors become accustomed to the quality range of student work and the grading process.

This method is usually implemented as content-focused and serves well for grading tests and assignments that require only knowledge or comprehension. However, it can and sometimes should include other dimensions as well: organization, trueness to specified format, quality of data/evidence, documentation, logic of reasoning, clarity, style (sentence structure, word choice, etc.), and mechanics (grammar, punctuation, spelling, etc.). You can easily keep track of four or five dimensions, and each one can take on a different point value or weight (e.g., 20 for content, 15 for organization, 10 for style, and 5 for mechanics, for a total of 50 points).

Do explain your general assessment dimensions and their point values to your class in advance, when you give the assignment or conduct a review for the test. Your students need to know and understand the criteria on which you will evaluate their work.

Analytical grading takes a great deal of time because it requires attention to detail and because some instructors feel obligated to write what is missing on each student's work. It is more efficient to give students a copy of the key when returning the test or paper. While analytical grading seems highly objective, it still invites grading protests and "point-mongering," especially for partial credit.

Holistic grading—also called global grading, single impression scoring, and Primary Trait Analysis. This method has gone under several labels over the years. Any differences among them are minor. This grading approach is based on implicit comparative evaluations of your students' responses and papers, but it does not involve curving. It is relatively quick, efficient, reliable, and fair when backed by experience and practice. (Holistic scorers of standardized essay tests undergo hours of training.) In addition, it is often the only suitable way to grade work that reflects higher-order cognitive thinking (application, analysis, synthesis, or evaluation).

In one holistic schema (suitable for small classes), you read quickly through all the responses or papers, put each above or below the ones you've already read, from best to worst, then group them for assigning grades. Finally, you write up descriptions of the quality of each group, and give them to students when you return their work. To personalize the feedback, either add appropriate comments to each student's sheet, or highlight the most applicable parts of your description of the grade.

In another scheme (suitable for any size class), you start by developing a ***rubric***—that is, listing the four or five dimensions on which you will grade the assignment or essay question. Four or five are easier to remember while grading than six or more. Here are just some of the many possible assessment criteria that may be important to you:

- Satisfying the assignment, following directions
- Memorization of facts, figures, definitions, equations, and/or text material
- Proper use of technical terminology
- Demonstration of accurate understanding of the materials and texts
- Proper references to texts and other sources
- Organization, conformity to the required organizing framework of format
- Precision of measurement, quality of data
- Specification of limits, qualifications to results and conclusions
- Clarity of expression and/or explanations
- Conciseness, parsimony
- Strength or tightness of arguments (e.g., internal consistency, evidence, logic)
- Mechanics (spelling, grammar, and punctuation)
- Writing style, as suitable to the discipline and assignment
- Creativity of thought, design, or solution.

Which dimensions you select or devise on your own for your rubric will depend upon your discipline, the level of your course, the nature of your material, and the specific assignment or essay-test question.

Then, referring to your rubric, you develop your **scoring guide**—that is, brief descriptions of what the answers earning various grades will look like or have in them. Of course, you can use numbers of points instead of letter grades. These descriptions can take the form of paragraphs, bulleted lists, or traits on a matrix or table, whichever your prefer. Usually, each description has one sentence or item for each dimension in the rubric.

A few examples should clarify. Let's say our assignment is to write a classic five-paragraph essay arguing in favor of norm-referenced grading or criterion-referenced grading, drawing on several readings on the topic. Let's assume our rubric focuses on satisfying the assignment (with an emphasis on following the classic five-paragraph essay format), demonstrating an accurate understanding of the readings, backing one's argument with evidence from the readings, and mechanics. Here is a suitable scoring guide done in paragraph form:

A   An "A" essay strictly follows the classic five-paragraph essay format, stating the thesis (position) in the first paragraph, providing evidence in each of the next three paragraphs, and concluding with a summary and/or synthesis. It consistently makes appropriate and accurate references to the readings. It also provides all the evidence available in the readings to support its argument. Finally, it contains no more than two spelling, punctuation, or grammatical errors.

B   A "B" essay follows the classic five-paragraph essay format with no more than one minor deviation. While generally accurate in referring to readings, it shows a thin, incomplete, or shaky understanding of some readings in a couple of places. It also misses some parts of the readings that would lend evidence to the argument. It contains no more than several spelling, punctuation, or grammatical errors.

C   A "C" essay breaks significantly from the classic five-paragraph essay format—perhaps failing to state a clear position in the first paragraph, mixing arguments across paragraphs, and/or closing with a new argument or information. While it refers to the readings, it demonstrates a spotty or superficial understanding of them. It also misses opportunities to use them for evidence. It contains quite a few spelling, punctuation, and/or grammatical errors, though not enough to make parts of it incomprehensible.

D   A "D" essay does not follow the classic five-paragraph essay format—failing either to state a clear position or to use the rest of essay to bring evidence from the readings to support it. It demonstrates little understanding or knowledge of the readings. In addition, it draws little relevant evidence from them. The frequent errors in spelling, punctuation, and grammar are distracting or render the essay incomprehensible in places.

F An "F" essay fails to address the assignment in topic or format, *or* the frequent errors in spelling, punctuation, and grammar render the essay incomprehensible, *or* it is not turned in.

It is important not to abbreviate the descriptions of the "B," "C," and "D" products because students are likely to focus only on the description of their own grade. The description of the "F" paper is often briefer because its shortcomings usually transcend the rubric.

In bulleted-list form, this same scoring guide starts out like this:
"A" Essay
• Strictly follows the classic five-paragraph essay format
• Makes appropriate and accurate references to readings
• Provides all the evidence available in the readings to buttress its argument
• Contains no more than two spelling, punctuation, or grammatical errors

As you can see, bulleting the key features may ease reading.

In matrix or table form, the scoring guide lists the rubric dimension down the left side of the page to define rows, and the possible letters grades or numbers of points across the top to create columns. You then fill in the cells with your standards on each dimension for each grade or point allocation.

To extend the example above, we would identify the first row in our matrix as "Satisfies the assignment, with an emphasis on following the classic five-paragraph essay format." Under the "A" grade column, we would write something like "Perfect"; under "B," "≤ 1 minor deviation"; under "C," "Significant deviations" perhaps with examples; under "D," "Does not follow format"; and under "F," "Does not satisfy the assignment." A matrix (or table) can be the easiest to read if you can fit all the rubric dimensions, grading or scoring levels, and descriptors on one piece of paper.

The literature offers examples of rubrics and scoring guides, mostly in paragraph and list forms, for many types of assignments: papers (Montgomery, 2002; Leahy, 2002); letters, group presentations (Montgomery, 2002); solo presentations, class participation, journals (Baughlin, Brod, and Page, 2002); essay tests, web page designs (Brookhart, 1999); mathematical problem solving (Montgomery, 2002; Baughlin, Brod, and Page, 2002; Benander et al, 2000); and lab reports, in a rare example of the matrix form (Rodgers, 1995).

One criticism of holistic grading is that the feedback to students is too general. However, you can most easily make it more specific by marking or highlighting on each student's scoring guide the features that are most important in determining his grade. You also can combine features of the analytical and the holistic methods and write personalized comments on the scoring guide or the student's paper. However, in doing so, you sacrifice much of the efficiency and time-saving advantages of this grading method.

In any case, holistic grading is designed strictly for *summative* assessment—i.e., grading a final (if only) version of a piece of work. In itself, it does not give enough detailed and individualized feedback to make it helpful in a formative way, nor does it suggest improvement strategies.

With a little experience using rubrics and scoring guides, you will be able to develop them at the same time that you design an assignment or write a essay-test question. At

218

this point, you can add student-centered value to the method by distributing your scoring guide to students along with the assignment. You can even give your students a generic scoring guide—one that doesn't give away the question—when preparing them for an essay test. A scoring guide explicates the intricacies of your assignment or test question, as well as the expectations you have of your students. Still, it is not a "key" with the "right answers" to keep secret. When students can work on an assignment with the scoring guide in front of them, they are less likely to explain away a poor performance with "I didn't know what he wanted."

Grading Lab Reports

While this is a specialized kind of grading for a specialized kind of writing, all guidelines for grading constructed responses still apply. The questions below are also important to take into consideration:

1) How well is the problem understood and how properly is it addressed?
2) How clearly stated is the hypothesis?
3) How are the results presented? According to the instructions? Are all the results included?
4) How clear are the logic and organization of the assignment?
5) How strong are the analytical skills shown in the results and discussion?
6) How solid is the student's grasp of the scientific method?

In lower-level science courses, you can help your students write better lab reports by providing them with samples of quality scientific writing—perhaps model lab reports from other courses—to familiarize them with the proper format and content. You can also have them organize their reports with an outline or flow chart and practice-write the various sections.

Another excellent way to help your students produce good reports is to give them the scoring guide in advance. Rodgers (1995) developed a detailed holistic scoring guide, presented in an easy-to-read matrix, to grade his students' chemistry lab reports. His rubric has a daunting 21 dimensions, but they fall within four general categories—focus, appearance, content, and structure—and he has only three levels of point allocations.

For example, under "Focus," Rodgers has nine rubric dimensions (1995, p. 21):

1. "Understanding experimental objectives"
2. "Abstract describes what was done and major results."
3. "Unnecessary statements or observations in the procedure"
4. "Depth of introduction"
5. "Tone"
6. "Suggestions for improvement, further study in conclusions"
7. "Effort to relate the experiment to other known chemical principles"
8. "Shows detailed understanding of scientific method"
9. "Student distinguishes between a theory and a proof."

Many of the cells have only one- or two-word descriptors—for #1, "Very clear," "Demonstrated," or "Unsophisticated"; for #7, "Clear," "Vague," or "None"; for #9, "Yes," "Yes," or "No." Even when the descriptor is considerably longer, it is very easy to simply check, circle, or highlight the most appropriate option. At the end, the grader totals the points accumulated across all 21 dimensions.

Rodgers conducted a timing study of how long it took to grade a lab report using his old analytical method versus his new holistic method. He timed both himself and his trained teaching assistants. The results were quite startling. Analytical grading required 15 to 20 minutes per report, while holistic took only 3.5 minutes (for him) to 4.0 minutes (for his TAs) per report. In other words, analytical grading took *four to five times longer* than holistic, and Rodgers was pleased with the reliability and overall grading results.

General Cautions for Grading Constructed Responses and Papers

With any grading method involving multiple criteria, do be careful to distinguish among your various evaluative dimensions. For example, try not to let a poor grammatical construction devalue a good idea—assuming, of course, you can decipher the idea despite the construction.

Another word of caution: Don't let yourself become a copy editor. If mechanics are important to you, point out and correct the errors only on the first page of the student's work. Let the student find the rest of them. If you use proofreading marks, be sure to define them to your class in a handout. Refer students with serious writing problems to your institution's writing program.

Identify students who are not native English speakers and be more patient in grading their responses and papers. If advisable, refer them to your institution's writing program for special help.

Returning Students' Work

Grade and return tests and assignments as promptly as you can; students can't learn from your feedback on a piece of work they've long forgotten. To protect their privacy, return their work in an any order *except* grading rank, and record scores and grades inside the test packet or paper—never where they can be seen. Under the provisions of the Buckley Amendment (the Family Educational Rights and Privacy Act), it is illegal to publicly display scores or grades with any identifying information, including Social Security numbers.

Allow class time for review, questions, and problem-solving exercises so students can learn what they didn't know for the test or assignment. It is best not to proceed to new material until students assure you that they understand what they did wrong.

When returning quizzes and exams, some instructors give a statistical grading summary showing the distribution of scores, the class mean, the standard deviation, and the cut-off lines for grades (already built into the CRG system). No doubt these data increase students' interest in elementary statistics, but they also encourage "point mongering" around cut-off lines.

This brings us to the unpleasant topic of grade disputes. No matter how carefully you grade, a few students will be dissatisfied with their scores. Never discuss a grade protest with an emotional student. Rather, require students to submit their case in writing. Those who cannot make one in two or three days probably don't have one.

The Real Meaning and Limits of Grades

In the best of all possible worlds we wouldn't give grades at all. We'd give our students individual feedback on how to improve their

220

work. So we should keep grades in perspective and see them for what they are: an institutionally mandated shorthand used to screen, sanction, motivate, and reward. What they can't do is *inspire* students to *want to learn*. That admirable task is ours, and our success depends on our teaching strategies, our enthusiasm, our rapport with students, and other qualities and behaviors that we will examine in the next and final chapter.

For further reading:

Brookhart, S.M. 1999. *The Art and Science of Classroom Assessment: The Missing Part of Pedagogy.* ASHE-ERIC Higher Education Report Vol. 27, No. 1. Washington, D.C.: The George Washington University, Graduate School of Education and Human Development.

Ory, J.C. and K.E. Ryan. 1993. *Tips for Improving Testing and Grading.* Vol. 4. Thousand Oaks, CA: Sage Publications.

Walvoord, B.E. and V.J. Anderson. 1998. *Effective Grading: A Tool for Learning and Assessment.* San Francisco: Jossey-Bass.

EVALUATING AND DOCUMENTING TEACHING EFFECTIVENESS

Teaching effectiveness weighs more and more heavily in the faculty review process, including tenure and promotion decisions, at an increasing number of colleges and universities. By definition, teaching effectiveness is an instructor's degree of success in facilitating student learning. The more students learn, the deeper the cognitive levels at which they learn, and the better they can communicate what they have learned, the more effective an instructor's teaching.

While we measure our students' learning in tests and assignments, we rarely use standardized assessment instruments across different sections and terms of the same course—and for good reason. First, being required to do so would impinge upon academic freedom and autonomy as we currently define them. Second, it would induce instructors to teach to the test—a good consequence only if the tests were designed to assess higher-order cognitive processes and deep learning at a high level of accuracy. But typically these instruments are too objective and fact-heavy to test and measure all the cognitive, affective, ethical, and social skills that so many courses aim to develop in students.

A third and final reason against assessing learning with standardized tests is the complexity of the learning process. The instructor is only one among many factors that affect the depth and breadth of student learning in a given course. Beyond her influence are the student's intelligence, energy level, attitudes towards work, extracurricular commitments, family background, and previous schooling (Arreola, 2000).

However, since institutions eschew standardized assessments, they cannot directly measure teaching effectiveness nor directly compare the relative effectiveness of different instructors. Therefore, they rely instead on student ratings and written comments about the course and the instructor. Numerical ratings in particular permit quick and easy analysis and comparison.

Relying on students' opinions to assess their learning may seem like a foolish leap of faith. But a vast literature on the various types of teaching evaluations—research with which few instructors are familiar—supports the claim that *student* evaluations are relatively reliable and valid proxies for direct measures learning.

This chapter summarizes the major research findings, clarifying where student ratings are and are not biased and suggesting how to use your prior student ratings to improve them. Then we will provide guidelines for documenting your teaching effectiveness in teaching and course portfolios. Finally, we will consider two recently developed systems for evaluating teaching effectiveness in formal faculty reviews, both of which take more than student ratings into account.

Peer, Administrative, and Self-Evaluations

Dozen of studies conducted in the 1970s and 1980s (e.g., Centra, 1975, 1979; Bergman, 1980; Greenwood and Ramagli, 1980; Aleamoni, 1982) came to these conclusions about self-evaluations of teaching and peer and administrative evaluations based on classroom visits:
1) All three relate very little or not at all to student learning/achievement and only mildly to student ratings.
2) Among peer evaluators making classroom visits, interrater reliability (that is, consensus) is low.
3) Self-evaluation and peer evaluations based on classroom visits are much more generous than student ratings.
4) Peer and administrative evaluations based on classroom visits are so highly correlated as to be almost redundant
5) Self-evaluations do not correlate much with any other type of evaluation.

The literature also consistently argues that *none* of these three types of evaluations should be used as the *sole* teaching evaluation tool, nor should they replace student ratings and comments. In fact, peer and administrative evaluations based on classroom visits shouldn't be used for promotion and tenure reviews *at all*, unless:
1. The observers are formally trained in classroom observation and the use of the evaluation form.
2. They meet with the instructor beforehand to discuss his student learning objectives, teaching philosophy, preferred methods, the characteristics of the course, etc.
3. They observe the instructor's class at least seven or eight times during the term.
4. They schedule the classroom visits with the instructor in advance.

Some of these conditions are very difficult for busy faculty, department chairs, and deans to meet, but such a professional observation program has been developed and tested (Millis, 1992).

The research indicates that the feedback from more casual peer and administrative classroom visits is not only harmless but potentially useful for *formative* purposes. Peers in particular have the expertise to advise on the course content, book selections, and the technical aspects of instructional design, such as the syllabus and assignments. However, students are the more relevant judges of instructional delivery (communication and presentation skills, clarity, organization, etc.)

Student Evaluations: How Reliable?

Since administrators started adding them to faculty and TA dossiers in the early 1970s, student evaluations have been under considerable scrutiny. Numerous studies document that student ratings provide meaningful assessment data that should be used in faculty reviews. But they also recommend that other data be included as well (Cashin, 1988;

Aleamoni, 1999; Arreola, 2000).

In assessing *reliability*, three criteria are very important: *consistency, stability,* and *generalizability.* First, how consistent are student ratings? Interrater reliability increases from moderately high to very high with class size. In Cashin and Perrin's (1978) study, average item reliability in a class of ten students was .69, but increased to .89 in a class of 40. Thus more raters yield higher consistency.

Stability indicates the agreement between raters over time. In a longitudinal study conducted by Marsh and Overall (1979; Overall and Marsh, 1980), student ratings collected at the end of a semester were compared against ratings collected at least one year after graduation. The average correlation of the ratings was .83, showing a high level of stability.

Finally, generalizability is the apparent accuracy of the data as indicators of instructor teaching effectiveness. Marsh (1982) examined the ratings of instructors teaching the same course in different semesters and teaching different courses. He also looked at different instructors teaching the same course as well as different instructors teaching different courses. The correlations for the same instructor/same course were quite high (.71) as opposed to the same course/different instructor (.14). An instructor's effectiveness apparently crosses course boundaries as well, since the same instructor/different course correlation was .52 vs. the different instructor/different course correlation of .06. More recent research (Albanese, 1991; Havita, 1996) has found even higher correlations of .87 to .89 between an instructor's student ratings from one year to the next.

Cashin (1988) recommends using data from multiple semesters and multiple courses to obtain a more reliable picture of teaching effectiveness. If an instructor teaches only one course, then consistent ratings from two terms may be sufficient. For instructors with more responsibilities, however, ratings from two or more courses for every term taught over the past two or more years provide a better assessment. For fair and comprehensive instructor reviews, evaluations of courses with fewer than 15 students should be supplemented with other assessment material.

Student Evaluations: How Valid?

To assess *validity* means to find out how well we are measuring what we intend to measure. Two concerns are paramount in determining the validity of student ratings:

1) How effectively do they serve as an indicator of student learning/achievement?

2) What biases may reduce that effectiveness?

Many dozens of studies conclude that student ratings (not necessarily the written comments) are sufficiently valid to be used in faculty reviews. This assumes, of course, that an institution is using a statistically solid student-rating instrument that is known to be valid and reliable (Arreola, 2000).

The evidence is found in the two meta-analyses conducted by Cohen (1981) and Feldman (1998). Synthesizing the results of dozens of rigorous studies, they both reported that student achievement on an external exam correlates decently with student ratings of teaching effectiveness (mean r = .57 to .38)—in particular, instructor's preparation, course organization, clarity, students' perceived learning gains, instructor's stimulation of interest in the subject, and her ability to motivate students to do their best. Instructor friendless and personality relate only weakly to achievement.

Instructors often wonder how their grading may affect their ratings. Actually, there is no statistically respectable method to draw definitive conclusions. The research finds that student grades (individual and class), motivation, and learning are not only all related to instructor/course ratings; they are also highly *inter*related— so much so that we can't say which truly explains their relationships to instructor/course ratings (Howard and Maxwell, 1982). One study that claims to find a causal link between the instructor's grading leniency (expected grades) and student ratings (Greenwald and Gillmore, 1997) fails to control for any of the *real* biases in student ratings, such as course level, students' prior interest in the subject matter, and their reason for taking the course (see below).

What about other biases? Cashin (1988) and Aleamoni (1999) separate myth from reality in their comprehensive literature reviews. First presented are the variables that have been found **not** to affect student ratings in a statistically significant *and* consistent way.

Instructor characteristics:
1) Gender (also see Centra and Gaubatz, 1999)
2) Age and experience
3) Personality (as measured by a personality inventory)
4) Research productivity (r=.12)

Student characteristics:
1) Gender
2) Age
3) Level (freshman to senior)
4) Grade point average
5) Personality (as measured by a personality inventory)

Course and administrative variables:
1) Class size
2) Time of day the course is taught
3) Time during the term the evaluations are collected

But some biases **do** exist (Cashin, 1988; Aleamoni, 1999):

Instructor characteristics:
1) Instructor status. Regular faculty are usually rated higher than are TAs.
2) Expressiveness—if it can be considered a bias. Expressiveness is related to greater student learning, even in the absence of tests and other extrinsic incentives.

Student characteristics:
1) Prior interest in the subject matter. The higher the students' prior interest in the subject matter, the higher their ratings of the course and the instructor.
2) Reason for taking the course. Holding course and instructor characteristics constant, students give higher ratings to courses they take voluntarily (e.g., as an elective) and lower ratings to those they take to fulfill a requirement (e.g., a required general education course).

Course and administrative variables:
1) Course level. Higher level courses, especially graduate level, tend to receive higher ratings.
2) Discipline. Humanities courses receive higher ratings than social science courses, which in turn receive higher ratings than science and mathematics courses. But research only suggests the reasons for

these differences. We know that humanities instructors exhibit a broader range of teaching behaviors that are positively related to student ratings (e.g., interactivity, rapport with class, making the material relevant) than do social and natural science instructors, who focus more on structuring and pacing the subject matter (Murray and Renaud, 1998).

3) Content, workload, and course difficulty. Contrary to popular belief, more *demanding* courses receive *higher* ratings—findings that strongly support the validity of student ratings.

4) Student anonymity. Signed ratings are higher than anonymous ones for obvious reasons.

5) Presence of the instructor. The instructor's presence while students are filling out the forms biases ratings upward.

6) Perceived purpose of the evaluation. Students rate more generously if they believe their ratings will be used for personnel decisions than if they believe their ratings are only for instructor self-improvement.

Improving Your Student Ratings

You might start by reviewing the statistical summaries and student comments from your previous evaluations and identify areas where you would like to improve. It is best to do this with your department chair, a trusted colleague, or a staff member from your institution's teaching center. This book, of course, presents a wealth of teaching formats and techniques that can enhance your ratings as well as your students' learning. However, it is wise to give a major innovation two or more terms to show positive results.

Secondly, consider getting student feedback far enough in advance of the official evaluation process to fine-tune your courses early in the term. You can write up, administer, and analyze your own midterm student evaluations, including items similar to those on your institution's or department's official student ratings form, as well as others of concern to you.

Alternatively you can ask your teaching center to conduct a small group instructional diagnosis (like a class interview) in your classes. Research shows that soliciting early student feedback and having an interpretive consultation with a specialist result in significantly higher student evaluations at the end of the term (Cohen, 1981).

Students seem to take that opportunity to give instructors midterm feedback more seriously than they do end-of-term teaching evaluations. After all, they stand to benefit from the former, while the latter come too late to improve their learning experience.

Documenting Your Effectiveness

The Teaching Philosophy. This one-to-two-page statement is often a required part of an academic job application and a teaching portfolio. It doesn't document your teaching effectiveness as much as it proves you have reflected on your teaching and are committed to an effective strategy.

There's no formula for writing a teaching philosophy, but certain conventions apply. It is a personal statement written in the first person. While non-technical, it requires your showing some understanding of how students learn and some knowledge of student-active teaching options.

Chism (1997-98) recommends developing the narrative around these four or five components:

1) How you think learning occurs.
2) How you think you as an instructor can promote it.
3) What general content, process, and lifelong learning goals you have for your students.
4) How you translate the three abstract elements above into action—that is, learning experiences for your students. Here you explain your teaching methods of choice, the instructional resources you've developed or adapted, and your assessment strategies.
5) How you have grown as an instructor, and how you plan to grow in the future (optional).

Berke and Kastberg (1998) suggest a slightly different framework focused on answering these questions:

- Why are you an instructor?
- What desires, beliefs, and values drive your teaching?
- What notions about learning make you teach the way you do?
- Why do you choose the teaching methods, assignments, and learning experiences for your students that you do?
- What is your conception of a great teacher and what are you doing to become one?
- What do you want your students to gain from your teaching?

The Teaching Portfolio. This is a collection of materials that you assemble to highlight your major teaching strengths and achievements. It is comparable to your publications, grants, and scholarly honors in your research record (Seldin, 1997). It provides a comprehensive, factual base to develop self-assessment and improvement

efforts and for peers and administrators to make sound hiring, promotion, and tenure decisions. Your purpose will influence what you include and how you organize it.

At various times in your teaching career, you will be preparing a portfolio for your reviews. As the teaching evaluation literature consistently cautions, student ratings alone cannot furnish a sufficiently complete assessment of your teaching effectiveness (Arreola, 2000). After all, current students are in no position to judge your course content, most of your course documentation, and the longer-term impact of your teaching. Student ratings should be supplemented with additional data and materials, and it is *your responsibility* to supply them.

To ensure objectivity in your selection of materials, it is best to prepare your portfolio in consultation with a mentor, a trusted colleague, your department chair, or teaching center consultant. Your objective partner can help you focus on the important questions: What is the purpose of the portfolio? What information will your audience find useful? Which teaching/learning areas best serve your purpose? What is the best way to present and analyze the information? What additional information do you need, and how can you obtain it?

Seldin (1997) suggests five steps to producing a good portfolio:

1) Summarize your teaching responsibilities. In two or three paragraphs, describe the types of courses you teach, your student learning objectives, your course design, your expectations for student progress, and your learning assessment tools.
2) Describe your criteria for teaching effectiveness and give reasons from your own experience

for your choosing these criteria. They should reflect your own teaching style and coincide with your teaching responsibilities.

3) Prioritize your criteria according to your purpose. For instance, if you particularly want to demonstrate your improvement, then rank your participation in teaching workshops and seminars high.

4) Assemble and make a list of the materials and data that support your criteria. You might provide copies of student assignments, journals, test results, student ratings, and the like.

5) Attach the portfolio to your curriculum vita. A document of five to seven pages should be sufficient to document your teaching commitment and achievements.

Aside from a summary of your responsibilities, you might also include at least some of the following materials:

- The statement of your teaching philosophy.
- A statement of your teaching goals for the next five years.
- Syllabi and other course materials.
- A brief self-evaluation with your teaching improvement strategies and efforts.
- Descriptions of improvements and updates in your course assignments, materials, and activities.
- Professional activities related to teaching, such as instructional research, writing, presentations, or journal editing.
- Names of students you advise or supervise in research projects.

If your department is interested in more documentation, consider adding support materials from other sources, such as:

- Statements from peers or administrators who have observed you teaching.
- Statements from peers who have reviewed your course materials.
- Student feedback or evaluation summaries that reflect improvement or overall satisfaction—aside from those automatically included in a review.
- A statement from your chair or supervisor about your past and projected departmental contributions.
- Statements from your advisees.
- Teaching awards, honors, and other types of recognition such as teaching committee appointments.
- Invitations to conduct teaching workshops/programs.
- Abstracts or reprints of your research on teaching.
- A videotape of one of your class periods.
- Student scores on standardized tests or your own tests.
- Samples of student work on graded assignments. It is wise to include samples of varying quality and your reasons for the grades you assigned.
- Records of student success in higher level courses following your course.
- Information on how you have influenced students' career choices.

The Course Portfolio. This collection of materials summarize how you planned, taught, managed, and evaluate a particular course. So you might assemble a portfolio on every course you regularly teach. Not as widely used as a teaching portfolio, a course portfolio assembles many of the same materials but organizes them around a course rather than your teaching career.

It also serves the same purposes of promoting self-assessment and improvement and encouraging more sound hiring, promotion, and tenure decisions, at least with respect to teaching effectiveness (Cerbin, 1994; Hutchings, 1998).

These are the kinds of documents that belong in a course portfolio (Cerbin, 1994; Hutchings, 1998):

- Course syllabus, with student learning objectives/outcomes.
- Brief description of course's content and its place in the curriculum.
- Helpful handouts.
- Annotated list of teaching methods.
- Descriptions of assignments (if not in the syllabus).
- Laboratory exercises and/or problem sets.
- Descriptions of special class activities, such as simulations, role plays, case studies, problem-based learning projects, service learning assignments, guest speakers, field trips, etc.
- Samples of graded student work.
- Assessment instruments (major CATs, quizzes, and tests).
- Results of midterm student feedback.
- Summaries of services and consultations conducted by your institution's teaching center.
- End-of-term students ratings and written comments.
- Any class visit feedback from peers or administrators.
- A reflective narrative/analysis.

This last element is the most important and will require your writing a number of pages. The documents will incorporate some of the materials above and will refer to others. It will be helpful to organize it around these course topics (Cerbin, 1994, 1995):

- *Design.* Why did you organize the course the way you did? How does it reflect your teaching philosophy and serve your student learning objectives? How does it help you meet the course's major challenges?
- *Enactment.* What do the students experience during the course? What are the reasons behind your important assignments, class activities, and assessment strategies? (Including a videotape of your major class activities is optional.)
- *Results.* What do students learn in the course? How are students changed? What have they not achieved that you hoped they would?
- *Analysis.* What is your overall assessment of the course and your teaching of it? What will you change to improve it?

A good teaching or course portfolio cannot guarantee you a faculty position, tenure, or promotion. But these portfolios do make the academic reward system more responsive to teaching achievements (Seldin, 1997). Their use is gaining acceptance because they complement the student ratings data and fit easily into current hiring and review procedures. Perhaps most important, they motivate instructors and administrators to talk about teaching, thereby promoting instructional innovation and improvement.

Comprehensive Approaches to Faculty Evaluation

Traditional faculty performance appraisal has developed a reputation for weighing research too heavily, relying too much on student ratings to assess teaching effectiveness, and in general being unsystematic and capricious. Some colleges and universities have responded by adopting one of two comprehensive systems for evaluating faculty performance, both suitable for promotion and tenure.

Glassick et al (1997) build their system around six standards for judging *all* forms of scholarship—discovery, integration, application, and teaching:

1) Clear and realistic goals, objectives, purpose to the work.

2) Adequate preparation in skills, resources, and background knowledge.

3) Appropriate methods, properly and flexibly implemented, to meet the goals.

4) Significant results, impact, achievement of the goals.

5) Effective presentation, clear and honest communication to the intended audience.

6) Reflective critique, evaluation of the results with plans for improvement.

In fact, these standards are already used, if often implicitly, by funding agencies in evaluating grant proposals and by faculty review bodies in assessing published research. While Glassick et al (1997) do not develop their system down to the indicators and measures, they propose that we use these same standards in evaluating teaching. In fact, adapting the framework to teaching is easy.

1) To assess goals, peers examine the student learning objectives in the syllabi, the teaching philosophy, and/or the reflective narrative in the course portfolio.

2) To assess preparation, peers examine the currency and appropriateness of the course content and readings in the syllabi.

3) To assess methods, peers examine the appropriateness of the teaching and assessment methods chosen (in the syllabi, teaching philosophy, and/or course portfolio).

4) To assess results, peers examine student performance on assessment instruments and other available indicators of learning *and* students ratings on items relevant to perceived learning, challenge, interest, and motivation to learn.

5) To assess presentation, peers examine student ratings on communication-relevant items.

6) To assess reflective critique, peers examine the teaching philosophy, the reflective narrative in the course portfolio, and/or other relevant portfolio documents.

Arreola's (2000) system, now used in whole or part at hundreds of North American institutions, has detailed, step-by-step guidelines for implementing it on a comprehensive scale, starting with these departmental decisions:

Step 1. Determine and list all the faculty activities/roles worth evaluating at your institution (e.g., research, teaching, advising, community service, professional service, university service, etc.).

Step 2. Weight the importance of each activity/role in percentages that add up to 100%.

Step 3. Define each activity/role as a list of components—that is, observable or documentable products, performances, or achievements. For example, teaching may be defined as content expertise, instructional design skills, instructional delivery skills, and course management.

Step 4. Weight the components of each role, again in percentages.

Step 5. Determine the best sources of evaluation information (e.g., students, peers, department chair, etc.).

Step 6. Weight each information source by appropriate worth. (A spreadsheet can do all the arithme-

tic required in steps 2, 4, and 6).
Step 7. Determine how to gather
the information from each source
(e.g., forms, questionnaires, etc.).
Step 8. Select or design the appropriate policies, procedures, protocols, and forms for your system.
Model forms are readily available
in Chism (1999) and Arreola (2000).

After the parameters are set and
the system is implemented, each
faculty member under review receives a number (usually between
1.0 and 4.0 or 1.0 and 5.0) that
represents the collective judgment
of that individual's performance
success in each faculty role. These
numbers are weighted (as in step 2)
and added to create an "overall
composite rating" (OCR), to be compared against the evaluative standards or categories set by top administration. This system easily
adapts to any review—tenure, pro-
motions, raises, and post-tenure.

The key—and the challenge—to
instituting any comprehensive faculty evaluation system is forging a
departmental consensus—on the
range of appropriate faculty activities, their relative value, the relative value their components, and
the relative value of their information sources. The decision-making
process is all about values, bringing
them out from *under* table and laying them out *on* the table.
Some have complained that such
systems undermine professional
and administrative judgment, but
all they really do is eliminate a review party's discretion to say one
thing and do another—e.g., to claim
to value teaching and service but to
decide careers on the research record. By demanding integrity and
making the review process trans-
parent, such systems can only benefit those who value, practice, and
document teaching at its best.

For further reading:

Arreola, R.A. 2000. *Developing a
Comprehensive Faculty Evalua-
tion System.* 2nd ed. Bolton, MA:
Anker Publishing.

Centra, J.A. 1999. *Reflective Faculty Evaluation: Enhancing
Teaching and Determining Faculty Effectiveness.* San Francisco:
Jossey-Bass.

Chism, N.V.N. 1999. *Peer Review of
Teaching: A Sourcebook.* Bolton,
MA: Anker Publishing.

Glassick, C.E., M.T. Huber, and G.
I. Maeroff. 1997. *Scholarship
Assessed: Evaluation of the Profes-
soriate.* San Francisco: Jossey-
Bass.

Hutchings, P. (ed.). 1998. *The
Course Portfolio: How Faculty Can
Examine Their Teaching to Ad-
vance Practice and Student Learn-
ing.* Washington, D.C.: American
Association for Higher Education.

Knapper, C. and P. Cranton (eds.).
2001. *Fresh Approaches to the
Evaluation of Teaching.* New
Directions for Teaching and
Learning 88. San Francisco:
Jossey-Bass.

Lewis, K.G. (ed.). 2001. *Techniques
and Strategies for Interpreting
Student Evaluations.* New Directions for Teaching and Learning
87. San Francisco: Jossey-Bass.

Seldin, P. 1997. *The Teaching Portfolio: A Practical Guide to Improved Performance and Promo-
tio/Tenure Decisions.* 2nd ed.
Bolton, MA: Anker Publishing.

Albanese, M.A. 1991. The validity of lecturer ratings by students and trained observers. *Academic Medicine* 66 (1): 26-28.

Albright, Michael J. and David L. Graf, eds. 1992. *Teaching in the Information Age: The Role of Educational Technology*. New Directions for Teaching and Learning 51. San Francisco: Jossey-Bass.

Aleamoni, L.M. 1982. Components of the instructional setting. *Instructional Evaluation* 7 (1): 11-16.

____. 1999. Student rating myths versus research facts: An update. *Journal of Personnel Evaluation* 13 (2): 153-166.

Allen, Deborah E. and Barbara J. Duch. 1998. *Thinking toward Solutions: Problem-based Learning Activities for General Biology*. New York: Saunders College Publishing.

Allen, Robert D. 1981. Intellectual development and the applications of William. *Journal of College Science Teaching* (November): 94-97.

Allen, Walker, Edgar Epps, and Nesha Haniff. 1991. *College in Black and White: African American Students in Predominantly White and Historically Black Public Universities*. Albany: University of New York Press.

Altman, Howard B. and William E. Cashin. 1992. Writing a syllabus. *Idea Paper* No. 27. Center for Faculty Evaluation and Development, Kansas State University.

Altschuler, G. 2001. Battling the cheats. *New York Times Magazine,* Education Life Section 4A (January 7): 15.

Ambron, Joanna. 1987. Writing to improve learning in biology. *Journal of College Science Teaching* 16 (February): 263-66.

Anderson, J.A. and M. Adams. 1992. Acknowledging the learning styles of diverse populations: Implications for instructional design. In *Teaching for Diversity*. New Directions in Teaching and Learning 49, edited by L. Border and N.V.N. Chism. San Francisco: Jossey-Bass.

Angelo, Thomas A. 1991a. Introduction and overview: From classroom assessment to classroom research. In *Classroom Research: Early Lessons from Success,* edited by T. A. Angelo. New Directions in Teaching and Learning 46. San Francisco: Jossey-Bass.

____. 1991b. Ten easy pieces: Assessing higher learning in four dimensions. In *Classroom Research: Early Lessons from Success,* edited by T.A. Angelo. New Directions in Teaching and Learning 46. San Francisco: Jossey-Bass.

Angelo, Thomas A. and K. Patricia Cross. 1993. *Classroom Assessment Techniques: A Handbook for College Teachers,* 2d ed. San Francisco: Jossey-Bass.

Arreola, Raoul A. 2000. *Developing a Comprehensive Faculty Evaluation System,* 2nd ed. Bolton, MA: Anker Publishing.

Astin, Alexander W. 1993. *What Matters in College: Four Critical Years Revisited*. San Francisco: Jossey-Bass.

Astin, Alexander W., Lori J. Vogelgesang, Elaine K. Ikeda, and Jennifer A. Yee. 2000. *How Service Learning Affects Students*. Higher Education Research Institute, University of California, Los Angeles.

Ballantine, Jeanne and Joanne Risacher. 1993. Coping with annoying classroom behaviors. Paper presented at the 13th Annual Lilly Conference on College Teaching, Oxford, OH. November 12.

Baldwin, Roger G. 1997-98. Academic civility begins in the classroom. *Essays on Teaching Excellence* 9 (8): 1-2.

Bandura, A. 1977. Self-efficacy: Toward a unifying theory of behavioral change. *Psychological Review* 84 (2): 191-215.

Barnett, David C. and Jon C. Dalton. 1981. Why college students cheat. *Journal of College Student Personnel* (November): 545-551.

Bartlett, Albert A. and Michael A. Thomason. 1983. Legibility in the lecture hall. *The Physics Teacher* (November): 531.

Baughin, Judith, Emily F. Brod, and Deborah L. Page. 2002. Primary trait analysis: A tool for classroom-based assessment. *College Teaching* 50 (2): 75-80.

Baxter, Magolda, M.B. 1992. *Knowing and Reasoning in College: Gender-related Patterns in Students' Intellectual Development*. San Francisco: Jossey-Bass.

Bean, John C. 1996. *Engaging Ideas: A Professor's Guide to Integrating Writing, Critical Thinking, and Active Learning in the Classroom*. San Francisco: Jossey-Bass.

Belanoff, P. and M. Dickson. 1991. *Portfolios: Process and Product*. Portsmouth, NH: Boynton/Cook and Heinemann.

Bergman, Jerry. 1980. Peer evaluation of university faculty. *College Student Journal* 14 (3): 1-21.

Benander, R., J. Denton, D. Page, and C. Skinner. 2000. Primary trait analysis: Anchoring assessment in the classroom. *Journal of General Education* 49 (4): 280-302.

Berke, Amy and Signe Kastberg. 1998. Writing a teaching philosophy: The beginning of a teaching portfolio. Session presented at the 19th annual sharing conference of the Southern Regional Faculty and Instructional Development Conference, Kennesaw, GA. March 16.

Bernhardt, Stephen A. 1992. Teaching English: Portfolio evaluation. *The Clearing House* 65 (6): 333-334.

Black, B. and E. Axelson. 1991. Teaching students to solve problems. In *The University of Michigan TA Guidebook*. Ann Arbor: University of Michigan.

Blandford, S. 2000. *Managing Professional Development in School*. London: Routledge.

Bloom, Benjamin. 1956. *Taxonomy of Educational Objectives*. New York: David McKay.

_____. 1984. The 2 sigma problem: The search for methods of group instruction as effective as one-on-one tutoring. *Educational Researcher* 13 (6): 4-16.

Bodner, George. 1987. The role of algorithms in teaching problem solving. *Journal of Chemical Education* 64 (6): 513-514.

Boice, B. 1996. Classroom incivilities. *Research in Higher Education* 37 (4): 453-485.

Boling, Elizabeth and Gerald A. Sousa. 1993. Interface design issues in the future of business training. *Business Horizons* (November/December): 50-54.

Bonwell, Charles C. and James A. Eison. 1991. *Active Learning: Creating Excitement in the Classroom. ASHE-ERIC Higher Education Report* No. 1. Washington, D.C.: School of Education and Human Development, George Washington University.

Bourland, Julie. 1996. Hollywood hustle. *Parenting* (March): 53.

Brauchle, Kenneth C. 2000. Plagiarism and the internet: Cut and paste your way to success. *The National Teaching and Learning Forum* 10 (1): 10-11.

Bridges, Edwin M. with Philip Hallinger. 1992. *Problem-Based Learning for Administrators*. Eugene, OR: ERIC Clearinghouse on Educational Management.

Bridgwood, Michael A. 1999. Guidelines for communication and engineering problem solving at the basic level. *IEEE Transactions on Professional Communication* 42 (3): 156-165.

Brinson, J. Dianne and Mark F. Radcliffe. 1996. *Multimedia Law and Business Handbook*. Menlo Park, CA: Ladera Press.

Brookhart, Susan M. 1999. *The Art and Science of Classroom Assessment: The Missing Part of Pedagogy*. ASHE-ERIC Higher Education Report. 27 (1). Washington, DC: The George Washington University, Graduate School of Education and Human Development.

Brookhart, Victoria. 1990. Problem solving in science. Unpublished manuscript, Teaching Assistant Development Program, University of California, Riverside.

Brooks, Robert P. 1987. Dealing with details in large classes. In *Teaching Large Classes Well*, edited by M.G. Weimer. New Directions in Teaching and Learning 32. San Francisco: Jossey-Bass.

Browne, M. Neil and Stuart M. Keeley. 2000. *Asking the Right Questions: A Guide to Critical Thinking*, 6th ed. Upper Saddle River, NJ: Prentice-Hall.

Bunn, Douglas N., Steven B. Caudill, and Daniel M. Gropper. 1992. Crime in the classroom: An economic analysis of undergraduate student cheating behavior. *Journal of Economic Education* 23 (3): 197-207.

Burns, E. Bradford. 1993. *Liberating the Imagination for Intellectual Discoveries*. 89 minutes. Produced by Vanderbilt University Center for Teaching. Videocassette.

Cameron, Beverly J. 1993. *Teaching at the University of Manitoba*. Manitoba, Winnipeg, Canada: University of Manitoba Teaching Services.

Campbell, Teresa Isabelle Danza. 2001. Personal email correspondence, September 27.

Carnevale, Dan. 1999. How to proctor from a distance: Experts say professors need savvy to prevent cheating in online courses. *Chronicle of Higher Education* (November 12): A47-A48.

Carrier, Carol A. 1983. Notetaking research implications for the classroom. *Journal of Instructional Development* 6 (3): 19-26.

Cashin, William E. 1979. Motivating students. IDEA Paper No. 1. Center for Faculty Evaluation and Development, Kansas State University.

_____. 1988. Student ratings of teaching: A summary of the research. IDEA Paper No. 20. Center for Faculty Evaluation and Development, Kansas State University.

Cashin, William E. and B.M. Perrin. 1978. Description of a standard form data base. IDEA Technical Report No. 4. Center for Faculty Evaluation and Development, Kansas State University.

Centra, John A. 1975. Colleagues as raters of classroom instruction. *Journal of Higher Education* 46 (1): 327-337.

____. 1979. *Determining Faculty Effectiveness.* San Francisco: Jossey-Bass.

____. 1999. *Reflective Faculty Evaluation: Enhancing Teaching and Determining Faculty Effectiveness.* San Francisco: Jossey-Bass.

Centra, John A. and N.B. Gaubatz. 1999. *Is There Gender Bias in Student Evaluations of Teaching?* Princeton, NJ: Educational Testing Service.

Cerbin, William. 1994. The course portfolio as a tool for continuous improvement of teaching and learning. *Journal of Excellence in College Teaching* 5: 95-105.

____. 1995. Connecting assessment of learning to the improvement of teaching. *Assessment Update* 7 (1): 4-6.

Chiaramonte, Peter. 1994. The agony and the ecstasy of case teaching. *Reaching Through Teaching* 7 (2): 1-2.

Chism, Nancy Van Note. 1997-98. Developing a philosophy of teaching statement. *Teaching Excellence* 9 (3): 1-2.

____. 1999. *Peer Review of Teaching: A Sourcebook.* Bolton, MA: Anker Publishing

Clute, Pamela S. 1994. Telephone interview, February. University of California, Riverside.

Cohen, P.A. 1981. Student ratings of instruction and student achievement: A meta-analysis of multi-section validity studies. *Review of Educational Research* 51: 281-309.

Collison, Michele. 1990a. Apparent rise in students' cheating has college officials worried. *Chronicle of Higher Education* (January 17): A33-34.

____. 1990b. Survey at Rutgers suggests that cheating may be on the rise at large universities. *Chronicle of Higher Education* (October 24): A31-32.

Connor-Greene, Patricia. 2000. Assessing and promoting student learning: Blurring the line between teaching and learning. *Teaching of Psychology* 27 (2): 84-88.

Cooper, J.L., P. Robinson, and M. McKinney. 1993. Cooperative learning in the classroom. In *Changing College Classrooms,* edited by D.F. Halpern and associates. San Francisco: Jossey-Bass.

Cross, K. Patricia. 1988. In search of zippers. *AAHE Bulletin* (June): 3-7.

____. 1992. Classroom assessment/classroom research: Four years into a hands-on movement. *The National Teaching & Learning Forum* 1 (6): 1-3.

Cross, K. Patricia and Thomas A. Angelo. 1988. *Classroom Assessment Techniques: A Handbook for Faculty.* Ann Arbor, MI: National Center for Research to Improve Postsecondary Teaching and Learning.

Crowley, Mary L. 1993. Student mathematics portfolio: More than a display case. *The Mathematics Teacher* 86 (7) (October): 544-547.

Daniel, J.S. 1975. Uses and abuses of slides in teaching. In *Teaching Aids in the College Classroom,* edited by L.P. Grayson and J.M. Biedenbach. Washington, D.C.: American Society for Engineering Education.

Day, R.S. 1980. Teaching from notes: Some cognitive consequences. In *Learning, Cognition, and College Teaching,* edited by W.J. McKeachie. New Directions for Teaching and Learning 2. San Francisco: Jossey-Bass.

Deming, W.E. 1993. *The New Economics for Industry, Government, and Education.* Cambridge, MA: MIT Center for Advanced Engineering Study.

Donald, Janet. 2002. *Learning to Think: Disciplinary Perspectives.* San Francisco: Jossey-Bass.

Duch, Barbara J. and Deborah E. Allen. 1996. Problems: A key factor in PBL. *About Teaching* 50 (Spring): 25-28.

Duch, Barbara J, Deborah E. Allen, and Harold B. White III. 1997-98. Problem-based learning: Preparing students to succeed in the 21st century. *Essays on Teaching Excellence* 9 (7): 1-2.

Edens, Kellah M. 2000. Preparing problem solvers for the 21st century through problem-based learning. *College Teaching* 48 (2): 55-60.

Ellis, Dave 2000. *Becoming a Master Student,* 9th ed. Boston: Houghton Mifflin.

Emett, Ray C. and Douglas A. New. 1997. Opening the world to your students without feeling like a criminal: Legal aspects of creating educational multimedia. Session presented at the annual meeting of the Professional and Organizational Development Network in Higher Education, Haines City, FL. October 18.

Ericksen, S.C. 1974. *Motivation for Learning: A Guide for the Teacher of the Young Adult.* Ann Arbor: University of Michigan Press.

Fagan, M.M. 1986. Do formal mentoring programs really mentor? In *Proceedings of the First International Conference on Mentoring* 2. Vancouver, B.C.: International Association for Mentoring.

Feichtner, Susan Brown and Elaine Actis Davis. 1984-85. Why some groups fail: A survey of students' experiences with learning groups. *The Organizational BehaviorTeaching Review* 9 (4): 58-73.

Felder, Richard M. and Rebecca Brent. 2001. Effective strategies for cooperative learning. *Journal of Cooperation and Collaboration in College Teaching* 10 (2): 67-75.

Feldman, Kenneth A. 1992. College students view of male and female college teachers: Part I—Evidence from the social laboratory and experiments. *Research in Higher Education* 33 (2): 317-75.

____. 1993. College students view of male and female college teachers: Part II—Evidence from students' evaluations of their classroom teachers. *Research in Higher Education* 34 (2): 151-211.

____. 1998. Identifying exemplary teachers and teaching: Evidence from student ratings. In *Teaching and Learning in the College Classroom*, edited by K.A. Feldman and M.B. Paulsen. Needham Heights, MA: Simon & Schuster.

Feldmann, Lloyd J. 2001. Classroom civility is another of our instructor responsibilities. *College Teaching* 49 (4): 137-141.

Ferris, William P. and Peter W. Hess. 1984-85. Peer evaluation of student interaction in organizational behavior and other courses. *The Organizational Behavior Teaching Review* 9 (4): 74-82.

Ferguson, M. 1989. The role of faculty in increasing student retention. *College and University* 69: 127-134.

Finkel, D.L. and G.S. Monk. 1983. Teachers and learning groups: Dissolution of the Atlas complex. In *Learning in Groups*, edited by C. Bouton and R.Y. Garth. New Directions for Teaching and Learning 14. San Francisco: Jossey-Bass.

Fleming, Neil D. and Colleen Mills. 1992. Not another inventory, rather a catalyst for reflection. *To Improve the Academy* 11: 137-155.

Fontana, L.A. 1991. The Civil War Interactive. *Instruction Delivery Systems* 5 (6): 5-9.

Friedman, Paul, Fred Rodriguez, and Joe McComb. 2001. Why students do and do not attend classes: Myths and realities. *College Teaching* 49 (4): 124-133.

Frierson, H.T. 1986. Two intervention methods: Effects on groups of predominantly black nursing students' board scores. *Journal of Research and Development in Education* 19: 18-23.

Frymier, J.R. 1970. Motivation is what it's all about. *Motivation Quarterly* 1: 1-3.

Gale, Richard A. and John D.W. Andrews. 1989. *A Handbook for Teaching Assistants.* Center for Teaching Development, University of California, San Diego.

Gallupe, R. Brent and William H. Cooper. 1993. Brainstorming electronically. *Sloan Management Review* (Fall): 27-36.

Gedalof, Allan J. 1998. *Teaching Large Classes.* Green Guide No. 1. Halifax, Ontario, Canada: Society for Teaching and Learning in Higher Education.

Gigliotti, Richard J. and Donald R. Fitzpatrick. 1977. An investigation into the factors accounting for college student interest in courses. *Educational Research Quarterly* 2 (1): 58-68.

Glassick, Charles E., Mary Taylor Huber, and Gene I. Maeroff. 1997. *Scholarship Assessed: Evaluation of the Professoriate.* San Francisco: Jossey-Bass.

Gogel, Howard K. 1985. Faculty office hours. *Journal of Medical Education* 60 (October): 242-245.

Gonsalves, Lisa M. 2002. Making connections: Addressing the pitfalls of white faculty/black male student communication. *College Composition and Communication Online* 53 (February): 435-465.

Gonzalez, Virginia and Estela Lopez. 2001. The age of incivility: Countering disruptive behavior in the classroom. *AAHE Bulletin* (April): 3-6.

Gordon, Larry. 1990. Study finds cheating joins 3 Rs as a basic college skill. *Los Angeles Times* (November 22).

Grant-Thompson, Sheila and Donald Atkinson. 1997. Cross-cultural mentor effectiveness and African American male students. *Journal of Black Psychology* 23: 120-134.

Greenwald, Anthony G. and Gerald M. Gillmore. 1997. No pain, no gain? The importance of measuring course workload in student ratings of instruction. *Journal of Educational Psychology* 89 (4): 743-751.

Greenwood, Gordon E. and Howard J. Ramagli, Jr. 1980. Alternatives to student ratings of college teaching. *Journal of Higher Education* 51 (6): 673-684.

Gronlund, Norman E. 1985. *Stating Objectives for Classroom Instruction*, 3rd ed. New York: Macmillan.

_____. 1999. *How to Write and Use Instructional Objectives,* 6th ed. New York: Prentice Hall.

Grunert, Judith. 1997. *The Course Syllabus: A Learning-Centered Approach.* Bolton, MA: Anker Publishing.

Hall, Roberta M. and Bernice Resnick Sandler. 1982. *The Classroom Climate: A Chilly One for Women?* Project on the Status and Education of Women. Washington, DC: Association of American Colleges.

Halpern, Diane F. and associates. 1994. *Changing College Classrooms.* San Francisco: Jossey-Bass.

Hammons, James O. and Janice R. Barnsley. 1992. Everything you need to know about developing a grading plan for your course (well, almost). *Journal on Excellence in College Teaching* 3: 51-68.

Harper, Georgia. 2002. *Crash Course in Copyright.* University of Texas System. http://www.utsystem.edu/OGC/IntellectualProperty/cprtindx.htm.

Hativa, N. 1996. University instructors' ratings profiles: Stability over time and disciplinary differences. *Research in Higher Education* 37 (3): 341-365.

Head, J.T. 1992. New directions in presentation graphics: Impact on teaching and learning. In *Teaching in the Information Age: The Role of Educational Technology*, edited by M.J. Albright and D.L. Graf. New Directions for Teaching and Learning 51. San Francisco: Jossey-Bass.

Hebert, Stephen W., M.D. 1984. A simple hypnotic approach to treat test anxiety in medical students and residents. *Journal of Medical Education* 59 (October): 841-842.

Heller, Patricia, Ronald Keith, and Scott Anderson. 1992. Teaching problem solving through cooperative grouping. Part 1: Group vs. individual problem solving. *American Journal of Physics* 60 (7): 627-636.

Heller, Patricia and Mark Hollabaugh. 1992. Teaching problem solving through cooperative grouping. Part 2: Designing problems and structuring groups. *American Journal of Physics* 60 (7): 637-644.

Hinkle, S. and A. Hinkle. 1990. An experimental comparison of the effects of focused freewriting and other study strategies on lecture comprehension. *Teaching of Psychology* 17 (February): 31-35.

Howard, George S. and Scott E. Maxwell. 1980. The correlation between student satisfaction and grades: A case of mistaken causation? *Journal of Educational Psychology* 72 (6): 810-820.

____. 1982. Do grades contaminate student evaluations of instruction? *Research in Higher Education* 16 (2): 175-188.

Hufford, Terry L. 1991. Increasing academic performance in an introductory biology course. *BioScience* 41 (2) (February): 107-108.

Hunter, Madeline. 1967. *Motivation Theory for Teachers.* El Segundo, CA: TIP Publications.

Hutchings, Patricia. 1998. Defining features and significant functions of the course portfolio. In *The Course Portfolio: How Faculty Can Examine Their Teaching to Advance Practice and Student Learning*, edited by P. Hutchings. Washington, DC: American Association for Higher Education.

Hyman, Ronald T. 1978. *Simulation Gaming for Values Education: The Prisoner's Dilemma.* Washington, DC: University Press of America.

____. 1981. Using simulation games in the college classroom. Idea Paper No. 5. Center for Faculty Evaluation and Development, Kansas State University.

Jacobs, Lucy Chester and Clinton I. Chase. 1992. *Developing and Using Tests Effectively: A Guide for Faculty.* San Francisco: Jossey-Bass.

Jalajas, David S, and Robert I. Sutton. 1984-85. Feuds in student groups: Coping with whiners, martyrs, saboteurs, bullies, and deadbeats. *The Organizational Behavior Teaching Review* 9 (4): 94-107.

Johnson, David, W. and others. 1981. Effects of cooperative, competitive, and individualistic goal structures on achievement: A meta-analysis. *Psychological Bulletin* 89: 47-62.

Johnson, David W. and Roger T. Johnson. 1989. *Cooperation and Competition: Theory and Research.* Edina, MN: Interaction Books.

Johnson, David W., Roger T. Johnson, and Karl A. Smith. 1991. *Active Learning: Cooperation in the College Classroom.* Edina, MN: Interaction Books.

Johnston, A.H. and W.Y. Su. 1994. Lectures—a learning experience? *Education in Chemistry* (May): 76-79.

Johnson, Carolyn and Connie Ury. 1998. Detecting internet plagiarism. *The National Teaching and Learning Forum* 7 (4): 7-8.

____. 1999. Preventing internet plagiarism. *The National Teaching and Learning Forum* 8 (5): 5-6.

Jonas, H., S. Etzel, and B. Barzansky. 1989. Undergraduate medical education. *JAMA* 262 (8): 1011-1019.

Jordan, Dan. 1996. Copyright and multimedia. Session conducted at the 17th Annual Sharing Conference of the Southern Regional Faculty and Instructional Development Consortium, Baton Rouge, LA. February 5.

Kagan, Spencer. 1988. *Cooperative learning.* San Juan Capistrano, CA: Resources for Teachers.

Kalman, Judith and Calvin S. Kalman. 1996. Writing to learn. *American Journal of Physics* 64: 954-956.

Karraker, Meg Wilkes. 1993. Mock trials and critical thinking. *College Teaching* 41 (4): 134-137.

Kaufman, A. 1985. *Implementing Problem-Based Medical Education.* New York: Springer Publishing Company.

Kaufman, A., et al. 1989. The New Mexico experiment: Educational innovation and institutional change. *Academic Medicine* (June Supplement): 285-294.

Kerkvliet, Joe. 1994. Cheating by economics students: A comparison of survey results. *Journal of Economic Education* 25 (2) (Spring): 121-133.

Kerkvliet, Joe and Charles L. Sigmund. 1999. Can we control cheating in the classroom? *Journal of Economic Education* 30 (4) (Fall): 331-334.

Kibler, William L. 1992. Cheating: Institutions need a comprehensive plan for promoting academic integrity. *Chronicle of Higher Education* (November 11): B1-B2.

Kiernan, Vincent. 2002. Nebraska researchers measure the extent of 'link rot' in distance education. *Chronicle of Higher Education* (April 10). http://chronicle.com/free/2002/04/2002041001u.htm.

Kimmel, Robert M. 2002. Undergraduate labs in applied polymer science. Session # 1526. In *Proceedings of the 2002 American Society for Engineering Education Annual Conference and Exposition*, American Society for Engineering Education.

Kingad, A.J. 1996. Time expenditure, workload, and student satisfaction in problem-based learning. In *Bringing Problem-Based Learning to Higher Education: Theory and Practice,* edited by L. Wilkerson and W. Gijselaers. San Francisco: Jossey-Bass.

Kirby, P. 1989. The Trinity College mentor program. Unpublished manuscript, Trinity College, Washington, DC.

Kirkpatrick, Larry D. and Adele S. Pittendrigh. 1984. A writing teacher in the physics classroom. *The Physics Teacher* 22 (March): 159-64.

Kleiner, Caroline and Mary Lord. 1999. The cheating game. *U.S. News and World Report* (November 22): 55-66.

Kloss, Robert J. 1994. A nudge is best: Helping students through the Perry schema of intellectual development. *College Teaching* 42 (4) (Fall): 151-158.

Knapper, C.K. 1982. Technology and teaching: Future prospects. In *Expanding Learning Through Communication Technologies*, edited by C.K. Knapper. New Directions for Teaching and Learning 9. San Francisco: Jossey-Bass.

Knowlton, Dave S., Heather M. Knowlton, and Camela Davis. 2000. The whys and hows of online discussion. *Syllabus* (June): 54-58.

Kobrak, Peter. 1992. Black student retention in predominantly white regional universities: The politics of faculty involvement. *Journal of Negro Education* 61: 509-530.

Kolb, David A. 1984. *Experiential Learning: Experience as the Source of Learning and Development.* Englewood Cliffs, NJ: Prentice-Hall.

Krathwohl, David R., Benjamin S. Bloom, and Bertram B. Masia. 1999. *Taxonomy of Educational Objectives Book 2/Affective Domain.* New York: Addison-Wesley Publishing.

Krupnick, Catherine G. 1985. Women and men in the classroom: Inequality and its remedies. *Journal of the Harvard-Danforth Center: On Teaching and Learning* 1 (May): 18-25.

Lacey-Casem, Merri Lynn. 1990. Testing students' learning and grading tests and papers. In *Teaching Techniques: A Handbook for TAs at UCR*, edited by L.B. Nilson. Teaching Assistant Development Program, University of California, Riverside.

Lamb, Annette C. 1992. Multimedia and the teaching-learning process in higher education. *In Teaching in the Information Age: The Role of Educational Technology,* edited by M.J. Albright and D.L. Graf. New Directions for Teaching and Learning 51. San Francisco: Jossey-Bass.

Langer, Judith A. 1992. Speaking of knowing: Conceptions of understanding in academic disciplines. In *Writing, Teaching, and Learning in the Disciplines*, edited by A. Herrington and C. Moran. New York: Modern Language Association of America.

Langer, Judith A. and Arthur N. Applebee. 1987. *How Writing Shapes Thinking.* Urbana, IL: National Council of Teachers of English.

Leahy, Richard. 2002. Conducting writing assignments. *College Teaching* 50 (2): 50-54.

Leamnson, Robert. 1999. *Thinking about Teaching and Learning: Developing Habits of Learning with First Year College and University Students*. Sterling, VA: Stylus.

_____. 2000. Learning as biological brain change. *Change* (November/December): 34-40.

Leatherman, C. 1996. Whatever happened to civility in academe? *Chronicle of Higher Education* (March 8): A21.

Lewis, R.J. and M. Wall. 1988. *Exploring Obstacles to Uses of Technology in Higher Education: A Discussion Paper*. Washington, DC: Academy for Educational Development.

Lieuz, Elizabeth M. 1996. Comparison study of learning in lecture vs. problem-based format. *About Teaching* 50 (Spring): 18-19.

Light, Richard J. 1990. *The Harvard Assessment Seminar, First Report: Explorations with Students and Faculty about Teaching, Learning, and Student Life*. Cambridge, MA: Harvard Graduate School of Education.

_____. 1992. *The Harvard Assessment Seminar, Second Report: Explorations with Students and Faculty about Teaching, Learning, and Student Life*. Cambridge, MA: Harvard Graduate School of Education.

Lowman, Joseph. 1987. Giving students feedback. In *Teaching Large Classes Well*, edited by M.G. Weimer. New Directions for Teaching and Learning 32. San Francisco: Jossey-Bass.

Lowther, M.A., J.S. Stark, and G.G. Martens. 1989. *Preparing Course Syllabi for Improved Communication*. Ann Arbor, MI: NCRIPTAL, University of Michigan.

MacGregor, J. 1990. Collaborative learning: Reframing the classroom. *Chalkboard* 2 (Fall): 1-2.

McCabe, Donald and Gary Pavela. 2000. Some good news about academic integrity. *Change* (September/October): 32-38.

McKeachie, Wilbert J. 1986. *Teaching Tips: A Guidebook for the Beginning College Teacher*, 8th ed. Lexington, MA: D.C. Heath and Company.

McKeachie, Wilbert J., Nancy Chism, Robert Menges, Marilla Svinicki, Claire Ellen Weinstein. 1994. *Teaching Tips: Strategies, Research, and Theory for College and University Teachers*, 9th ed. Lexington, MA: D.C. Heath and Company.

Madigan, Robert and James Brosamer. 1990. Improving the writing skills of students in introductory psychology. *Teaching of Psychology* 17 (February): 27-30.

Marsh, H.W. and J.U. Overall. 1979. Long-term stability of students' evaluations: A note on Feldman's "Consistency and variability among college students in rating their teachers and courses." *Research in Higher Education* 10: 139-147.

Marsh, H.W. 1982. The use of path analysis to estimate teacher and course effects in student rating of instructional effectiveness. *Applied Psychological Measurement* 6: 47-59.

_____. 1984. Experimental manipulations of university student motivation and their effects on examination performance. *British Journal of Educational Psychology* 54 (June): 206-213.

Mazur, Erik. 1997. *Peer Instruction: A User's Manual*. Upper Saddle River, NJ: Prentice Hall.

McKinney, Kathleen. 2001. Responses from POD (faculty development) discussion list on encouraging students to prepare for class. http://www.cat.ilstu.edu/teaching_tips/handouts/pod.shtml.

Mealey, Donna L. and Timothy R. Host. 1993. Coping with test anxiety. *College Teaching* 40 (4): 147-150.

Menges, Robert J. 1988. Research on teaching and learning: The relevant and the redundant. *Review of Higher Education* 11: 259-68.

Michaelsen, Larry K. 1997-98. Three keys to using groups effectively. *Teaching Excellence* 9 (5): 1-2.

Mierson, Sheella. 1998. A problem-based learning course in physiology for undergraduate and graduate basic science students. *Advances in Physiological Education* 20 (1): S16-S27.

Mierson, Sheella and Anuj A. Parikh. 2000. Stories from the field: Problem-based learning from a teacher's and a student's perspective. *Change* 32 (1) (January/February): 20-27.

Miller, J. and M. Chamberlin. 2000. Women are teachers, men are professors: A study of student perceptions. *Teaching Sociology* 28: 283-298.

Millis, B.J. 1990. Helping faculty build learning communities through cooperative groups. In *To Improve the Academy* 10, edited by L. Hilsen. Stillwater, OK: New Forums Press.

_____. 1992. Conducting effective peer classroom observations. In *To Improve the Academy* 11, edited by D. Wulff and J. Nyquist. Stillwater, OK: New Forums Press.

238

Millis, Barbara J. and Philip G. Cottell, Jr. 1998. *Cooperative Learning for Higher Education Faculty.* Phoenix, AZ: American Council on Education and Oryx Press.

Mitchell, P. David. 1982. Simulation and gaming in higher education. In *Expanding Learning Through New Communications Technologies,* edited by C.K. Knapper. New Directions for Teaching and Learning 9. San Francisco: Jossey-Bass.

Mixon, Franklin G., Jr. 1996. Crime in the classroom: An extension. *Journal of Economic Education* 27 (3): 195-200.

Montgomery, Kathleen. 2000. Authentic tasks and rubrics: Going beyond traditional assessments in college teaching. *College Teaching* 50 (1): 34-39.

Murray, Harry C. and Robert D. Renaud. 1998. Disciplinary differences in classroom teaching behaviors. In *Teaching and Learning in the College Classroom*, edited by K.A. Feldman and M.B. Paulsen. Needham Heights, MA: Simon & Schuster.

Murray, Margo with Marna A. Owen. 1991. *Beyond the Myths and Magic of Mentoring: How to Facilitate an Effective Mentoring Program.* San Francisco: Jossey-Bass.

Murrell, Kenneth L. 1984-85. Peer performance evaluation: When peers do it, they do it better. *Organizational Behavior Teaching Review* 9 (4): 83-85.

Naveh-Benjamin, Moshe, Wilbert J. McKeachie, and Yi-Guang Lin. 1987. Two types of test-anxious students: Support for an information processing model. *Journal of Educational Psychology* 79 (2): 131-136.

Neel, Jasper P. 1993. Teaching and grading writing. Workshop presented in the Center for Teaching Master Teaching Fellows Training Program, Vanderbilt University, Nashville, TN. August 12-13.

Nelson, Craig. 1993. Fostering critical thinking and mature valuing across the curriculum. Workshop presented at the 13th Annual Lilly Conference on College Teaching, Oxford, OH. November 12-13.

Nettles, Michael. 1988. *Towards Black Undergraduate Student Equality in American Higher Education.* New York: Greenwood Press.

Newell, George E. 1984. Learning from writing in two content areas: A case study/protocol analysis. *Research in the Teaching of English* 18 (October): 265-87.

Nicholls, Gill. 2002. Mentoring: The art of teaching. In *The Theory and Practice of Teaching*, edited by P. Jarvis. Sterling, VA: Stylus Publishing.

Nilson, Linda B. 1981. *The TA Handbook: Teaching Techniques and Self-Improvement Strategies.* TA Training Program, Department of Sociology, University of California, Los Angeles

____, ed. 1990. *Teaching Techniques: A Handbook for TAs at UCR.* Teaching Assistant Development Program, University of California, Riverside.

____. 1992. Publishing research on teaching. In *The Grad Student's Guide to Getting Published*, edited by A. Allison and T. Frongia. New York: Prentice Hall.

____. 2002. The graphic syllabus: Shedding a visual light on course organization. In *To Improve the Academy* 20, edited by D. Liberman and C. Wehlburg. Bolton, MA: Anker Publishing.

____. 2002-03. Helping students help each other: Making peer feedback more valuable. *Teaching Excellence* 14 (8): 1-2.

____. 2003. Improving student peer feedback. *College Teaching* 51 (1): 34-38..

Nilson, Linda B. and John T. Lysaker. 1996. The gender factor in teaching evaluations: Beyond economics. *American Economics Association 1996 Committee on the Status of Women in the Economics Profession Newsletter* (Spring/May): 5-7.

Norden, Jeanette J. 1994. Prozac and other psychoactive drugs: What they tell us about the relationship between the brain and the "self." Lecture given in Anatomy and Physiology, School of Nursing, Vanderbilt University. January 28.

Nosich, Gerald. 1993. *Motivating Students To Think Critically By Teaching For Discovery.* 59 minutes. Produced by the Foundation for Critical Thinking. Videocassette.

Nowell, Clifford and Doug Laufer. 1997. Undergraduate student cheating in the fields of business and economics. *Journal of Economic Education* 28 (1): 3-12.

Nurrenbern, Susan and Pickering, Miles. 1987. Concept learning versus problem solving: Is there a difference? *Journal of Chemical Education* 64 (6): 508-510.

Odom, Chris D. 2002. Advances in instructional physics laboratories at Clemson University. Colloquium presented in the College of Engineering and Sciences, Clemson University. April 19.

Office of Educational Development. 1985. Preventing student academic dishonesty. *Tools for Teaching.* University of California, Berkeley.

Orlans, Harold. 1999. Scholarly fair use: Chaotic and shrinking. *Change* (November/December): 53-60.

Ory, John C. and Katherine E. Ryan. 1993. *Tips for Improving Testing and Grading*, Vol 4. Thousand Oaks, CA: Sage Publications.

Overholser, James C. 1992. Socrates in the classroom. *College Teaching* 40 (1): 14-19.

Overall, J.U. and H.W. Marsh. 1980. Students' evaluations of instruction: A longitudinal study of their stability. *Journal of Educational Psychology* 72: 321-325.

Owens, R.E. 1972. How important is motivation in college learning? *Kansas State University Teaching Notes* 2: 2-3.

Penick, John E. and Linda W. Crow. 1989. Characteristics of innovative college science programs. *Journal of College Science Teaching* (September/October): 14-17.

Perry, William G. 1968. *Forms of Intellectual and Ethical Development in the College Years: A Scheme.* New York: Holt, Rinehart & Winston.

_____. 1985. Different worlds in the same classroom. *Journal of the Harvard-Danforth Center: On Teaching and Learning* 1 (May): 1-17.

Pollio, Howard R. and W. Lee Humphreys. 1988. Grading students. In *Assessing Students' Learning*, edited by J.H. McMillan. New Directions in Teaching and Learning 34. San Francisco: Jossey-Bass.

Pregent, Richard. 1994. *Charting Your Course: How To Prepare To Teach More Effectively.* Madison, WI: Magna Publications.

Rhem, James. 1992. Conference report: Cooperative learning as a teaching alternative. *The National Teaching and Learning Forum* 2 (1): 1-2.

Roach, K. David. 1997. Effects of graduate teaching assistant attire on student learning, misbehaviors, and ratings of instruction. *Communication Quarterly* 45 (3): 125-142.

Rodgers, M.L. 1995. How holistic scoring kept writing alive in chemistry. *College Teaching* 43 (1): 19-22.

Rogers, Kathy A. 1993. Using the overhead. *The Toastmaster* (August): 27-29.

Rowe, Mary Budd. 1980. Pausing principles and their effects on reasoning in science. In *Teaching the Sciences*, edited by F.B. Brawer. New Directions for Community Colleges 31. San Francisco: Jossey-Bass.

Royce, Anya Peterson. 2000. *A Survey of Academic Incivility at Indiana University: Preliminary Report.* Bloomington, IN: Center for Survey Research, Indiana University.

Ruhl, Kathy L., Charles A. Hughes, and Patrick J. Schloss. 1987. Using the pause procedure to enhance lecture recall. *Teacher Education and Special Education* 10: 14-18.

Samples, J.W. 1994. We want them to learn; sometimes we need to teach them how. *Connexions* 6 (2): 2.

Schneider, Alison. 1999. Why professors don't do more to stop students who cheat. *Chronicle of Higher Education* (January 22): A8-A10.

Schoenfeld, Alan H. 1985. *Mathematical Problem Solving.* San Diego: Academic Press.

Schroeder, Charles C. 1993. New students—New learning styles. *Change* (September/October): 21-26.

Seldin, Peter. 1997. *The Teaching Portfolio: A Practical Guide to Improved Performance and Promotion/Tenure Decisions*, 2nd ed. Bolton, MA: Anker Publishing.

Seymour, Elaine and Nancy M. Hewitt. 1997. *Talking About Leaving: Why Undergraduates Leave the Sciences.* Boulder, CO: Westview Press.

Sherer, Pamela and Timothy Shea. 2002. Designing courses outside the classroom: New opportunities with the electronic delivery toolkit. *College Teaching* 50 (1): 15-20.

Simon, Jamil. 1992. *Thinking Together: Collaborative Learning in the Sciences.* 18 minutes. Derek Bok Center for Teaching and Learning, Harvard University. Videocassette.

Smith, Karl A. 1993. Cooperation in the classroom. Unpublished seminar notes. Minneapolis: University of Minnesota.

_____. 1994. *Cooperation in the College Classroom.* 70 minutes. Produced by Vanderbilt University Center for Teaching. Videocassette.

Spence, Larry D. 2001. The case against teaching. *Change* (November/December): 11-19.

Stage, Frances K., Jillian Kinzie, Patricia Muller, and Ada Simmons. 1999. *Creating Learning Centered Classrooms: What Does Learning Theory Have to Say?* Washington, DC: ERIC Clearing House on Higher Education.

Stark, Joan S. and others. 1988. *Reflections on Course Planning: Faculty and Students Consider Influences and Goals.* Ann Arbor, MI: NCRIPTAL, University of Michigan.

Stenmark, Jean K. 1989. *Assessment Alternatives in Mathematics: An Overview of Assessment Techniques That Promote Learning.* Berkeley, CA: EQUALS, Lawrence Hall of Science and California Mathematics Council.

_____. 1991. *Mathematics Assessment: Myths, Models, Good Questions, and Practical Suggestions.* Reston, VA: National Council of Teachers of Mathematics.

Teaching Notes. 1992. *Chronicle of Higher Education* (February 26): A35.

Thompson, Brad. 2002. If I quiz them, they will come. *Chronicle of Higher Education* (June 21): B5.

Tigner, Robert B. 1999. Putting memory research to good use: Hints from cognitive psychology. *College Teaching* 47 (4): 149-152.

Tobias, Sheila. 1990. *They're Not Dumb, They're Different: Stalking the Second Tier.* Tucson, AZ: Research Corporation.

Toombs, W. and W. Tierney. 1992. *Meeting the Mandate: Renewing the College and Department Curriculum.* ASHE-ERIC Higher Education Report No. 91-6. Washington, DC: Association for the Study of Higher Education.

Topping, Kenneth. 1998. Peer-assessment between students in colleges and universities. *Review of Educational Research* 68: 249-276.

Toulmin, Stephen, Richard Rieke, and Allan Janik. 1984. *An Introduction to Reasoning,* 2nd ed. New York: Macmillan.

Treisman, Philip Uri. 1986. A study of the mathematics performance of black students at the University of California, Berkeley. Doctoral dissertation. Berkeley, CA: University of California.

Trower, Cathy A. and Richard P. Chait. 2002. Faculty diversity: Too little for too long. *Harvard Magazine* 104 (4): 33-43.

Vella, J. 1994. *Learning to Listen, Learning to Teach: The Power of Dialogue in Educating Adults.* San Francisco: Jossey-Bass.

Weaver, Barbara. 2002. Personal interview, June 20.

Walvoord, Barbara E. and Lucille Parkinson McCarthy. 1991. *Thinking and Writing in College: A Naturalistic Study of Students in Four Disciplines.* Urbana, IL: National Council of Teachers of English.

Walvoord, Barbara E. and Virginia Johnson Anderson. 1998. *Effective Grading: A Tool for Learning and Assessment.* San Francisco: Jossey-Bass.

Warmington, Eric H. and Philip G. Rouse, eds. 1984. *The Great Dialogues of Plato.* Translated by W.H.D. Rouse. Markham, Ontario, Canada: Penguin Books.

Watson, David L. and Nancy A. Stockert. 1987. Ensuring teaching and learning effectiveness. *Thought and Action: The NEA Higher Education Journal* 3 (2): 91-104.

Wergin, Jon F. 1988. Basic issues and principles in classroom assessment. In *Assessing Students' Learning,* edited by J.H. McMillan. New Directions for Teaching and Learning 34. San Francisco: Jossey-Bass.

Wilhoit, Stephen. 1994. Helping students avoid plagiarism. *College Teaching* 42 (4): 161-164.

Wlodkowski, R.J. 1993. *Enhancing Adult Motivation to Learn: A Guide to Improving Instruction and Increasing Learner Achievements.* San Francisco: Jossey-Bass

Woods, Donald R. 1989. Developing students' problem-solving skills. *Journal of College Science Teaching* (November): 108-110.

____. 1996. Problem-based learning for large classes in chemical engineering. In *Bringing Problem-Based Learning to Higher Education: Theory and Practice,* edited by L. Wilkerson and W. Gijselaers. San Francisco: Jossey-Bass.

Wright, W. Alan, Eileen M. Herteis, and Brad Abernehy. 2001. *Learning Through Writing: A Compendium of Assignments and Techniques.* Halifax, Nova Scotia, Canada: Office of Instructional Development, Dalhousie University.

Young, Art. 1997. *Writing Across the Curriculum,* 2nd ed. Upper Saddle River, NJ: Prentice Hall

Young, Art and Todd Fulwiler. 1986. *Writing Across the Disciplines: Research into Practice.* Upper Montclair, NJ: Boynton/Cook Publishers.

Zoller, Uri. 1987. The fostering of question-asking capacity. *Journal of Chemical Education* 64 (6): 510-512.

INDEX